THE Spice BOOK

THE
Spice
BOOK

An A–Z reference and cook's kitchen bible

SALLIE MORRIS & LESLIE MACKLEY

H H
HERMES
HOUSE

This edition is published by Hermes House, an imprint of Anness Publishing Ltd, Blaby Road, Wigston, Leicestershire LE18 4SE

Email: info@anness.com
Web: www.hermeshouse.com; www.annesspublishing.com

If you like the images in this book and would like to investigate using them for publishing, promotions or advertising, please visit our website www.practicalpictures.com for more information.

Publisher: Joanna Lorenz
Senior Cookery Editor: Linda Fraser
Copy Editors: Bridget Jones and Jenni Fleetwood
Indexer: Hilary Bird
Designer: Annie Moss
Mac Artist: John Fowler
Photographer: William Adams-Lingwood assisted by Louise Dare
Home Economist: Lucy McKelvie assisted by Alison Austin

Previously published as *The Spice Ingredients Cookbook*

ETHICAL TRADING POLICY

Because of our ongoing ecological investment programme, you, as our customer, can have the pleasure and reassurance of knowing that a tree is being cultivated on your behalf to naturally replace the materials used to make the book you are holding. For further information about this scheme, go to www.annesspublishing.com/trees

NOTES

Bracketed terms are intended for American readers.
For all recipes, quantities are given in both metric and imperial measures and, where appropriate, in standard cups and spoons.
Follow one set of measures, but not a mixture, because they are not interchangeable.
Standard spoon and cup measures are level. 1 tsp = 5ml, 1 tbsp = 15ml, 1 cup = 250ml/8fl oz.
Australian standard tablespoons are 20ml. Australian readers should use 3 tsp in place of 1 tbsp for measuring small quantities.
American pints are 16fl oz/2 cups. American readers should use 20fl oz/2.5 cups in place of 1 pint when measuring liquids.
Electric oven temperatures in this book are for conventional ovens. When using a fan oven, the temperature will probably need to be reduced by about 10–20°C/20–40°F. Since ovens vary, you should check with your manufacturer's instruction book for guidance.
Medium (US large) eggs are used unless otherwise stated.

Abbreviations: FR. (French), G. (German), SP. (Spanish), IT. (Italian), AR. (Arabic), DU. (Dutch), ETH. (Ethiopian), FIL. (Filipino), IN. (Indian), IND. (Indonesian), JAP. (Japanese), MAL. (Malaysian), SINH. (Sinhalese).

PUBLISHER'S NOTE

Contents

In the Spice Index the spices
are arranged by botanical name.

Introduction

Spices have played a major influence in our lives and in the economic development of many countries for centuries. Exotic and aromatic spices give us pleasure in our enjoyment of food, they are invaluable in folk medicines and modern medications, they sweeten our rooms as well as our bodies and enliven our language with sayings like 'the spice of life' and 'spicing things up'. The spice trade has brought romance and drama into history, with the adventures of the sea captains and explorers who went in search of these sought-after and expensive prizes.

THE SPICE TRADE

As long ago as 3500 BC, the Ancient Egyptians were using spices for flavouring their food, in cosmetics and in lotions for embalming their dead. They believed that the spirit returned to the body of the deceased, so the bodies of their pharaohs, queens and nobility were mummified and entombed with their worldly treasures. From biblical references, we know that the Queen of Sheba travelled from her homeland, Ethiopia, to visit King Solomon in Jerusalem. His enormous wealth was due to the 'traffick of the spice merchants' and gifts of spices added to his treasure: 'All those who sought to hear him brought costly presents, including spices'. (1 Kings 10:25)

The story of Joseph, he with the coat of many colours, is also related to the spice trade. His jealous brothers resolved to kill him, 'but a company of Ishmaelites came down from Gilead with their camels bearing spicery, and balm and myrrh, going to carry it down to Egypt'. The brothers sold Joseph for twenty pieces of silver and returned to their father, Jacob, with the bloodstained coat. Jacob was consumed with grief. In reality, Joseph was sold to an officer of Pharaoh and

Left: *Spices were once brought into the Middle East by camel caravans, today spices can easily be bought fresh in the marketplace.*

he eventually became a high-ranking official at court. His ability to interpret Pharaoh's dreams saved his adopted country from famine. Later he had the enormous satisfaction of selling corn to his brothers, who did not recognize him. They brought appropriate gifts of balm, honey, spices, myrrh, nuts and almonds.

The spice trade, controlled by the Arabs for at least 5,000 years, grew through the Middle East to the Eastern Mediterranean and to Europe. Donkey or camel caravans, carrying precious cargoes of cinnamon, cassia, cardamom, ginger, turmeric, frankincense and jewels, travelled hazardous routes.

Below: *Brightly coloured, fragrant spices tempt buyers in an Egyptian bazaar.*

Their journeys may have started in China, Indonesia, India or Ceylon (now Sri Lanka). Very often, enterprising Chinese merchants sailed to the Spice Islands (now Maluku, a group of islands in Indonesia), then brought their cargoes of spices and perfumes to the Indian or Sri Lankan coast, where they dealt with the Arab traders. The Arabs were anxious to conceal both the sources of their supplies and the overland spice routes. The classic route crossed the River Indus, through Pesharwar, over the Khyber Pass, through Afghanistan and Iran, then south to the city of Babylon on the Euphrates. From there the spices were taken to the most powerful city or town of the day. The Phoenicians, great seafarers and traders, thrived on the lucrative spice trade, and they set up their city of Tyre as a major distribution centre, serving the whole of the Mediterranean from 1200 to 800 BC.

As seats of power switched from Egypt to Babylon and Assyria, the Arabs maintained their hold on the supply of spices from the East, throughout the development of the Greek and Roman civilizations. Clearly, the stories the Arabs related about the origins of the spices were impressive and believed: they told of cinnamon from deep snake-infested valleys and of cassia from shallow lakes protected by fierce and enormous

winged birds with nests built high on limestone cliffs. When the nests collapsed, the traders collected the cassia.

The Romans were prolific in their use of spices, and the demand increased the pressures to find a route to India so that they could break the Arab monopoly on the spice trade. Understanding the weather patterns and the monsoons provided the answer: soon Roman ships, laden with precious spices, were sailing into Alexandria, in Egypt, their chief port. The Romans were great gourmets and lovers of the good things of life, they used spices in cooking, scented their rooms with 'strewings' of spices and used the distilled spice oils for bathing and keeping their lamps alight. Wherever their legions marched they introduced a wealth of spices and herbs, and for the first time

the exotic flavourings were taken to Northern Europe. The fall of the Roman Empire in the 5th century and the dawning of the Dark Ages heralded a long period of cultural stagnation, including knowledge of spices.

Above: *A market seller in India sits surrounded by a vibrant array of spices.*

Mohammed, the prophet and founder of the Muslim faith, married the wealthy widow of a spice merchant. The missionary zeal in the spread of the faith through the East was inextricably linked with the trading of spices. Whilst Western Europe slept, the spice trade in the East expanded aggressively. The religious crusades from 1000 AD for three hundred years broadened the appreciation of spices from the East as the Christians tried to wrest power from the Muslims in the unholy trade. Venice and Genoa became trading centres, and ships travelling to the Holy Land with the crusaders returned with cargoes of spices, silks and jewels. Spices, because they were

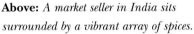

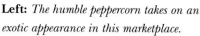

Left: *The humble peppercorn takes on an exotic appearance in this marketplace.*

scarce, became as precious as silver and gold and the trade began to flourish once more.

Marco Polo was born in 1256 AD into a family of jewel merchants who were fascinated with the East. They travelled as far as China, known as Cathay, staying at the court of the Mongol Emperor, the Great Khan, and, during a journey, which lasted twenty-four years, Marco travelled throughout China, Asia and India. His story *The Adventures of Marco Polo* was written on parchment while he was taken prisoner after a sea battle between Venice and Genoa. His book recalled the spices he had seen growing on his travels and dispelled the fearsome tales and myths told by the early Arab traders. He wrote poetically of Java: 'it abounds with rich commodities. Pepper, nutmeg ... cloves and all other valuable spices and drugs are the produce of the island which occasion it to be visited by many ships laden with merchandise, that yields to the owners considerable profit'. His book was to inspire the next and following generations of sailors and travellers who were keen to make their names and their fortunes.

The Age of Discovery (1400 AD) dawned and the epic history of spices

Above: *Cassia bark in a Cairo street bazaar.*

Below: *Dried red chilli peppers available by the sackful.*

continued. European seafarers became obsessed with the dream of finding the best sea route to India and the East. Vasco de Gama, the Portuguese navigator, was the first to discover the sea route to India by rounding the Cape of Good Hope, Africa's southernmost tip. He was not kindly received but he managed to load his ships with nutmegs, cloves, cinnamon, ginger and peppercorns. He was welcomed home as a hero in 1499 and, more importantly, he had a letter from the Indian rulers of Calicut agreeing to a trading partnership.

Lisbon took over the role of spice capital, a position so jealously guarded and enjoyed by Venice in the past. Prior to this, Christopher Columbus had a novel approach to the idea of sailing east: he sailed west. In 1492 he thought he had reached Japan but in fact it was San Salvador (now known as Watling Island), one of the islands near the Bahamas, Haiti and Cuba. He had discovered the New World and he was the first Westerner to taste the fiery chilli. On his second voyage, Columbus left Spain with 1,500 men to establish Spanish power in the New World hoping that he would find gold and Oriental spices; instead he discovered allspice and vanilla, and, from the

great South American continent, he introduced potatoes, chocolate, maize, peanuts and turkeys to Europe.

The Portuguese made a fundamental mistake in hiring the Dutch as their merchants in Europe, requesting them to sail to the Spice Islands to collect

cloves, nutmegs and cinnamon. After a century of complete dominance, the Portuguese were overthrown by the Dutch. The Dutch East India Company was formed in 1602 in response to the formation of the British East India Company, which had been given a Royal Charter by Queen Elizabeth I in 1600. Meanwhile, Sir Francis Drake circumnavigated the world, sailing his ship, the *Golden Hind*, through the Magellan Straits and across the Pacific to the Spice Islands. These islands were the focus for the whole of Europe with each nation aiming for monopoly of the spice trade, which they knew to be the source of riches beyond compare. The Dutch approach was to restrict the growing of nutmegs and cloves to the islands of Amboyna and Banda in the Moluccas. This was foiled by a French missionary, Pierre Poivre, who found saplings on a nearby island, to which the seeds had been carried by birds, and he transported them to

Above: *Indonesian women offer a wide range of spices in the daily markets.*

Mauritius. The cloves were taken on to Zanzibar, which is still a major producer today, and the nutmegs to Grenada, in the West Indies, known as the 'Nutmeg Isle'. About the same time, the British were experimenting with the planting of nutmegs and cloves in Penang; later they cultivated spices in Singapore, under the direction of Sir Stamford Raffles, a famous employee of the East India Company and founder of Singapore.

The struggle between the British and the Dutch became very bitter and bloody and lasted almost two hundred years. The conflict was resolved when Britain took over India and Ceylon and the Dutch were left with Java and Sumatra, which remained under their jurisdiction until the Second World War. By this time, spices were more plentiful and cheaper than ever before.

The late 18th century brought another nation on to the spice stage, the United States of America. The clipper ships of New England were successful in tracking down peppercorns. Trading and bartering as they went, the clipper skippers returned to Salem in Massachusetts with bulging holds of the best Sumatran pepper. Salem became the centre of the pepper trade and, with a potential profit of 700 per cent, the owners of the ships became the first millionaires. These journeys were not, however, without their difficulties: the round trip might take two to three years, the possibility of being killed by pirates or natives was extremely high, and the storms and tempests on the high seas were equally threatening.

Today we take the commonplace availability of exotic ingredients for

Below: *Spices cover every inch of space in this shop in Singapore.*

granted. It is difficult for us to imagine that a handful of cardamoms was the equivalent of a poor man's annual wage; that slaves were sold for a few handfuls of peppercorns; that a pound of mace could buy three sheep and a cow; or that a pound of ginger was worth the same as a sheep. Dockers in London were made to sew up their pockets to discourage them from stealing even a single peppercorn.

Modern international travel has created a market for foods from all over the globe, and the principal spice markets are London, Hamburg, Rotterdam, Singapore and New York. Spices are inspected before being stored in huge warehouses, then they are sold and sent for processing and packaging. The spice trade is worth millions of dollars per annum: black pepper tops the list, followed by chillies and cardamom. India is the principal producer, followed by Indonesia, Brazil, Madagascar and Malaysia; spices are vital to the economies of all these countries. As cooks we depend on the spices they produce to enliven our daily meals and to bring fragrance to our lives. Empires have been won and lost in the historic battles for the seasoning on our kitchen shelves.

Spices in the Kitchen

Throughout the world, the cooking of every country is distinguished by the way in which spices are used to give it a unique character. With so many spices now readily available, cooking can be a great adventure that will transport you to any part of the world that takes your fancy.

Imagine the smoky scent of grilled lamb infused with cumin and garlic or the fragrance of coriander and garlic from a gently simmering curry. Even before you taste the food the evocative aroma of spices stimulates the appetite and heightens the antici-pation of what is to come. Indian cooking, though not necessarily hot, is distinctively spicy and is characterized by the use of a greater range of dried spices than any other cuisine in the world. Up to fifteen spices may be blended to flavour one dish.

India is a vast country and the style of cooking varies enormously from region to region, but the spices most often used include coriander, cumin, turmeric, black pepper, mustard seeds, fennel seeds, cardamom, cloves, garlic and ginger. Chillies are valued for both fire and flavour; some Indian dishes are extremely hot, but in others spices are used with rare subtlety.

Chinese cooks use liberal quantities of fresh ginger and garlic. They favour spices such as sesame seeds and star anise, which is the predominant flavour in their famous five spice blend. The spices in this blend are finely ground so that they release their flavour quickly in stir-fried dishes.

Thai food tends to be very hot, with the tiny – and fiery – Thai chillies appearing in many dishes. The heat, however, is tempered by the fresh light flavours of lemon grass and kaffir lime leaves and the soothing effect of coconut milk. In the recipes in this collection, some authentic Thai dishes, such as Hot and Sour Prawn Soup, have been marginally modified for Western tastes; if your taste buds can take the heat, just add more chillies.

Below: *An increasing range of formerly exotic spices and aromatics are becoming familiar to the Western cook.*

Mexican food is also characterized by the liberal use of chillies. Several different types are often combined in the same dish. Each chilli contributes its own distinctive flavour as well as the fire for which they are famous.

Mexican chillies had already travelled to the Caribbean islands by the time Columbus arrived, and their use characterizes all island cooking. All-spice and cayenne are also widely used in Caribbean dishes. Traditional recipes such as Jerk Pork and Caribbean Fish Steaks typically combine these with a pungent fresh herb such as thyme.

Around the Mediterranean it is the warm spices such as cinnamon, coriander, saffron and cumin that create the typical flavours that so readily conjure up memories of holidays in Turkey, Greece or Morocco. These spices are frequently combined with fruit and nuts in dishes like Moroccan Harissa-spiced Roast Chicken or Lamb Tagine. In North Africa, harissa (an explosive chilli sauce) is added to many dishes or handed separately, to add fire to fragrant spice combinations.

Many European dishes are flavoured with spices like caraway, dill, cardamom and fennel. These spices are equally at home in sweet or savoury dishes.

Although Europe has had a long tradition of using spices, particularly in preserves, pickles and sauces, their use in everyday cooking has been moderate until comparatively recently.

Only twenty years ago, although most kitchens probably had a spice rack on display, the ground spices in the jars would have been used sparingly – if at all – until they were so stale that they would have been of scant use as a flavouring. Cooks may have sprinkled a little ground nutmeg on a milk pudding, or added a clove or two to an apple pie, but that was a long way from the days of the 17th century, when expensive spices were used in Europe as a means of dis-

Above: *Chillies by the cupful in Brazil.*

playing wealth and food was heavily spiced and scented with ginger, pepper, cinnamon, cloves and nutmeg.

In recent years, however, we have been rediscovering the wealth of ways in which spices and aromatic flavourings can enhance all types of dishes from soups to sweetmeats. As we travel more and explore increasingly exotic locations, and as restaurants spring up in every town offering food from all over the world, we are becoming familiar with a wide variety of different cuisines. We are taking the tastes home, too, becoming more adventurous in what we attempt to re-create in our own kitchens.

Fortunately, it is no longer necessary to seek out ethnic shops for more unusual ingredients. Supermarkets and grocers' shops now stock everything from turmeric to tamarind juice. Stale spices rapidly lose their flavour and can become musty, so it is important to buy small amounts from a shop with a rapid turnover, and use spices soon after purchase, particularly if they are ready ground.

Cooking, like other arts, is constantly evolving, and one of the most exciting developments that has followed the rediscovery of spices is the

way in which classic dishes can be transformed by innovative use of familiar (and unfamiliar) flavourings. While many of the recipes in this book are entirely authentic, an equal number take a fresh look at old favourites by introducing new and sophisticated spice blends. For example, try Salmon Marinated with Thai Spices, a dish based on the traditional Scandinavian gravadlax, or enjoy Pear Tart Tatin, which owes its fragrance to the unusual addition of cardamom.

Don't be afraid of spices. This comprehensive collection will tell you all you'll ever need to know about these fascinating flavourings, from advice on selection and storage to suggestions for making a wide range of powders and pastes. Mixing and blending spices is part of the pleasure. Quantities of spices given in recipes are only a guide, so experiment to discover the combinations you prefer. That way, you can personalize your own cooking – and prove that spices can make a world of a difference.

Above: *A bountiful display – spices as far as the eye can see.*

13

Choosing and Preparing Spices

What is a spice? Spices are the dried seeds (cumin, coriander, cardamom, mustard), buds (cloves), fruit or flower parts (peppercorns, allspice), bark and roots (cassia, cinnamon and ginger) or leaves (kaffir lime leaves, curry leaves) of plants. They are usually of tropical origin, and almost all are native to the Orient. There are exceptions: allspice, vanilla and chillies were originally found in tropical Central America and the West Indies.

CHOOSING SPICES

When buying spices, select whole seeds, berries, buds and bark, such as cumin seeds, cardamoms, peppercorns, allspice, cloves, cassia and cinnamon sticks, if you can, as these keep their flavour and pungency far longer than the powdered spices, and can be ground easily as needed. Fresh roots, such as ginger and galangal, and fresh lemon grass are essential for some dishes and have an entirely different flavour than the dried versions.

PREPARATION TECHNIQUES

Spices are prepared in many ways, depending on the form of the spice and the dish in which it's being used – the point though is always the same: to release the optimum amount of flavour and aroma.

Dry-frying

This process, sometimes called dry roasting, and often used in Indian cookery, increases the flavour of such spices as cumin, coriander, fennel, mustard and poppy seeds.

Heat a small heavy-based pan over a medium heat for about 1 minute, put in the whole spices and cook for 2-3 minutes, stirring or shaking the pan frequently to prevent the spices burning, or until the spices start to give off a warm, rich aroma.

Remove the pan from the heat and tip the spices into a bowl and grind finely in a mortar with a pestle.

Frying in Oil

Whole spices are sometimes fried in oil, either at the beginning of a recipe, before other ingredients are added, or simply to flavour the oil.

Grinding

Spices are frequently crushed or ground to release their flavour and aroma. Only a few, notably mace, dried ginger and turmeric, cinnamon and cassia, are hard to grind at home and usually bought in powdered form. For the best flavour, grind spices as you need them. Don't grind them more than a day or two in advance.

For small, easily ground dried spices, such as cumin, fennel, ajowan and caraway seeds and cloves, use a china pestle and mortar. Grind only a small amount at a time – don't put more than a tablespoon or two in the bowl at a time, and grind in a circular motion.

Coriander seeds and allspice, and some harder spices, such as fenugreek, can be ground successfully in a peppermill. Special nutmeg grinders, similar to pepper mills are also available and work fairly well.

An easier and quicker method of grinding these harder spices is to use an electric coffee grinder. Don't overfill the bowl and grind in short bursts.

Fresh ingredients, such as ginger and garlic, and larger spices, such as chillies, can be easily ground using pestles and mortars. Traditional Indian and Oriental mortars have pitted or ridged bowls and are good for making wet spice mixtures and pastes.

Wet spice mixtures can also be made in a food processor. Use the metal blade, add the ingredients and purée to a rough or smooth paste as required. Slicing the ingredients into small pieces before adding to the processor will result in a smoother paste. If the ingredients are all dry, add a little of the oil from the recipe to help the processing.

PREPARING CHILLIES

Chillies need to be handled carefully. If you have sensitive skin, or are preparing a lot of chillies, it is worth wearing rubber gloves. Don't touch your eyes or mouth while you work, and always wash your hands and cooking implements after preparing chillies. It is easier to seed chillies before chopping: cut the chilli in half and scrape out the seeds using the point of a knife.

Grating

Fresh root spices, such as horseradish and ginger, and whole nutmegs are grated before use.

To grate ginger or horseradish, peel the root, then grate it on the fine blade of a stainless steel grater.

Grate nutmegs on a special nutmeg grater or on the finest blade of a standard grater.

Bruising and Crushing

Some spices, such as cardamom, juniper, ginger and lemon grass, are often lightly crushed to release their aroma or, in the case of cardamom, to release the seeds for crushing. Garlic is often crushed rather than chopped.

Juniper berries and cardamoms are easily crushed using a pestle and mortar. (Alternatively, place them in a sturdy polythene bag and crush them with a rolling pin.)

Fresh ginger, galangal or lemon grass, which are to be added whole to a recipe during cooking for a subtle flavour and then removed before serving, can be bruised with one or two sharp blows, until the fibres are crushed, on a chopping board using the flat blade of a large knife, or a large pestle.

A simple and effective way of crushing garlic cloves is to trim off the root end and place the unpeeled clove cut-end down in a garlic press. After the garlic is crushed, the skin can simply be removed, making cleaning the press very easy.

Shredding and Chopping

Some fresh spices, such as ginger, garlic and kaffir lime leaves, are cut into fine slices or pieces before use to maximize the flavour and aroma.

Kaffir lime leaves are usually shredded rather than chopped. Hold one or two leaves together on a chopping board and cut into fine strips using a small sharp knife.

To chop ginger, cut the peeled root lengthways into fine slices then slice again into long strips. Hold a few strips together at a time and chop finely.

Infusing

One or two spices are always infused in a warm liquid before use. When saffron is infused it imparts not only a wonderful aroma, but also a vibrant yellow colour. Tamarind is infused to produce a tangy juice that is used in a similar way to lemon juice or vinegar to add sharpness to a dish.

To infuse saffron strands, warm a little milk, water or liquid from the recipe. Add the saffron and leave to infuse for about 5 minutes. Don't strain the liquid, both strands and liquid are used in the recipe.

To infuse tamarind pulp, place a small piece of the pulp in a jug or bowl, add 4 tbsp warm water and leave to infuse for 10 minutes.

Mix with the fingers to loosen the purée from the seeds, then strain through a nylon sieve. Discard the pulp and seeds and use the juice as directed in the recipe.

PREPARING BLACHAN

Blachan, also called trassi or terasi, is not a spice, it is a strong smelling, firm paste made of fermented shrimps that is used in South-east Asian cookery. It can be bought in Oriental shops. Unless it is to be fried as part of a recipe, blachan is always lightly cooked before use. If you have a gas cooker, simply mould the blachan on to the end of a metal skewer and rotate over a low to medium gas flame, or heat the piece of blachan under the grill of an electric cooker, until the outside begins to look crusty but not burnt. To avoid the strong smell filling the kitchen, wrap the blachan in foil and fry in a dry frying pan over a gentle heat for 4-5 minutes, turning from time to time.

Equipment for Preparing Spices

Spices are often ground, crushed, pounded or puréed to create powders and pastes. Although these processes are simple, there are a few useful items of equipment that make these tasks much easier.

Nutmeg graters come in a variety of shapes and sizes. They have very fine rough holes and produce a fine powder. The one on the left doubles as a storage container.

Smooth china pestles and mortars come in a variety of sizes and are excellent for grinding small amounts of dry spices.

Traditional Indian and Oriental granite or stone pestles and mortars are generally fairly large, with deep, pitted or ridged bowls. They are ideal for pounding fresh spices, such as ginger, galangal and lemon grass, as the rough surface seems to grip the pieces and prevents them flying out of the bowl as you pound the mixture.

Bigger, flat-bowled pestles and mortars are particularly good for making spice pastes that include large amounts of fresh spices, herbs, onion and garlic.

A simple garlic press makes quick work of crushing garlic cloves.

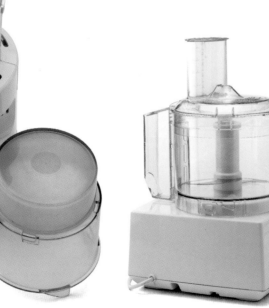

An electric coffee grinder is excellent for grinding dry spices. If you are going to do a lot of spice cooking, it is worth keeping a separate grinder purely for this purpose.

Electric food processors come into their own for making larger quantities of spice pastes and purées.

Nutmeg mills work by rotating the nutmeg over a blade – different models grate with varying degrees of success.

This small clear perspex mill can be used to grind both cinnamon and cassia bark.

Traditional wooden Japanese ginger graters make light work of grating ginger and are easy to clean. A stainless steel box grater works equally well – use the finest grating surface and work over a flat plate to catch the juices.

How to Store Spices

Very few cooks store spices correctly. Dried spices are usually displayed in glass jars on the kitchen shelf or in wall racks, and fresh spices, such as ginger or lemon grass, are often kept on a kitchen shelf or in a vegetable rack, sometimes in a sunny spot or under bright lights. Here are some tips on how to preserve the flavour and aroma of your spices.

STORING FRESH SPICES

Unless you are going to use fresh spices the day they are bought, they should be chilled rather than stored at room temperature. Lemon grass, kaffir lime leaves and curry leaves are best wrapped in a piece of kitchen paper and stored in the salad drawer of a fridge for up to 2 weeks. Fresh galangal, ginger and chillies will keep for up to 3 weeks in a sealed container, lined with kitchen paper, in the fridge. If you would like to keep them longer, fresh spices can be pounded to a paste, then put in small sealed containers and frozen for up to 6 months.

STORING DRIED SPICES

Both ground and whole dried spices should be stored in airtight containers in a cool, dark cupboard or drawer as light, heat and moisture lessen their quality. Whole spices will keep for 6 months or even longer, if stored carefully. However, most ground spices lose their colour, flavour and aroma within 5 or 6 months. If you are unsure just how long the spices have been stored for, check the aroma – if the spice smells musty, or if there is little aroma, it is likely that the flavour will be impaired, too. It's a good idea to label new jars of spices with the date of purchase.

Opaque jars made of either china or metal don't need to be stored in a dark place, but they are still better kept in a cool cupboard out of the heat of the kitchen.

STORING OTHER SPICES

Bottles or tubes of spice pastes and purées, such as ginger and garlic purée, will keep unopened until the best-before date. However, once opened, they should be stored in the fridge and used within 6 weeks. Both dried and ready-made mustard will keep for up to a year even when opened. Dried tamarind and vanilla pods will keep in a cool dark place for up to 2 years.

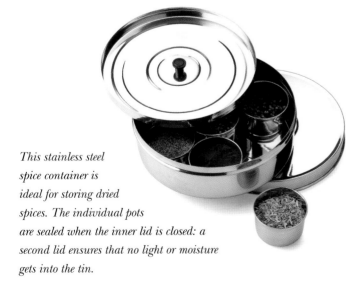

This stainless steel spice container is ideal for storing dried spices. The individual pots are sealed when the inner lid is closed: a second lid ensures that no light or moisture gets into the tin.

Small glass jars with airtight seals or screw tops are perfectly good containers for storing dried spices, providing they are kept in a cool dark cupboard and not in a rack on the wall, or on a kitchen shelf.

THE SPICE INDEX

Garlic

BOTANICAL NAME: *Allium sativum* • FAMILY NAME: *Alliaceae*

FR. *ail*; G. *Knoblauch*; SP. *ajo*; IT. *aglio*

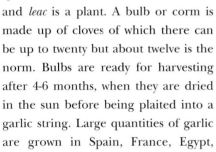

Garlic features in the mythology, religion and culture of many nations. For example, Arab legend has it that garlic grew from one of the Devil's footprints and onion from the other as he left the Garden of Eden, and there are many references to this noble plant in the Bible. Workers constructing the pyramids were given garlic, and it was found in the tomb of the young Pharaoh Tutankhamen. Roman labourers and soldiers chewed on garlic, the soldiers did so before battle, especially when they anticipated hand-to-hand fighting – it is little wonder they were so successful. In Chinese mythology, garlic has been considered capable of warding off the Evil Eye, the symbol of misfortune and ill fate. Culpeper, the famous herbalist, suggested chewing cumin or green beans to get rid of the smell of garlic on the breath; modern answers include drinking several glasses of red wine or, less drastically, eating fresh parsley, mint, thyme or celery leaves.

CULTIVATION

Garlic, a perennial of the lily family, grows like a leek to the height of about 0.6 metres/2 feet. The name garlic comes from the Anglo Saxon *garleac* in which *gar*, a spear, refers to the leaves and *leac* is a plant. A bulb or corm is made up of cloves of which there can be up to twenty but about twelve is the norm. Bulbs are ready for harvesting after 4-6 months, when they are dried in the sun before being plaited into a garlic string. Large quantities of garlic are grown in Spain, France, Egypt,

purple garlic

Bulgaria, Hungary, USA, Mexico and Brazil.

There are many different types of garlic, the most common being the white papery-skinned variety. Pink- or purple-skinned garlic has a less papery outer skin and wonderfully fleshy, plump cloves. A giant variety comes from California, while in South-east Asia there is a miniature type with only four to six cloves in each bulb.

Some gardeners believe that planting garlic under roses encourages the flowers to produce even more perfume, at the same time preventing black spot and greenfly.

AROMA AND FLAVOUR

Garlic is indispensable in many cuisines. Before preparation, a whole clove has only a mild bouquet; it is only marginally stronger when sliced, but it has a very powerful flavour with a lingering aftertaste and aroma once chopped or crushed. The flavour is sharp, with a lot of punch for such a small ingredient. When frying, never allow the garlic to brown or else it will taste bitter.

garlic paste

There are different schools of thought on how best to crush garlic; here are three suggestions.

Trim the root end from a garlic clove, place it in a mortar and give it one blow with a pestle to release the skin. Discard the skin, then crush the flesh with a tiny amount of salt to absorb the juices that might otherwise be lost. The salt also prevents the garlic from flying out of the mortar.

Place the unpeeled clove on a chopping board, cover with the flat blade of a knife and press hard. This releases the skin, which should be removed, then press again before finely chopping the flesh with a tiny amount of salt. Wash the chopping board and knife with hot soapy water to remove any odour.

If you have a garlic press, leave the garlic clove unpeeled and cut off the root end. Place the clove cut end down in the press.

Crush the garlic clove into a small bowl, or directly into the cooking pot. The garlic skin can be removed from the press in one neat piece, making the press easier to clean.

garlic granules

garlic salt

smoked garlic

coarse garlic granules

garlic flakes

minced garlic

white garlic

CULINARY USE

Garlic is an essential ingredient in thousands of dishes from around the globe. Along with ginger and onion it forms a 'trinity' of flavours that is familiar in Oriental and Asian cuisines.

Garlic is also widely used in Western cooking – roasted as whole cloves (up to forty may be used) or cut into slivers and inserted into meat, or cooked in sauces and casseroles. It flavours savoury butters, dressings and sauces for pasta, fish, poultry, meat, game and vegetables.

Garlic butter is the classic accompaniment for snails, and it is served with shellfish or fish steaks. Alternatively, it can be spread on sliced French bread and baked in foil.

Raw garlic is used in salad dressings and some sauces, particularly in aïoli and rouille. For just a hint of garlic in a salad, rub the inside of the salad bowl with a cut clove of garlic.

Garlic products include purée, dried flakes and garlic salt, but it's best to use fresh garlic wherever possible.

MEDICINAL AND OTHER USE

Garlic is thought of as a wonderful tonic and is the subject of all manner of health-giving claims. It is said to purify the blood and lower blood pressure, which is enough encouragement for many people to take a garlic capsule on a daily basis. It is said to aid digestion and prevent flatulence. It is considered to be beneficial in the treatment of diabetes and to lower cholesterol. Garlic juice is used in cough medicines and it helps to alleviate asthma. An old country remedy for whooping cough was to put a clove of garlic in the shoe or the clog of the patient.

STORAGE

Peeled cloves should be a clean creamy white without blemish. Make sure that the bulbs are closely packed and firm; store them in a cool dry place, away from strong light.

Dill

BOTANICAL NAME: *Anethum graveolens* • FAMILY NAME: *Umbelliferae*

OTHER NAMES: *dill seed, garden dill;*
FR. *aneth;* G. *Dill;* SP. *eneldo;* IT. *aneto*

The name is believed to come from an ancient Norse word 'dilla' meaning to lull, refer-ring to the calming effect an infusion of dill has on crying babies. Dill was widely used in Greek and Roman times; in the Middle Ages it was thought to have magical properties and was used in witchcraft, love potions and as an aphrodisiac.

fresh dill

CULTIVATION

Native to Southern Europe and West-ern Asia, dill grows wild in Spain, Portugal and Italy. It thrives in warmer regions of the Northern hemisphere and is particularly associated with Scandinavian cuisine. It is now grown in India and North and South America as a commercial crop and much of this is used to obtain dillweed oil. The plant is an annual of the parsley family and it grows to about 1.2 metres/4 feet. It has feathery, fern-like leaves with yellow flowers. The oval seeds are unusually convex on one side, with three ridges, and flat on the reverse, with two ridges.

AROMA AND FLAVOUR

Dill has a sweet and aromatic bouquet; the taste has a hint of caraway and is slightly, but by no means unpleasantly, bitter. Buy the whole seeds, which have a long shelf life if kept away from strong light. Indian or Japanese dill is thinner and paler than its Western counterpart.

CULINARY USE

Dill seeds are invariably found in jars of pickled cucumbers. Crushed dill seeds marry well with almost all fish dishes: add a little to a creamy sauce for a fish pie, or stir some into thick yogurt with a teaspoon of chopped chives and serve as a sauce with grilled fresh salmon or cod fillet. Dill is also good with egg dishes such as egg may-onnaise. Use dill vinegar or crushed seeds to make a dressing for a mixed seafood salad, coleslaw or potato salad, adding a few feathery leaves as a garnish. Flavour home-made bread with dill to serve with veg-etable soups, such as carrot or tomato soup.

MEDICINAL AND OTHER USE

As well as its power to soothe crying babies, dill is used widely as a treatment for stomach and digestive troubles, and to cure insomnia and hiccups. The Ancient Greeks believed that carrying dill in the left hand could prevent epilepsy.

COOKING TIP

Gravadlax (Scandinavian marinated salmon) can be made successfully using crushed dill seeds when dill leaves are unavailable.

PREPARATION TIP

Dill vinegar is easy to make at home.

Place 2 tbsp dill seeds in a small preserving jar. Top up with white wine vinegar and close the lid. Leave the vinegar in a cool dark place for 2-3 weeks, then strain and use in salad dressings and sauces.

Indian or Japanese dill seed

dill seed

dried dill

Celery

BOTANICAL NAME: *Apium graveolens* • FAMILY NAME: *Umbelliferae*

FR. *céléri;* G. *Stangensellerie;* SP. *apio;* IT. *sedano*

celery sticks

ground celery seeds

Celery was developed by Italian gardeners in the 17th century from the wild celery of the European salt marshes, a plant known as smallage. Celery seeds are small and grey-brown in colour, with fine ridges.

CULTIVATION

Celery is a herbaceous biennial plant of the carrot, parsley and caraway family which throws up a flower head in the second year producing masses of seeds. Like caraway, the fruit of the celery plant consists of two joined carpels, which divide into single seeds when harvested.

AROMA AND FLAVOUR

Celery seeds should be used with discretion as they have a fairly strong, and sometimes rather bitter, flavour. There is no mistaking their distinctive, celery aroma.

CULINARY USE

Whole celery seeds can be added to bread dough or when making cheese biscuits, and both may be served with soups and savoury dishes. A few seeds can be sprinkled over lightly boiled carrots, grilled tomatoes or salads and they are especially complementary to egg and fish dishes. Celery salt and celery pepper are both made by grinding the seeds with either salt or peppercorns in the required proportions. Use these seasonings judiciously as their flavours are strong. Celery salt or pepper is best made when required.

MEDICINAL AND OTHER USE

The oil from the seeds is used medically to treat asthma, flatulence and bronchitic conditions.

celery seeds

celery leaves

> ### COOKING TIPS
>
> *Always buy whole seeds, rather than ready ground seeds, and crush them just before use if necessary.*
> *To make a 'pick-me-up' sprinkle celery seeds into a glass of tomato juice, chilled with plenty of crushed ice.*

Horseradish

BOTANICAL NAME: *Armoracia rusticana, syn Cochlearia armoracia,*
Armoracia lapathifolia • FAMILY NAME: *Cruciferae*

FR. *cranson de Bretagne, raifort;* G. *Meerrettich;*
SP. *rábano picante;* IT. *rafano*

Horseradish has been used in the kitchens of
Europe since the Middle Ages. It is said to
have been one of the bitter herbs eaten by
the Jews at Passover.

powdered wasabi

wasabi paste

dried
horseradish

CULTIVATION

Horseradish is a perennial, a
member of the mustard and,
curiously, the wallflower family.
The plant has large, long leaves with
pronounced pale veins. It grows best in
cool to moderate
climates, flourish-
ing in Northern
and South-eastern
Europe and in
Scan-dinavia. Horse-
radish is an invasive
plant and, if you do not
take care to limit its
growth, it will take over
like a weed. Root sec-
tions are planted in the spring and harvested in autumn. The tubers can be
stored for the winter, in the same way as
potatoes, in a covering of sand.

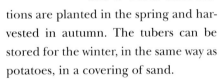

horseradish
cream

horseradish
relish

fresh
horseradish

AROMA AND FLAVOUR

Horseradish is a long, rough, tapering
root, not unlike a parsnip, with rings,
and tiny roots sprouting from the main
root. Its powerful smell and fiery taste
put even mustard in the shade. The
taste is very strong, very hot
and very sharp.

horseradish
sauce

CULINARY USE

There are no half measures
associated with horseradish: it
is a potent gastric stimulant and
is the perfect accompaniment for
rich or rather fatty foods. It is richer

WASABI

This is the Japanese answer to horse-
radish. Wasabi japonica by botanical
name, is also known as the mountain
hollyhock. It is cultivated near fast-
moving mountain streams. The peeled
root reveals delicate, apple-green flesh,
which is either grated or dried and pow-
dered. The dried powder is made into a
cream with a little soy sauce or water.

in Vitamin C than lemons or
oranges. To prepare fresh horseradish, peel only the amount
needed and grate, or shred in
a food processor. Once grated,
it quickly loses its pungency, so
prepare in small quantities. Horseradish sauce with a creamy consistency varies in strength according to
brand. Creamed horseradish, which is
milder, can be used for the same pur-
poses, as an accompaniment to beef,
steaks and venison or served with a
strong fish like mackerel, tuna or
smoked trout.

STORAGE

To store horseradish, brush excess soil
or dirt off the dry root, then wrap it in a
paper bag (not polythene) and place in
the vegetable box in the fridge; it can
also be frozen.

Annatto

BOTANICAL NAME: *Bixa orellana* • FAMILY NAME: *Bixaceae*

OTHER NAMES: *achiote, anatta, annotto;* FR. *roucou, rocou;* G. *Annatto;* SP. *achiote achote;* IT. *anotto,* DU. *rocou;* FIL. *achuete*

annatto seeds

The shrub, indigenous to both the Caribbean and tropical America, has heart-shaped, glossy leaves and spectacular, pink, rose-like flowers, which made it a favourite in colonial gardens, where it was planted to form a superior hedge. The plant produces a heart-shaped fruit capsule resembling a beech seed pod, with lots of spiky hairs that are its in-built protection from foraging animals. When ripe, the capsule splits exactly in half to reveal upwards of fifty seeds in a pulp. The Mayan Indians of Central America used the dye from the seeds, often described as 'the colour of fire', as war paint.

AROMA AND FLAVOUR

Choose brick-red, triangular annatto seeds for a rich colour, and for their slightly peppery flavour and bouquet, with just a hint of nutmeg in their aroma.

CULINARY USE

The seeds are washed and dried separately from the pulp for culinary use. An orange food colouring, made from the husk, is used as a colouring agent in dairy produce, such as Edam, Munster, Red Leicester and Red Cheshire cheeses. The famous Jamaican dish of salt cod and ackee is served in a vivid sauce, coloured with annatto. The Spanish introduced the spice to the Filipinos and it is used widely in their cuisine.

COOKING TIPS

The seeds can be infused in hot water until the colour is as intense as required. The water can be added to rice dishes and used as a substitute for saffron – but it lacks the beautiful aroma associated with saffron.

PREPARATION TIP

Annatto seeds impart a wonderful colour to oil when fried for a few minutes, but have a lid ready to cover the pan as they splutter and jump out when hot.

Heat a little oil in a heavy-based saucepan, add the seeds and shake the pan over the heat for a few minutes.

Cool and strain the oil, which will keep indefinitely.

MEDICINAL AND OTHER USE

Annatto was once widely used in medicines, and in Africa it is used to control fevers and dysentery; however, it is now used principally as a dye. The pulp surrounding the seeds is the main commercial source of ox-blood red dye used in textile manufacture. The ripe seeds are soaked in water, the dye settles and it is then dried into cakes. As a natural colouring, annatto is also quite safe when used in cosmetics or in food. In India the pulp is used as an insect repellent.

Red Leicester cheese

Mustard

BOTANICAL NAME: *Brassica alba, B. juncea, B. nigra,*
syn Sinapsis alba • FAMILY NAME: *Cruciferae*

WHITE OR YELLOW MUSTARD (USA)

> FR. *moutarde blanche;* G. *senf, weisser senf;*
> SP. *mostaza silvestre;* IT. *senape bianca, mostarda*

BLACK OR BROWN MUSTARD (UK)

> FR. *moutarde noire;* G. *schwarzer senf;*
> SP. *mostaza negra;* IT. *senapa nera*

BROWN OR INDIAN MUSTARD

> FR. *moutarde de Chine;* G. *Indischer senf;*
> SP. *mostaza India;* IT. *senape Indiana*

**English
mustard powder**

Mustard has featured in history and literature since early times. Pythagoras suggested a mustard paste as a treatment for scorpion stings, and Hippocrates, the father of medicine, recommended mustard for both internal and external use. Darius III of Persia was said to have sent Alexander the Great a bag of sesame seeds to indicate the numbers in his army and Alexander responded by sending mustard seeds to represent not only numbers but strength.

Mustard is mentioned many times in the Bible. From the New Testament: 'Another parable put he forth unto them saying, The kingdom of heaven is like to a grain of mustard seed, which a man took, and sowed in his field: Which indeed is the least of all seeds: but when it is grown, it is the greatest among herbs, and becometh a tree, so that the birds of the air come and lodge in the branches thereof'. (Matthew 13:31-32)

During the Middle Ages, mustard was introduced into Spain by Arab traders, and it was soon carried throughout Europe. The French mustard industry, in particular, has an impressive record, with Dijon, Meaux and Bordeaux all associated with mustard production and Dijon being referred to as the mustard capital of the world.

The word mustard comes from the Latin *mustum* or *must,* the name for the grape juice used to mix the ground seeds to a paste, which was known as *mustum ardens,* meaning the burning paste. There are three different types of mustard seed: white (alba), brown (juncea) and black (nigra). These are all part of the family of cruciferae (cross bearer) plants, which produce flowers in the shape of a cross.

English mustard

CULTIVATION

White mustard seeds are, in fact, sand or honey coloured and are slightly larger than the other two varieties. The pale outer husk is removed before the seeds are used. This is the type of mustard grown in mixed punnets of mustard and cress, though rape seed is sometimes subsituted for the mustard seed. *Brassica alba* is a native of the Mediterranean but it now grows throughout Europe and North America. It is a hairy annual plant growing to nearly 0.6 metres/2 feet. The bright yellow flowers form seed pods, which grow horizontally, each holding about six seeds.

Black mustard seeds *(Brassica nigra)* have been superseded in popularity by the brown seed for a very good reason: the black mustard seed plant grows tall and drops its seeds very easily when ripe. This makes harvesting by machine difficult so the plant is now grown only where harvesting by hand is the norm. The plant grows to over 0.9 metres/3 feet tall; its bright yellow flowers are smaller than those of the white mustard plant and it forms erect pods close to the central stem, each containing twelve seeds.

Brown mustard seeds (*Brassica juncea*) have largely replaced the black seeds, though they are not as intensively pungent as the black seeds. Their colour varies from light to darker brown. Native to, and grown throughout, India, the plant produces flowers, which are a pale yellow, and seed pods, which are larger than those on the other mustard plants.

brown mustard seeds

black mustard seeds

white mustard seeds

crushed yellow mustard

yellow mustard seeds

mustard oil

AROMA AND FLAVOUR

Mustard seeds have little or no smell. The hot taste which gives mustard its 'bite' is released only when the seeds are crushed and mixed with water. Crushing and moistening the mustard, or mixing powdered mustard with water, activates an enzyme present in the seeds, and it reacts with other natural constituents to develop the essential oil, which gives the characteristic taste. The white seeds have an initial sweetness with a mild taste. Brown seeds have an initial bitterness to their flavour, from the outer husk, and then the sharp biting flavour comes through; black seeds share these same characteristics: they are sharp, biting and pungent.

PREPARATION TIPS

It is recommended that English mustard powder is mixed 10 minutes before it is required to allow the clean pungent flavours to develop. The mustard loses its pungency in a few hours, so fresh mustard should be made daily or as required. For fiery results, mix mustard powder with cold liquids, never with boiling water or vinegar, as both kill the enzyme that gives the condiment its hot flavour, resulting in a mild, but bitter, mustard. Similarly when mustard powder is to be added to hot dishes such as sauces and stews, stir it in at the end of the cooking and heat gently on the lowest heat to retain its bite.

To make mustard, mix mustard powder with warm water, milk or beer.

French mustard

Dijon grey mustard

COOKING TIP

To bring out the flavour of mustard seeds, heat a little ghee or oil in a wide pan. Add the seeds and shake the pan over the heat, stirring occasionally, until the seeds start to change colour.

Have a pan lid ready to prevent the mustard seeds popping out of the pan.

CULINARY USE

Mustard is an indispensable ingredient in cooking: the different whole seeds, powdered or ground seeds, prepared pastes and oil are all used. The white seeds are used in pickling, and the brown seeds are used throughout India in curry powders and in spiced ghee (baghar or tadka). The seeds are cooked in hot oil until they pop and turn grey and are then stirred into a variety of vegetable or dhal dishes. Whenever frying mustard seeds, always have a lid ready for when they start to pop, to prevent them from flying out of the pan. Mustard oil, available in Asian and Oriental stores, is used in many Indian recipes. Mustard is used in salad dressings and mayonnaise, where it helps the emulsification of the egg yolk and the oil. It is also added to cheese sauce, Welsh rarebit and sauces for cabbage or cauliflower, Jerusalem artichokes or leeks.

MEDICINAL AND OTHER USE

A few spoonfuls of mustard powder in a footbath or bath are said to relieve and soothe muscular aches and pains. Mustard is a stimulant and it is used to relieve respiratory complaints and rheumatism. It also stimulates the kidneys. Mustard used to be given as a laxative and emetic (to induce vomiting). A gargle of mustard seed in hot water is helpful in the relief of sore throats and bronchitis.

CLASSIC MUSTARDS OF THE WORLD

English Mustard: This hot mustard is made from yellow mustard and is sometimes mixed with wheat flour, for bulk, and turmeric, for colour.

American Mustard: The obligatory accompaniment to the all-American hot dog, this is made from mild white mustard seeds, vinegar, sugar, spices and turmeric. Mild with a hint of sweetness.

German Mustard: This is a smooth, dark mustard made from black seeds and vinegar to give a sweet and sour flavour with just a hint of sharpness, which complements the huge range of German sausages. There are also extra-strong German mustards.

Dijon Mustard: Traditionally prepared from only black seeds, but Dijon mustard is now made from brown seeds. The seed husks are removed, resulting in a mustard with a pale blond colour. The mustard is blended with wine or verjuice (the sour juice from unripe grapes or wild apples), salt and spices. This is the classic French mustard, which is eaten with steaks and grills. It is smooth, salty and sharp with a good mustardy flavour.

Bordeaux Mustard: Referred to as French mustard, this is darker than Dijon mustard. It is also made from a blend of

tarragon mustard

provençale mustard

red grape mustard

honeycup mustard

old-style grey mustard

black and brown seeds and the husks are retained, which results in the darker colour. Bordeaux mustard is mixed with vinegar and sugar, plenty of tarragon, plus other herbs and spices to give a mild sweet-sour taste, which goes best with cold meats and sausages.

Meaux Mustard: For this mustard, the black seeds are part crushed and part ground to give the typical crunchy texture. Mixed with vinegar and spices, this mustard is medium to hot in flavour with an interesting spiciness; it is good with cold meats, meat pies or sausages. Meaux mustard is often sold in stoneware jars with a sealed cork stopper.

Other Mustards: There are dozens of different mustards, such as French Maille mustard, from a company established in 1747, and Provençal mustard, which is flavoured with garlic and red peppers. Tarragon, tomato, basil and honey are all examples of ingredients used to flavour mustard; for a touch of luxury, there is even a smooth, mild mustard blended with champagne.

COOKING TIP

To sprout mustard seeds, put about 2 tbsp of the seeds in a muslin-covered glass jar. Rinse and drain the seeds once or twice a day until they sprout.

mild wholegrain mustard

mustard seed sprouts

American mustard

German mustard

house neri karashi

Capers

BOTANICAL NAME: *Capparis rupestris, of which there are two types:*
C. spinos (spiny), C. inermis (no spines) • FAMILY NAME: *Capparidaceae*

caper berries

Capers are the flower buds of a low-growing bush with round, fairly thick leaves, which is easily identified by its beautiful pink, dog-rose-type flowers that have long tassels of purple stamens. The flowers open in the morning and are dead by midday. The flower buds have been used since biblical times.

nasturtium seeds

CULTIVATION

Capers grow in profusion all around the Mediterranean, with its warm dry climate. They have to be picked by hand, which is labour intensive and makes them expensive. The bushes are checked each morning for small hard buds that are just at the right stage for harvesting. The capers are washed and allowed to wilt for a day in the sun before being put into jars and covered with salted wine vinegar, brine or olive oil. Alternatively they can be preserved in salt alone.

AROMA AND FLAVOUR

Some would describe the taste of the pickled caper as like goat's milk cheese, with sour and salt flavours coming through when the bud is bitten.

CULINARY USE

Chopped capers are included in a huge range of classic sauces, including tartare, rémoulade and ravigote sauces, and Italian tonnato sauce, used in the famous dish of cold braised veal, Vitello Tonnato. In Britain, hot caper sauce is traditionally served with boiled mutton, but try it with salmon or pan-fried or grilled fish with the addition of a little grated lemon rind to complement the distinctive flavour.

Capers are widely used in other areas of Italian cooking, for example as a flavouring in antipasti salads and as a topping on pizza. They also feature in fish and vegetable dishes from Northern and Eastern Europe.

dry-salted capers

STORAGE

Capers should always be submerged in their pickling medium, otherwise they will develop an off-flavour.

nasturtium flowers and leaves

capers in brine

Chillies

BOTANICAL NAME: *Capsicum annuum or C. frutescens*
FAMILY NAME: *Solanaceae*

OTHER NAMES: *chilli pepper, chili;* FR. *piment, piment fort, piment rouge;* G. *roter Pfeffer, spanischer Pfeffer;* SP. *chile;* IT. *peperoncino*

Chilli is the most popular spice and throughout history: wherever it was used it transformed the previously bland cuisine. Latin American, Asian, African, Caribbean and certain regional Oriental cuisines make extensive use of this spice. The name chilli is believed to be derived from an ancient Indian word txile. *Chillies are native to Mexico. Evidence of chilli peppers is known from burial sites in pre-Colombian times in Peru. Christopher Columbus, who was searching the New World for pepper* (Piper nigrum), *came across these fruits, which, he discovered, were even hotter than peppercorns. He carried his prize to Europe and from there to Africa, India and the East where chilli became an integral part of each cuisine. The long shelf life of the seeds (it can be 2-3 years) was a bonus in the days of sea travel.*

small green chillies

caribe chillies

bird's eye chillies

Chillies have a chemical effect on our bodies which some of us enjoy more than others. Once you have got over the stage where the slightest hint of chilli makes you cry and splutter, you may find that the flavour becomes pleasurable and even addictive. Chillies are rich in Vitamin C, they stimulate the appetite and cool the body, especially in hot climates, by making the person sweat. The cooling effect also creates a feeling of calm and benignity. To relieve the burning sensation in the mouth, drink yogurt or milk, not water or beer.

CULTIVATION

Chillies are part of the potato, tomato, aubergine and nightshade family of plants. The chilli family is a minefield: there are at least 150 different types, so it is wise to assume that any unfamiliar chilli is HOT! The plant, which is bush-like, grows up to about 0.6 metres/2 feet and bears white flowers that produce fruits in a variety of sizes and shapes. Some chillies look like stout fingers (such as the cayenne),

others are tiny (like the bird's eye chilli, which is very tiny, explosive and often used in Thai cooking), and some look deceptively like mini sweet peppers (for example, habanero, which is the hottest). The plants grow at altitudes from sea level to 1,800 metres/ 6,000 feet in the tropics. Their pungency is influenced by several factors, such as high night temperatures and drought or over-watering. Green chillies are immature fruits and red chillies have been allowed to ripen for a further 4 weeks. Ripened chillies can also be orange-yellow, purple, dark brown or black.

India is the largest producer and exporter of chillies, with a significant part of the total crop used for home consumption. Travellers in Rajasthan and the south of India marvel at the acres of chillies, laid out to dry like a huge red carpet stretching as far as the eye can see.

Thailand, Mexico, Japan, Turkey, Nigeria, Ethiopia, Uganda, Kenya and Tanzania are also major producers, and they export chillies to other countries around the world.

The most common Mexican chillies, used in the cuisine to make fiery salsas, bean, fish and poultry dishes, are fresh green serrano, jalapeño and poblano chillies.

AROMA AND FLAVOUR

The characteristic pungency of chillies is caused by the presence of capsaicin. Research has indicated that the components of capsaicin (capsaicinoids) promote different taste sensations when eaten, giving either a short fiery flavour or lingering hot taste. The hotness is said not to come from the seeds but rather the placenta. This is the pithy white part of the fruit to which the seeds are attached, and it contains the most capsaicin so removal of both seeds and placenta should reduce the pungency of chillies, if required.

The heat of chillies is measured in Scoville units, ranging from 0 (for sweet bell peppers) to 300,000 (for the habanero). To provide a simple guide, the scale has been reduced to 0-10, with the habaneros having a scorching rating of 10.

CULINARY USE

The chilli flavour revolutionized the cooking of tropical countries with bland staple foods, like cassava in South America, West and East Africa; rice in India and South-east Asia; and beans in Mexico and the Southern States of America. Famous Mexican moles, chilli con carne and Tex-mex foods make extensive use of chillies. Curries from Thailand and Malaysia, and Indonesian sambals and satays all rely on chillies for their characteristic flavours. Many Szechuan dishes depend on the chilli flavour. Countries which do not use chillies as extensively in everyday dishes also depend on their heat for certain traditional preparations; for example, piquant pasta dishes from Italy use fresh and dried chillies, and prudent use of chillies is made in many of the pickles, relishes and cooked chutneys of the more Northern European countries.

FRESH CHILLIES

Fresh chillies are available almost everywhere, from independent greengrocers to Oriental stores and supermarkets. It is difficult to be specific about their heat: even fruits from the same plant can vary in strength.

Anaheim: These are about 10 cm/4 in long, red or green and mild to medium in flavour.

PREPARATION TIPS FOR FRESH CHILLIES

Cut away and discard the stalk end. Holding the chilli under cold running water to prevent the oils from affecting your eyes and throat, slit it from the stalk end to the tip. Scrape out the placenta and seeds. Afterwards, wash your hands, knife and chopping board thoroughly to clean off the oils. Do not rub your eyes or lips – even after washing your hands. Those with sensitive skin should wear rubber gloves when preparing chillies.

cayenne chillies

anaheim chilli

serrano chillies

small red chillies

Cayenne: Sometimes called finger chill-ies, these are slimmer than anaheim chillies, they are always red and hot.

Serrano: Slightly chunky, these red or green chillies can be hot or slightly milder.

Bird's Eye: These chillies are so hot that they taste explosive to the uniniti-ated. They can be green, red or orange in colour.

DRIED MEXICAN CHILLIES

New Mexico Red: HEATSCALE 2-4 This is a large red chilli with a clean heat and earthy, fruity flavour. Great for red sauces.

Ancho or Dried Poblano: HEATSCALE 3 Sweet, fruity and mild, these can be stuffed, cut into strips or added to mole sauces (sauces enriched with bitter chocolate or cocoa).

Guajillo: HEATSCALE 3 These are mild, with a green-tea flavour. Used in many classic salsas.

Mulato: HEATSCALE 3 Similar to ancho, but with a more smoked taste, and a hint of liquorice flavour. These can be stuffed, cut into strips or used in Mexi-can mole sauces.

Pasado: HEATSCALE 3 This crisp, roasted, peeled chilli has a toasted flavour com-bined with apple, celery and citrus flavours. Use in soups and stews.

Cascabel or Little Rattle: HEATSCALE 4 Nutty and woody in flavour, with a medium 'rounded' heat, these thick-fleshed chillies are great in sauces, soups, stews and salsas.

Pasilla or Little Raisin: HEATSCALE 4 These medium-hot chillies taste of berries and liquorice. Good with seafood and in mole sauces.

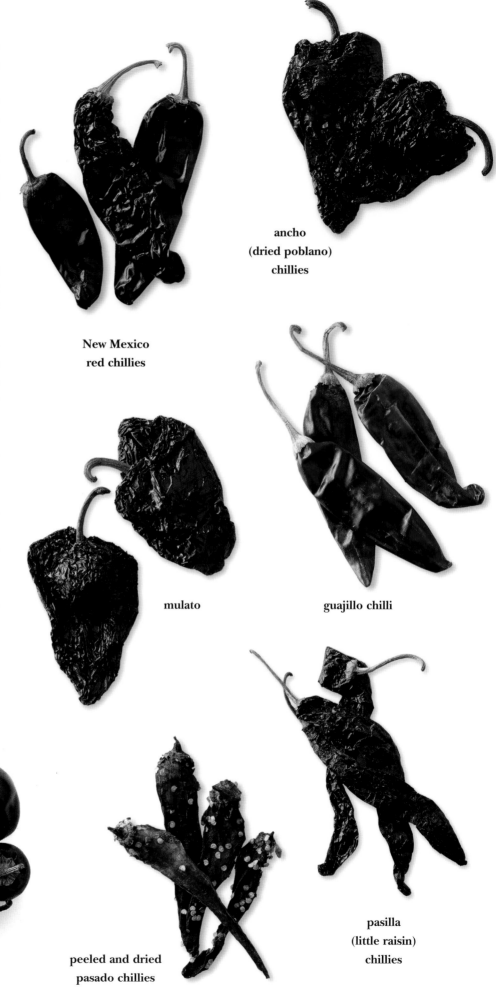

ancho
(dried poblano)
chillies

New Mexico
red chillies

mulato

guajillo chilli

cascabel
(little rattle)
chillies

peeled and dried
pasado chillies

pasilla
(little raisin)
chillies

guindilla chillies

chipotle chillies

nyora chillies

habanero chillies

arbol chillies

pequin chillies

bird's eye chillies

crushed caribe chillies

Chipotle or Smoked Jalapeño: HEATSCALE 6 This chilli is smoky and nutty in flavour, and fairly hot.

Tepin or Flea Chilli: HEATSCALE 8 This small, hand-picked chilli has a searing heat and it tastes of corn and nuts. Crush the chilli over food or use it to flavour bottles of vinegar or oils.

Habanero: HEATSCALE 10 With intense aroma and fiery taste, these are excellent in condiments, fish stews, curries and salsas.

DRIED SMOKED SPANISH CHILLIES

Dried, mild-smoked chillies are widely used in Spanish cooking.

Choricero: HEATSCALE 0-1 An extremely sweet and mild Spanish chilli, large enough to stuff or use to make well-flavoured sauces, soups and stews.

Nyora: HEATSCALE 1-2 A dried Spanish chilli with a sweet, fruity flavour; great for mild salsas, soups and stews.

Guindilla: HEATSCALE 3 A medium-hot Spanish chilli with a sweet flavour, this adds 'zip' to fish.

cherry chillies

Madras chillies

kashmiri chillies

PREPARATION TIPS FOR DRIED CHILLIES

Dried chillies can be soaked, then cut into thin strips and added to stir-fries, soups or other dishes. The strips can also be stored in a jar, covered with olive oil; herbs may be added to flavour the chilli strips.

To make chilli purée, remove the stem and seeds. Soak the chillies in boiling water for 20 minutes, then purée them with some of the soaking liquid. Sieve the purée to make a smooth sauce. Add to taste when cooking. Purées can be stored in a covered jar in the fridge for up to a week or frozen for up to a year.

COOKING TIPS FOR DRIED CHILLIES

To make chilli vinegar, fill a bottle with chillies, top up with vinegar and leave for two weeks before using.

Dry-roasting heightens the flavour of chillies. Heat a heavy frying pan without adding oil. Press the chillies on to the surface of the pan to roast them. Do not allow the chillies to burn, or their flavour will be bitter. When roasted, remove the chillies from the pan and grind them.

Larger, thick-fleshed and thin-skinned dried chillies (such as anchos or mulatos) can be stuffed with meat, rice or vegetable fillings. Make a small lengthways split in the chilli and remove the seeds. Leave the stem intact. Soak the chilli, then drain and pat it dry on kitchen paper. Stuff carefully and bake until heated through.

CHILLI PRODUCTS
Cayenne Pepper

This is a very fine ground powder from the *Capsicum frutescens* variety of chilli. The placenta and seeds are included in the powder, making it very hot, so it must be used judiciously. This is named on account of its origins in the Cayenne region of French Guyana but the chillies used in its preparation now come from India, Japan and East Africa. Cayenne is widely used as a seasoning (in tiny amounts), for example in savoury biscuits and cheese and egg dishes, and it is also added to some curries.

cayenne pepper

pickled sweet cherry peppers

pickled hot chilli peppers

pickled jalepeño peppers

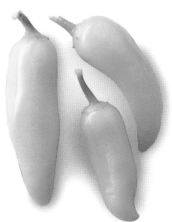

pickled hot banana wax peppers

chilli
powder

ancho
powder

pimenton
de la vera

chimayo
powder

pasilla
powder

mulato powder

hot
chilli paste

Chilli Powder

Milder than cayenne pepper and more coarsely ground, this is prepared from a variety of mild to hot chillies. Check the ingredients list, as some chilli powders (especially those of American type) contain a variety of other flavours, such as garlic, onion, cumin and oregano. They are added for convenience for use in chilli con carne. If the chilli powder is dark in colour, it may contain the rich-rust-coloured ancho chilli.

For best results make your own chilli powder. Deseed dried chillies, then dry-fry them and grind them to the required fineness.

Chilli Sauce

Tabasco sauce is a North American seasoning made from extremely hot tabasco or cone chillies, which are mixed with salt and vinegar and then matured in white oak casks for several years. Many of the islands of the Caribbean have their own style of chilli sauce. Most are, like Tabasco, made from steeping the chillies in vinegar and all are very hot indeed. Chilli sauces are widely used in small quantities as a general seasoning. Tabasco is served with tomato juice and used to flavour Bloody Mary cocktails.

Chilli Paste

Ready-made chilli paste is sold in small jars. However, it is easy to make at home. Simply seed fresh chillies, then purée them in a food processor to make a smooth paste. An onion can be added to the processor to add bulk to the paste. Store small amounts in the fridge for up to 1 week, or spoon into small containers, cover and freeze for up to 6 months.

Crushed Chillies

These dried chilli flakes contain both the flesh and seeds from red chillies and can be used in place of some or all of the chilli powder in a dish.

crushed
chillies

chilli sauce

West Indian hot
pepper sauce

Tabasco sauce

green
jalapeño
sauce

chilli oil

Paprika

BOTANICAL NAME: *Capsicum annuum* • FAMILY NAME: *Solanaceae*

OTHER NAMES: *Hungarian pepper, sweet paprika, rose paprika, pimento pepper;* FR. *piment;* G. *Paprika;* SP. *pimentón, pimento colorado;* IT. *paprica*

Hungarian paprika

Spanish paprika

A fine powder made from specially mild varieties of pepper, the fruit from the Capsicum annuum, *which were originally taken to Hungary by the Turks. The core and seeds are removed, then the flesh is dried and powdered, which results in the characteristic rich red colour. Paprika is mild to pungent and sweet with a hint of bitterness: always check the label, which will give a guide to its pungency.*

Hungarians have adopted this as their national spice, using it generously in their famous goulashes, stews and chicken dishes. Paprika also has an affinity with Spanish and Portuguese cuisines. Crops are grown in Andalucía and Extremadura in Spain, and in Portugal. About half the Spanish crop, which can often be quite pungent, is exported to the USA.

If you find the true fresh paprika peppers, which are very like ordinary or sweet red peppers, but more pointed, try stuffing them with minced lamb seasoned with oregano or thyme, cooked in a tomato sauce – they are excellent.

Papaya Seeds

BOTANICAL NAME: *Carica papaya, syn Papaya carica*
FAMILY NAME: *Caricaceae*

OTHER NAMES: *pawpaw, papaw;* FR. *papaye;* G. *Melonenbaum Papaia;* SP. *papaya;* IT. *papaia*

The jet-black or grey-black seeds from papaya look like giant caviar when the fruit is first cut open. The colour of the seeds depends on the tree; white seeds indicate an unripe fruit. The tree now grows in most tropical and sub-tropical countries worldwide.

fresh papaya

CULTIVATION

The tree, a fast-growing herbaceous perennial, is found in the tropics, but not above 1,500 metres/5,000 feet. The stem or trunk is straight, with a cluster of large, maple-shaped leaves on top. The fruits, which are called berries, can weigh up to 9 kg/20 lb each. They are ovoid in shape and are attached to the trunk just under the leaves. The seeds are enclosed in the hollow centre of the fruit, arranged in five rows.

AROMA AND FLAVOUR

Papaya seeds are slightly aromatic when fresh but their aroma is less pronounced as they dry. Fresh seeds have a sparky taste, strongly resembling that of mustard and cress. They can be used fresh or allowed to dry in the sun, when their smell and taste are somewhat diminished.

CULINARY USE

The plant sap, which is tapped from the trees like rubber, is rich in the enzyme papain which is an efficient meat ten-

crushed papaya seeds

fresh papaya seeds

derizer of commercial value. Both fruit and seeds also contain papain. Rub tough meat with the seeds and the skin of the fruit, or wrap it in papaya leaves (if available) and leave to marinate for several hours. Remove the papaya leaf wrapping before cooking. Crushed papaya seeds can be added to minced meat for koftas (spicy meatballs) or to a marinade for meat. Some of the pounded flesh of the fruit can also be added. When cooked, the meat will be tender, with an interesting, peppery flavour.

Crushed papaya seeds can be added to salad dressings or sauces to serve with fish. They also add texture and flavour to a fruit salad. The fresh fruit can be served in slim wedges with the seeds still intact. Next time you cut a papaya, remember the many interesting ways in which the seeds can be used before you discard them.

MEDICINAL AND OTHER USE

In India, papaya seeds are chewed to freshen the breath, and they are widely used as pessaries, also as a medicine for flatulence and piles. Australian aborigines have a more romantic approach to the seeds, and consider them to be of value as an aphrodisiac.

Ajowan

BOTANICAL NAME: *Carum ajowan, Ptychotis ajowan, Carum copticum* • FAMILY NAME: *Umbelliferae*

OTHER NAMES: *carom, bishop's weed, ajwain, omum, ajwan;* FR. *ajowan;* G. *Ajowan;* SP. *ajowan;* IT. *ajowan;* ETH. *cumin*

The celery-type, striped seeds (similar to caraway and cumin seeds in appearance) are used as the spice. They are sold whole – when crushed, they have a rather strong and distinctive thyme-like bouquet; indeed, they can be used as a substitute for thyme, but add them sparingly as they are stronger in flavour than thyme. In some Indian recipes ajowan is referred to as lovage.

Bombay mix

CULTIVATION

Part of the *Umbelliferae* family, ajowan (pronounced aj'owen) looks like wild parsley. A native Indian plant, and usually a cool-weather crop, it is also grown in Pakistan, Afghanistan, Iran and Egypt. It is grown mainly for export, for the extraction of its oil, which contains a high percentage of thymol.

PREPARATION TIP

Before using ajowan seeds, crush them to release the aroma by rubbing between your finger tips.

CULINARY USE

Ajowan is particularly popular in savoury Indian recipes: savoury pastries, snacks (including Bombay mix) and breads (especially parathas), bean and pulse recipes, all of which illustrates the affinity ajowan has for starchy foods. Ajowan can be crushed in the hand, when it releases a powerful thyme aroma and flavour.

MEDICINAL AND OTHER USE

The medicinal properties of ajowan are numerous. In India, the seeds are used to ease asthma and indigestion. A liquid product of ajowan is widely used to treat diarrhoea and wind; ajowan seeds are popular in recipes for beans and lentils due to their properties in relieving flatulence. Its thymol content makes ajowan a potent fungicide.

ajowan seeds

ground ajowan

Caraway

BOTANICAL NAME: *Carum carvi*
FAMILY NAME: *Umbelliferae*

**caraway
seeds**

OTHER NAMES: *caraway fruit or seed, carvies (Scottish),
wild cumin, Roman cumin, Persian caraway;* FR. *carvi,
graines de carvi;* G. *Cumich, Kümmel;* SP. *alcaravea;*
IT. *caro, carvi;* AR. *karawya*

*This is one of the world's oldest culinary spices, with evidence
of seeds found in the remains of food from the Mesolithic age,
about 5,000 years ago. Caraway was used to flavour bread
eaten by Roman soldiers and its popularity spread as their
empire grew. The Ancient Egyptians always placed a container
of caraway in tombs to ward off evil spirits. It was later considered
to be an important ingredient in love potions, to prevent fickleness.
In 16th-century Britain, caraway was used in breads, pastries
and cakes.*

**ground
caraway**

CULTIVATION

A member of the parsley family, caraway has feathery leaves. It grows to
about 0.6 metres/2 feet in height and
blooms every two years to produce
large creamy flowers. Caraway is
widely grown in Europe, but principally in Holland, where this hollow-
stemmed biennial thrives particularly
well in the heavy clay soil and humid
conditions. The oil extracted from
Dutch caraway is said to be superior
because the crops are grown quite
close to the sea. It is also grown in
Russia and India.

Caraway seeds are mericarps, that
is, they split into two on harvesting.
Each single seed, or carpel, is slightly
crescent shaped and pale to dark
brown, with five ribs. They are best
harvested early in the morning when
the seeds are less likely to fall off the
flower head. The cut plants are
stacked to dry and ripen for over a
week and then the seeds are threshed.

AROMA AND FLAVOUR

Caraway seeds have a warm, sweet and
slightly peppery aroma. Their distinct
flavour has a hint of fennel or aniseed.

Caraway seeds have a slight eucalyptus-
like tang to their flavour and are
chewed to sweeten the breath.

CULINARY USE

Caraway is used extensively in Eastern
European, German and Austrian cooking. It features in savoury, as well as
sweet, dishes, including sauerkraut,
cabbage soups, coleslaw, goulash,
potato- and cheese-based dishes. Caraway flavours breads, especially rye
bread, cakes, including old-fashioned
British seed cake, and biscuits. Caraway
seed cake was traditionally baked by
farmers' wives to celebrate the end of
planting and distributed among the
farm workers. Caraway has also long
been used to flavour cheese, with
medieval recipes for caraway-
flavoured Dutch cheese still in
use today. In Alsace, Munster cheese is always served
with a saucer of caraway
seeds to sprinkle on to slices
before eating – a delicious combination of flavours.

Sausages and other meat preparations are seasoned with caraway. The
leaves can be snipped into salads or

used as a garnish.
The carrot-shaped
root has the same
flavour as the
seeds and it can
be cooked in the same
way as parsnips, either by
baking or boiling.

Caraway is also a vital ingredient
in the liqueur Kümmel, in Aquavit,
a favourite tipple of the Scandina-
vians, and as an ingredient in gin
and schnapps. To round off a
meal, the seeds can be infused in
water which is just off the boil and
served as a tisane.

MEDICINAL AND OTHER USE

Oil of caraway was recommended as
a tonic for pale girls by Dioscorides, a
Greek physician in the 1st century: it
was rubbed into the skin to improve
the complexion. In more recent times,
caraway in gripe water was used to
settle babies with wind. It is used as a
flavouring in children's medicines.
Caraway is a useful antidote for flatulence and an aid to digestion. It is used
in a multitude of ways for its flavour and
aroma, for example in mouthwash
and gargle preparations as well as in the
perfume industry.

**caraway
cheese**

Cassia

BOTANICAL NAME: *Cinnamomum cassia* • FAMILY NAME: *Lauraceae*

OTHER NAMES: *bastard cinnamon, canel, canton cassia, casia bark, Chinese cinnamon;* FR. *casse, canefice;* G. *Kassia, Kaneel;* SP. *casia;* IT. *cassia*

This ancient spice was known to the Chinese as early as 3000 BC and mentioned in the early books of the Bible. Cassia was also mentioned in the Psalms and used by the Pharaohs. It came into Europe over the spice routes from the East.

CULTIVATION

Cassia is a native of Burma and it should not be confused with cinnamon, which originates from Sri Lanka. The bulk of the world's cassia comes from China, Indochina, Indonesia, the East and West Indies and Central America. Both cassia and cinnamon grow on small, evergreen laurel-like trees of the same family. Growing to 3 metres/ 10 feet high in warm tropical conditions, the cassia tree has yellow flowers. The tree is cut down when the bark is ready to harvest and trimmed into workable lengths. Long slits are made in the greyish bark and inside this the pieces of cassia are a deep rust-brown colour. The cassia curls slightly on drying, but not into the neat quills associated with cinnamon.

AROMA AND FLAVOUR

The bouquet and the taste share similar characteristics. Cassia is coarser, more pungent and less fragrant than cinnamon; in America cassia is substituted for the finer-tasting cinnamon.

CULINARY USE

Cassia is generally used in savoury dishes, while cinnamon is preferable in sweet and delicately flavoured recipes. Cassia is an ingredient in mixed spice, pickling spices and Chinese five spices, and in Germany it is used as a flavouring for chocolate. Cassia is good with stewed fruits such as rhubarb and apple. Cassia buds resemble cloves and are used in the East for pickles, in curries and spicy meat dishes where they impart a warm aromatic flavour.

MEDICINAL AND OTHER USE

The volatile oil is used in some inhalants, in tonics and as a cure for flatulence, sickness and diarrhoea.

cassia bark

ground cassia

Cinnamon

BOTANICAL NAME: *Cinnamomum zeylanicum*
FAMILY NAME: *Lauraceae*

FR. *cannelle;* G. *Ceylonzimt, Kaneel, Zimt;* SP. *canela;* IT. *cannella;* SINH. *cinnamon*

Cinnamon and cassia, a relative spice, have long been associated with ancient rituals of sacrifice or pleasure. The Ancient Egyptians used the spice in embalming. Hieroglyphics discovered on a temple built around 1489 BC by Hapshepsut, a formidable Pharaoh queen, indicate that she sent ships to Punt, now Somalia, to bring back, among other things, cinnamon, frankincense and myrrh trees. Throughout the Old Testament in the Bible, references to cinnamon illustrate that it was more precious than gold. The Roman Emperor Nero is said to have murdered his wife in a fit of rage, then he ordered that a year's supply of cinnamon be burned at her funeral as a sign of remorse.

ground cinnamon

The trade for cinnamon was first documented by the 13th-century Arab writer Kazwini. Waves of traders and merchants profited from this special aromatic crop: first the Portuguese in 1500, followed by the Dutch and then the British East India Company. When traders were taking European travellers to the island of Ceylon (Sri Lanka) they would spread cinnamon on the decks of their ships just before sighting the island and amuse their passengers by telling them, 'Now you can smell it, soon you will see it'. It was true, for the very best cinnamon grew at low altitudes on poor white sands. In the Victorian language of flowers, cinnamon is translated as meaning 'my fortune is yours'. In Austria lovers would exchange a posy containing cinnamon, reflecting warmth and love.

CULTIVATION

Cinnamon is native to Sri Lanka, Burma and the southern coastal strip of India. Sri Lanka still produces the best-quality spice. Cinnamon now thrives in South America and the West Indies. A substantial crop also grows in the Seychelles and Réunion, taken there from Sri Lanka by Pierre Poivre, an enterprising missionary.

Cinnamon is a bushy evergreen tree of the laurel family, cultivated as low bushes to ease the harvesting process. The bushes like shelter and moderate rainfall without extremes in temperature. Eight or ten lateral branches grow on each bush and, after three years, they are harvested in the rainy season, when the humidity makes the bark peel more easily. The slim branches are first peeled, then the inner bark is bruised with a brass rod to loosen it. Long incisions are made in the branch, the bark lifts off and the drying process begins. The quills of bark are rolled daily by hand until neat and compact, and any off-cuts are used to fill the longer quills.

cinnamon sticks

AROMA AND FLAVOUR

The bouquet of cinnamon is delightfully exotic, sweet and fragrant, and its flavour is sweet and warm.

CULINARY USE

Cinnamon is appreciated in a multitude of dishes from around the world. The quills or cinnamon sticks are added whole to casseroles, rice dishes, mulled wines and punches, and to syrups for poaching fruit. In Mexico, they are used to stir mugs of hot steaming chocolate. Ground cinnamon is used in cakes, pastries and biscuits.

MEDICINAL AND OTHER USE

Cinnamon is a stimulant, astringent and carminative, used as an antidote for diarrhoea and stomach upsets. It is also given to women in labour as a sedative. Oil is extracted from the leaves, which are long, dark, glossy and beautifully aromatic. Oil from the leaves is used as a substitute for clove oil; oil from the broken bark is used in the manufacture of perfume. In Mexico, cinnamon is added as a flavouring in the manufacture of chocolate.

STORAGE

Store cinnamon in an airtight jar, in a cool dark cupboard. Buy little and often for the best flavour.

COOKING TIPS

Cinnamon sticks and ground cinnamon are widely used in all kinds of sweet and savoury dishes.

To make mulled wine add one or two cinnamon sticks to other flavouring ingredients and heat gently.

Sprinkle prepared fruit, such as peaches, nectarines, pears and apples, with cinnamon-flavoured sugar and grill until the sugar is golden. Serve hot, with chilled crème fraîche.

To make cinnamon toast, toast bread on one side, then butter the untoasted side, sprinkle it with cinnamon sugar and toast it until golden.

Add cinnamon to bread dough to make savoury buns to serve with tomato or pumpkin soup.

Stir a cup of hot, sweet, fresh coffee with a cinnamon stick or sprinkle ground cinnamon over frothy, milky cappuccino coffee.

Mexican chocolate

41

Kaffir Lime Leaves

BOTANICAL NAME: *Citrus hystrix* • FAMILY NAME: *Makrut, Magrut*

IND. *daun jeruk purut;* THAI *bai makrut*

The leaves of this member of the citrus family are responsible for the distinctive lime-lemon aroma and flavour that are an indispensable part of Thai and, to a lesser extent, Indonesian cooking. These dark green, glossy leaves grow in pairs and look like a figure of eight. The citrus fruit from this bush fruit looks like a gnarled lime or lemon.

fresh kaffir
lime leaves

kaffir
limes

CULINARY USE

Apart from the leaves of the bush, only the fruit rind is used, finely grated, in Thai and Indonesian dishes. The leaves are torn or finely shredded and used in soups and curries – they also give a distinctive flavour to fish and chicken dishes.

dried kaffir
lime leaves

MEDICINAL AND OTHER USE

The citrus juice used to be included in Thai ointments and shampoo, and in tonics in Malaysia.

AROMA AND FLAVOUR

The haunting bouquet is unmistakably citrus and scented. The full citrus flavour is imparted when the leaves are torn or shredded.

STORAGE

Buy fresh lime leaves in Oriental stores and freeze them for future use. Dried lime leaves are now available.

grated kaffir
lime peel

Coriander

BOTANICAL NAME: *Coriandrum sativum* • FAMILY NAME: *Umbelliferae*

OTHER NAMES: *Chinese parsley, cilantro;* FR. *coriandre;*
G. *Koriander;* SP. *coriandro, culantro;* IT. *coriandolo*

Coriander has been used as a flavouring and medicine since ancient times. Seeds have been found in the tombs of the Pharaohs, and the Roman legions carried coriander as they progressed through Europe, using it to flavour their bread. The origin of the name is rather off-putting – it comes from koris, *the Greek word for a bed bug, so given because of the similarity between the smell of coriander leaves and the offending bug.*

CULTIVATION

Coriander is a slender, solid-stemmed plant, growing to 0.6 metres/2 feet high, with branching stems, compound leaves and small white flowers, which have a pink tinge. It is part of the parsley and carrot family, native to the Mediterranean and Middle East.

The seeds are tiny globes, about the size of peppercorns, and they are a pale, creamy-brown colour. Coriander grows wherever there is warmth. It needs a sunny position in well-drained soil and grows easily in boxes and pots. It is grown extensively as a crop in India, Russia, Brazil, South America, North Africa and Holland.

AROMA AND FLAVOUR

Dry-fried seeds have a heady, slightly 'burnt orange' aroma, which is very appealing. The ground seeds give a pleasing, mild and sweet taste. The seeds have a long shelf life and are easily ground to a powder: the freshly ground spice is to be recommended because it has a more pronounced flavour than ready ground coriander. The latter loses flavour and aroma quite quickly.

CULINARY USE

Every Indian household uses huge quantities of ground coriander in curry powders, garam masala and other spice mixes. Coriander seeds are frequently combined with cumin seeds, the two spices being dry-fried together before being ground. This combination is common in Middle Eastern dishes too. Whole coriander may be added to chicken and pork casseroles, and it is one of the ingredients in pickling spice. Whole or ground coriander may be used in chutneys, particularly with green tomatoes. Whole or coarsely ground coriander may be used in dishes 'à la Grecque'.

MEDICINAL AND OTHER USE

Coriander seed oil has myriad medicinal uses. It has antibacterial properties and is also included in treatments for colic, neuralgia and rheumatism. The oil also counteracts unpleasant odours in pharmaceutical preparations and tobacco; and it is used in perfumes, liqueurs and gin. The seeds are ground into a paste for application to skin and mouth ulcers. Before toothpaste was commonly used, coriander seeds were chewed as a breath sweetener.

COOKING TIPS

Add freshly ground coriander to home-made tomato or béchamel sauces or include it as a seasoning in carrot, parsnip or pumpkin soups. Try adding ground coriander to savoury bread dough with sun-dried tomatoes or olives.

PREPARATION TIP

The flavour of the seeds is greatly enhanced by dry-frying. Heat the frying pan without oil, add the seeds and toss them over a gentle heat until they begin to give off a rich aroma. Cool the seeds slightly before grinding them.

coriander seeds

roasted coriander flakes

coriander roots

ground coriander

fresh coriander

43

Saffron

BOTANICAL NAME: *Crocus sativus*
FAMILY NAME: *Iridaceae*

FR. *safran;* G. *Safran;* SP. *azafrán;*
IT. *zafferano;* IN. *kesar, khesa, kesram*

saffron strands

The name saffron comes from the Arabic za'faran, *which
means yellow – a sacred colour chosen by Buddhist monks for their robes. Saffron is
hugely expensive: consider that 200,000 flowers have to be harvested by hand to obtain
450 g/1 lb saffron and no further explanation for cost is necessary.*

Saffron has been highly prized as a dye, medication and culinary spice since Greek and Roman times. One of the more extravagant Roman Emperors, Heliogabalus, is said to have bathed in saffron-scented water. Arab traders introduced saffron to Spain, where its richness of colour and flavour were appreciated, then rapidly assimilated in the cuisines all along the Mediterranean. From there saffron spread to Britain, where it was extensively grown in Essex, with the town of Saffron Walden as a centre for cultivation. Early British saffron growers were known as 'crokers'.

Buy true saffron in fine, bright orange-red ragged strands for preference, as they are less likely to have been adulterated. Look out for tell-tale light patches on the strands. Ready ground (powdered) saffron is also a candidate for adulteration, so buy from a reputable source.

CULTIVATION

The *Crocus sativus* is a bulbous, autumn-flowering, perennial of the iris family. The flowers have three bright, orange-red stigmas which are the true saffron. These are toasted, or dried, in sieves over a very low heat. Nowadays, the very best saffron comes from Valencia or La Mancha in Spain; however, it is grown also in Greece, Turkey, Iran, Morocco and Kashmir.

AROMA AND FLAVOUR

Saffron has a distinctive and lasting aroma with a certain warmth. Use saffron sparingly to avoid a medicinal flavour. The spice is so expensive that cheating is quite common.

CULINARY USE

Appreciated for its delicate, yet distinctive, flavour and striking colour, saffron is added to special dishes in many cuisines. Celebration pilaus from India are scented with saffron, as are rice dishes from the Mediterranean, particularly Spanish paella and Italian risotto Milanese. Bouillabaisse, the famous seafood soup-stew, is flavoured with saffron.

This spice is also widely used in sweet recipes: milky rice or vermicelli puddings and sweet custard-like desserts from India. Baked goods flavoured with saffron include yeasted breads as well as cakes. It is one of the ingredients in the liqueur Chartreuse.

Chartreuse

MEDICINAL AND OTHER USE

Saffron is used in sedatives, as an antispasmodic and for flatulence. It is also used in perfumes and dyes and, being so expensive, it is considered to be an aphrodisiac in some cultures.

STORAGE

Store saffron, wrapped in its cellophane or paper sachet, in airtight tins, to keep it away from strong light.

SUBSTITUTES FOR SAFFRON

There are a number of substitutes for saffron: in India turmeric is often referred to as saffron. Turmeric does not have the fine flavour or bright colour of true saffron. Safflower, known as Mexican or bastard saffron, is another saffron look-alike: the same comments apply, it can be used but does not compare well with the real thing.

saffron powder

Cumin

BOTANICAL NAME: *Cuminum cyminum*

FAMILY NAME: *Umbelliferae*

FR. *cumin*; G. *Kreuzkümmel romische*;
SP. *comino*; IT. *cumino*; IN. *jeera, jira, zeera, jeera safed (white), jeera kala (black)*

black cumin seeds

Cumin has a long and fascinating history. Evidence shows that it was known to the Egyptians 5,000 years ago and it was found in the pyramids. There are biblical references to threshing cumin with a rod, and this practice is still carried on today in remote regions of the Eastern Mediterranean. Theophrasatus, a Greek philosopher and celebrated botanist, was of the opinion that 'cumin must be cursed and abused while sowing if the crop is to be fair and abundant'. In ancient times cumin was a symbol of greed and meanness. Curiously, by the Middle Ages this derogatory reputation had changed and cumin was regarded as a symbol of faithfulness. For example, in Germany, where cumin is still a popular spice, a bride and groom would carry a little of the seed to represent their commitment to being faithful.

white cumin seeds

CULTIVATION

Cumin is a small, annual herbaceous plant of the parsley family, growing to a height of about 25 cm/10 in. It is a native of Eastern Mediterranean countries and upper Egypt, but it is now cultivated in Morocco, Iran, Turkey, India, China and the Americas. Cumin flourishes best in sunny climes with some rainfall. The small white or pink flowers grow on small compound umbels, like many of the plants in the *Umbelliferae* family.

Harvesting takes place about 4 months after planting. The small, boat-shaped seed has nine ridges, and it is brown-yellow in colour. Cumin seeds are sometimes confused with caraway, but the cumin seeds are lighter in colour. There is a type of black cumin,

ground cumin

which grows in Iran. The seeds are smaller and they have a sweeter aroma. Black cumin is occasionally confused with nigella, which is sometimes called black caraway in Indian cooking.

AROMA AND FLAVOUR

Cumin has a strong, spicy, sweet aroma with a slightly bitter and pungent taste. The pungency and bitterness are particularly noticeable in the ground spice; however, as it is frequently used with coriander, the bitterness is counteracted. Dry-frying before grinding brings out a toasted, nutty flavour, making the spice less harsh. Buy the seeds and grind them as required for superb flavour. Black cumin seeds have a slightly sweeter, more delicate, flavour than the white seeds.

CULINARY USE

On account of its strong flavour, ground cumin is most popular in cuisines which are generally highly spiced; for example in Indian, Middle Eastern, North African and Mexican cooking. Cumin is an essential ingredient in most Indian curry powders and garam masala. It is added to soups and stews, especially Moroccan lamb dishes and Mexican meat dishes, such as chilli con carne. Cumin seed contributes a lighter flavour, without the distinctive bitterness, and it is valued in Indian vegetable, rice and dhal recipes. Black cumin is particularly associated with Indian rice preparations.

Cumin features widely in German cookery, in classics like sauerkraut, pickles, sausages and Munster cheese. It is also used in Dutch cheese, based on an old medieval recipe.

MEDICINAL AND OTHER USE

Cumin is regarded as an appetite stimulant, and it is widely used to ease stomach disorders, flatulence, colic and diarrhoea. It is also used in veterinary medicines. Cumin oil is used in perfumes.

COOKING TIP

Dry-fry cumin seeds in a heavy-based pan for a few minutes to bring out the flavour before using them whole or grinding them.

Turmeric

BOTANICAL NAME: *Curcuma domestica, syn C. longa*
FAMILY NAME: *Zingiberaceae*

FR. *curcuma;* G. *Gelbwurz;* SP. *cúrcuma;*
IT. *curcuma;* IN. *haldi*

The name turmeric is believed to have come from the Latin terra merita, *merit of the earth. Marco Polo was intrigued by the turmeric he found in Southern China: 'There is also a vegetable which has all the properties of true saffron, as well the smell and the colour, and yet it is not really saffron'. Turmeric is much revered by Hindus and associated with fertility. During Hindu wedding ceremonies, a sacred thread dipped in turmeric paste is tied around the bride's neck by the bridegroom. In Malaysia, a paste of turmeric is spread on the mother's abdomen and on the umbilical cord after childbirth, not only to warn off evil spirits, but also for its medicinal value, as turmeric is known to be antiseptic.*

CULTIVATION

Turmeric is a robust, bright, deep yellow rhizome, similar in size and form to ginger, and it belongs to the same family of plants, which thrive in hot, moist tropical conditions. Huge quantities are grown and consumed in, as well as being exported from, India, the world's greatest source of supply. Today, turmeric crops are also harvested in China, Taiwan, Indonesia, Sri Lanka, Australia, Africa, Peru and the West Indies.

The spice is propagated by planting pieces of the previous season's rhizome, which grow to form plants of about 0.9 metres/3 feet, with long-stemmed hosta- or lily-like leaves and pale yellow flowers. Turmeric is ready for harvesting after about 9 months, when the whole underground system of rhizomes is carefully lifted. The rhizomes are boiled, peeled and dried for a week in the sun before they are graded for quality. The superior grade is referred to as 'fingers', then there are 'rounds' and 'splits'. The rhizome loses about three-quarters of its original weight during drying. Almost all the turmeric crop is ground and sold as powder.

PREPARATION TIP

Fresh turmeric is available from some Oriental stores. Peel it in the same way as ginger, with a sharp knife. The vibrant colour will stain heavily, so it is a good idea to wear rubber gloves. Once peeled, the fresh turmeric can be sliced, grated, chopped or ground to a paste with other ingredients and cooked in the same way as fresh root ginger. Fresh turmeric is superb in fish curries.

**fresh turmeric
root slices**

fresh turmeric root

ground turmeric

curry powder

**dried
turmeric root**

AROMA AND FLAVOUR

Turmeric has a peppery aroma and flavour with a hint of wood. It has a warm, musky flavour with a slightly bitter aftertaste.

CULINARY USE

Where a recipe calls for saffron some might suggest substituting turmeric, but it is a misconception that turmeric is regarded only as a second-rate alternative to the most expensive of spices. In Indian cooking, turmeric is often used as an everyday alternative to saffron. It may be added to dishes usually spiced with saffron for its colour, but not for the flavour, and it is sometimes referred to as saffron in this context. Using turmeric in place of saffron is in the interest of economy; saffron would be reserved for celebration dishes: pilaus for weddings, for example.

Turmeric is, perhaps, best appreciated as an ingredient in curries (especially fish curries) and curry powders, contributing flavour as well as the characteristic yellow colour. It is also used in chutneys and pickles, particularly piccalilli, kedgeree and many Indian rice, vegetable and dhal dishes. Turmeric is popular in many North African dishes to spice lamb and vegetables.

MEDICINAL AND OTHER USE

Turmeric is aromatic and a mild digestive, and in Asian countries it is taken to ease liver complaints and stomach ulcers. Boiled with milk and sugar, it is said to be a cure for colds. The role of turmeric as a dye was mentioned in an ancient Assyrian herbal recipe from 600 BC, and it is still used as a dye for cotton and silk. It is widely used in the food industry as an edible colouring in mustards, butter, cheese and liqueurs.

STORAGE

The powder should be bought in small quantities and stored in an airtight container away from strong light to preserve its colour and flavour. Whole pieces of dried turmeric are sometimes used in pickling. It is difficult to grind the dried spice and therefore best to buy ready ground turmeric.

Zedoary

BOTANICAL NAME: *Curcuma zedoaria, C. zerumbet*
FAMILY NAME: *Zingiberaceae*

OTHER NAMES: *wild turmeric;* FR. *zedoaire;*
G. *Zitwer;* SP. *cedoaria;* IT. *zedoaria*
IND. *kentjur;* IN. *amb halad, garndhmul*

Native to India and China, zedoary was transported to Europe in the Middle Ages by Arab traders, but over the years its popularity waned and it is now used mainly in countries where it is grown.

CULTIVATION

A member of the ginger and turmeric family of plants, like turmeric, it is bright yellow in colour and propagated in the same way, by planting pieces of the rhizome. Zedoary takes two years to mature before it can be harvested, which possibly has some bearing on its decline in popularity. The plant grows well in wet tropical forest areas. The rhizomes are similar in size to turmeric and ginger, and the leaves are similar to turmeric, but larger, growing to about 0.9 metres/3 feet. The plant bears yellow flowers with red and green bracts. Powdered or dried zedoary is occasionally available from Oriental food stores under its Indonesian name of kentjur.

AROMA AND FLAVOUR

Zedoary has a musky aroma with a hint of camphor. It has a ginger-like flavour but a bitter aftertaste.

CULINARY USE

Although its use is primarily medicinal, the peeled and chopped root might be pounded with turmeric and ginger to make a spice paste for goat, lamb or chicken curries.

MEDICINAL AND OTHER USE

Used as an aid to digestion, to relieve flatulence and colic. The starch, *shoti*, obtained from the root is easily digested and nutritious, and it is therefore used as a food in the East for the sick and young. Zedoary is also used as a dye.

chopped dried zedoary root

Lemon Grass

BOTANICAL NAME: *Cymbopogon citratus, syn*
Andropogon schoenanthus • FAMILY NAME: *Gramineae*

**lemon grass
paste**

OTHER NAMES: *citronella;* FR. *herbe de citron;*
G. *Zitronengras;* SP. *hierba de limón;*
IT. *erba di limone;* IND. *sereh;* MAL. *serai*

This tropical and sub-tropical scented grass flourishes all over South-east Asia. It was described by Tennant on Ceylon *in 1860: 'These sunny expanses ... are covered with tall lemon grass'.*

**chopped dried
lemon grass**

CULTIVATION

Lemon grass is a perennial tufted plant with long, sharp-edged leaves. It grows in dense clumps in sunny climates with some rainfall. Propagation is by dividing the root stock. The mother plant will grow for 3-4 years and the bulbous stems are cut three times a year. Lemon grass is cultivated on a commercial scale in South-east Asia, Southern India, Africa, Brazil, Guatemala, the USA and the West Indies. The cut stems are about 20 cm/8 in long, and they look like thick spring onions.

Lemon grass can be grown as an ornamental houseplant in colder regions. Fresh stems from an Oriental supermarket sometimes have little buds at the root: place them in water until roots begin to sprout. Dust the developing growth with rooting powder, place in a pot of compost and keep in a sunny place.

AROMA AND FLAVOUR

Lemon grass stems do not have an identifiable aroma until they are cut, then they have a distinctive citrus bouquet. Lemon grass contributes a 'bright' lemon flavour to dishes – lemon rind is sometimes recommended as an alternative, but it does not match the lively flavour of the grass.

CULINARY USE

Lemon grass features in many dishes, including soups, marinades, stir-fries, curries, salads and pickles. It is a perfect partner for coconut milk, especially in those dishes using fish, seafood and chicken. Sereh powder (ground dried lemon grass) can be used in place of fresh – 1 tsp is equivalent to one stalk. In South America, a refreshing tea is made by infusing the leaves in water.

MEDICINAL AND OTHER USE

The medicinal and cosmetic value of lemon grass was recognized centuries ago by the Egyptians, Greeks and Romans. The essential oil from lemon grass is used in soaps and perfumes and for aromatherapy. An ointment containing the oil is said to be good for rheumatism, lumbago and sprains.

**fresh
lemon
grass**

Trim and discard the root end, then cut the low bulbous end to 7.5 cm/3 in long and slice it finely.

Bruise the tough, top end of the stem in a pestle and mortar and add to gravies and soups for extra flavour but always remove before serving.

Alternatively, the stem end can be bruised at one end to make a brush, and used to baste meats with oil, marinade or coconut cream.

STORAGE

When wrapped in a paper bag, lemon grass stems will keep in the vegetable compartment of the fridge for 2-3 weeks. The lower part of the stem can be sliced or pounded and frozen along with the top half of the stems, tied in a separate bundle. Freeze the equivalent of two stems in separate portions and label them for future reference.

**sereh
powder**

Cardamom

BOTANICAL NAME: *Elettaria cardamomum* • FAMILY NAME: *Zingiberaceae*

FR. *cardamome;* G. *Kardamome;* SP. *cardamono;*
IT. *cardamomo, cardamone;* IN. *elachi*

It is said that cardamoms grew in the gardens of the King of Babylon in 720 BC. The Ancient Egyptians chewed cardamoms to whiten their teeth and simultaneously sweeten their breath. Even earlier, in 4 BC, Indian Ayurvedic medicine (of Hindu tradition) used the spice to 'remove fat' and as a cure for urinary and skin complaints. Cardamom was used in perfumes by ancient Greeks and Romans, and also recommended by Apicius, a famous Roman epicure, to counteract over-indulgence.

Although there are various similar types of cardamom-like spices, *Elettaria cardamomum* is the true spice. Buy unsplit pods from a reputable source to be sure of the best quality. Green cardamoms are the most common and useful; white cardamoms are the same type of pods which have been bleached (they are used in Indian desserts); and black cardamoms are quite different. The black spice is used in long-cooked, highly flavoured, savoury Indian dishes. The pods are large, hairy and brown-black, with a coarse, strong flavour. Black cardamoms are too crude for light dishes or sweet mixtures; it is best to use the green pods for all cooking.

CULTIVATION

Cardamom is a herbaceous perennial bush of the ginger family. It flourishes in areas which have a constant warm temperature with moderate rainfall, and grows wild in the forests of Southern India. Commercially, the bulk of the crop is grown in India. Unsuccessful attempts were made to grow the crop in Singapore and Penang late in the last century. India grows 80 per cent of the world's crop, exports half its production and makes domestic use of the remainder.

The bush bears fruit pods after three years and continues cropping for ten to fifteen years. The bush has elegant, long, oval leaves of 2.4-3 metres/ 8-10 feet. The stalks, which bear the seeds are near the base of the plant. The seed pods appear over a long period, and they do not ripen at the same time. They are triangular in cross-section and oval in shape. When opened the papery pod reveals three segments, each with a row of tiny, brownish-black seeds. The pods are removed carefully with scissors before they

green cardamoms

cardamom seeds

black cardamoms

white cardamoms

are ripe. If the pods ripen and split, the flavour and aroma are diminished. Hand picking is therefore essential to avoid damaging both pods and plants. This is very labour-intensive and it accounts for the fact that cardamom is one of the most expensive spices, along with saffron and vanilla. The pods are also dried slowly in the sun, in kilns or hot rooms to prevent splitting.

AROMA AND FLAVOUR

The pungent and warm bouquet of cardamom seeds with their distinct aroma is unforgettable. Cardamoms have a pleasing, warm, slightly lemon-like flavour, with a distinct element of eucalyptus and camphor that will sweeten the breath if the seeds are chewed – the perfect antidote to garlic or alcohol.

CULINARY USE

Cardamom plays an essential role in both sweet and savoury dishes, worldwide. It is essential in a wide range of Indian dishes: curries, pilaus, garam masala and other spice mixtures. It is also vital to the flavour of many Indian sweetmeats and desserts, such as the popular ice cream kulfi and milk puddings. Cardamom is used extensively in Scandinavian cooking, in pickles, with herrings, cakes and pastries.

**ground
cardamom**

It also flavours Aquavit.

Arab traders became addicted to the cardamom-flavoured coffee known as *gahwa*, and it is still served today, with much ceremony, as a symbol of Arab hospitality. The curved spout of the coffee pot is stuffed with a few opened cardamom pods which flavour the strong coffee as it is poured: good manners dictate that you must drink at least three cups.

MEDICINAL AND OTHER USE

The seeds and pods contain a volatile oil which is used in perfumes and as a stimulant. Cardamom features often in *The Arabian Nights*, where its aphrodisiac properties are extolled; that belief is still held in the Middle East today. Additionally it is held that cardamom is a stimulant, that it cools the body in extreme heat and that it aids digestion.

STORAGE

Always buy whole, unsplit cardamom pods in small quantities as they lose their flavour as they grow stale. Ready ground cardamom is rarely available, extremely costly and not to be recommended as the seeds lose their flavour very quickly once removed from the pods; also, the powder may well have been adulterated. Store the pods in a small, airtight jar in a cool dark place.

Cloves

BOTANICAL NAME: *Eugenia caryophyllus* • FAMILY NAME: *Myrtaceae*

FR. *clou de girofle;* G. *Gewürznelke;*
SP. *clavo de especia;* IT. *chiodo di garofano*

The name clove is believed to be derived from the French word clou *meaning nail, which is an apt description of the appearance of this spice. There may be a lot of truth in the saying, 'nutmegs must be able to smell the sea but cloves must see it', as clove crops appear to flourish best on islands. The people of the Moluccas or Spice Islands (now Maluku, a group of islands in Indonesia) used to plant a clove tree to celebrate the birth of a child. If the tree flourished, this was a good omen for the child, who would wear a necklace of cloves as a protection from evil spirits and illness. Chinese physicians appreciated the medicinal benefits of cloves as early as 3 BC. Dignitaries visiting the emperor were expected to suck cloves to sweeten their breath; today eugenol, extracted from clove oil, is used in toothpastes and gargles.*

whole cloves

COOKING TIPS

Place an onion studded with cloves in the body cavity of a duck before roasting it. Alternatively, stud an orange with cloves and bake it briefly, then use it to flavour mulled wine.

CULTIVATION

The tree, part of the myrtle family, with fragrant, rich green leaves, is native to the Moluccas, part of the Indonesian archipelago. It was grown exclusively in the Moluccas until the early 18th century, when the French decided to break the monopoly by asking Pierre Poivre, who had taken cinnamon to the Seychelles, to carry seedlings to Mauritius. The trees flourished in Mauritius, and subsequently further seedlings were taken to the islands of Zanzibar and Pemba on the East African coast, now the world's largest producer of cloves. The cloves, the unopened flower buds of this 12 metre/40 foot tree, are harvested when the tree is 6-8 years old. The crop can be sporadic: one year heavy and the next light.

The cloves are hand picked to avoid damaging the branches which would jeopardize subsequent crops. If the pink buds are not picked, small purple or crimson flowers develop. The buds change from a pale russet colour to a darker brown as they dry slowly in the sun. This process cannot be hastened or the cloves become dry, brittle and withered, rather than plump.

AROMA AND FLAVOUR

Approaching a clove tree is a heady experience, as the warm, pungent

**ground
cloves**

aroma drifts towards you. Cloves have a slightly astringent, sweetly pungent and strongly aromatic flavour.

CULINARY USE

Cloves are included in many classic spice mixtures, including Chinese five spice powder; Indian and Oriental curry powders; European whole pickling spices; spices for mulling wine; and ground mixed spice for baking.

Whole cloves are frequently used to flavour cooking liquids for simmering fish, poultry, game or meat. They feature in classic sauces and are a festive flavouring and garnish for baked hams.

Cloves have a particular association with apples and are added to apple sauce, tarts and pies or other apple puddings. Ground cloves are used to spice rich cakes, biscuits, gingerbreads and satisfying puddings from all over the world.

MEDICINAL AND OTHER USE

Oil of cloves, which is distilled from the buds, leaves and stalks, is a valuable commodity: it is a strong antiseptic and preservative, and it is used in toothpastes, mouthwashes and gargle preparations. Additionally it is used to treat flatulence, colic, indigestion and nausea. A cotton bud soaked in oil of cloves eases toothache when applied to the tooth.

STORAGE

Buy whole cloves which have a long shelf life if kept in a cool place away from strong light. To make your own powder when just a small amount is required, grind the central bud at the top of the nail (this should still be intact if the cloves are reasonably fresh). Powdered cloves are available, but buy the powder in small quantities as required as the flavour and colour soon dissipates.

Asafoetida

BOTANICAL NAME: *Ferula asafoetida* • FAMILY NAME: *Umbelliferae*

OTHER NAMES: *asafetida, assafoetida, devil's dung, food of the gods;* FR. *assa foetida, férule perisque;* G. *Asafotida, stinkender Asant;* SP. *asafétida;* IT. *assafetida*

Early records mention that Alexander the Great carried this 'stink finger' west in 4 BC. Used as a flavouring in the kitchens of ancient Rome, this pungent, resinous gum is used widely in Indian vegetarian cooking.

asafoetida resin

CULTIVATION

Ferula asafoetida, a perennial of the carrot family, grows wild to 3.6 metres/ 12 feet high in huge natural forests. The plant is indigenous to Iran, Afghanistan and in the north of India. There is a smaller species called *Ferula narthax.* The whole plant exudes the characteristic strong smell, described by some as a stink. The milky resin comes from both the thick stems and the root, and it dries into asafoetida.

AROMA AND FLAVOUR

In its raw state, the resin or the powder has an unpleasant smell. This completely disappears when the spice is added to a variety of vegetable, fish, pulse and pickle ingredients.

CULINARY USE

Used mostly in Indian vegetarian cooking, in which the strong onion-garlic smell enhances many dishes, especially those of the Brahmin and Jain castes where onions and garlic are prohibited. Also used in curries, and pickles from the West and South of India. The lump of resin would only be acceptable to keen Indian cooks who use a very small piece at a time. For most of us, the powdered version is easier to handle. Buy asafoetida in small quantities. The powdered resin is usually mixed with flour to provide bulk and is often sold in a bright yellow tub.

asafoetida powder

asafoetida powder

MEDICINAL AND OTHER USE

Asafoetida is a useful antidote for flatulence, hence its popularity with Indian vegetarian cooks, who make generous use of pulses. There are claims for it being used to cure bronchitis and even hysteria.

Fennel

BOTANICAL NAME: *Foeniculum vulgare*

FAMILY NAME: *Umbelliferae*

OTHER NAMES: *common fennel, sweet fennel, Florence fennel*; FR. *fenouil, anet douce*; G. *Fenchel*; SP. *hinojo*; IT. *finocchio*

fennel flower heads

The name comes from the Latin foenum, *a variety of fragrant hay. Fennel has been known to herbalists and doctors since time immemorial: it was believed to be the total cure and to have the power to make people young, strong and healthy. The American poet Longfellow summarized opinions about fennel in his poem* The Goblet of Life:

Above the lowly plants it towers,
The fennel with its yellow flowers,
And in an earlier age than ours,
Was gifted with the wondrous powers,
Lost vision to restore.

It gave new strength, and fearless mood;
And gladiators, fierce and rude,
Mingled it in their daily food;
And he who battled and subdued,
A wreath of fennel wore.

CULTIVATION

Fennel is a tall, leggy, aromatic perennial of the parsley family, native to Southern Europe and the Mediterranean, where it grows particularly well near the sea. It is extensively cultivated in India and Argentina, and grown throughout Europe, North Africa, Romania, Bulgaria, Russia, Japan and the USA. Fennel has fine feathery leaves and yellow flowers. The seeds are harvested when the fruits are mature and sage green in colour. The fruit splits into two seeds, which are oval in shape with five ridges. It is wise to avoid planting dill and fennel near each other to prevent cross fertilization.

AROMA AND FLAVOUR

Fennel has a delightfully sweet and warm aroma with a flavour of mild anise. Fennel is best bought in seed form and ground or dry-fried as required.

CULINARY USE

Fennel has a great affinity with fish, especially oily fish like mackerel, herring and salmon. Dried stems of fennel may be burned on the barbecue when grilling fish, to impart a unique flavour to the food. It also complements pork and lamb. The crushed seeds are used in salad dressings and in mayonnaise to serve with fish. Ground fennel is used in many curry powders and in Chinese five spice powder. Crushed seeds are used in savoury and sweet baking: in breads, doughs, cakes and biscuits. Try sipping fennel tea for a jaded palate – infuse 1 tsp seeds in about 300 ml/½ pint/1¼ cups water that is just off the boil. Then strain the liquid into a tall glass.

PREPARATION TIP

Dry-frying and crushing fennel seeds before using them heightens the flavour.

Dry-fry the seeds first in a heavy-based pan for 1-2 minutes until they release their aroma, then crush the seeds in a mortar with a pestle.

MEDICINAL AND OTHER USE

Fennel is said to cure earache, toothache, asthma and rheumatism. It is meant to help stop hiccups and coughs, and improve eyesight. It has even been thought of as a good slimming agent. Fennel oil is used in cough medicine, liquorice sweets, perfumes and soaps.

fennel seeds

Liquorice

BOTANICAL NAME: *Glycyrrhiza glabra*

FAMILY NAME: *Leguminosae*

OTHER NAMES: *licorice (US);*
FR. *réglisse;* G. *Lakritze, Süssholz;*
SP. *regaliz;* IT. *liquirizia*

liquorice powder

The name comes from the Greek glyks *or* glukus, *meaning sweet, and* rhiza, *meaning root. Liquorice is particularly well known for its use in confectionery, particularly for the famous British sweets, Liquorice Allsorts.*

It has been grown in the UK since the 16th century, when it was cultivated by Dominican monks in Pontefract, Yorkshire, where the confectionery trade began. Liquorice was used in the famous Pontefract cakes before the children's sweets were manufactured.

liquorice allsorts

CULTIVATION

Liquorice, a perennial of the pea family, native to the Middle East and South-east Europe, grows to over 0.9 metres/3 feet. Above ground, the plant has long stems with pinnate leaves, made up of nine to seventeen leaflets, and blue flowers, which produce pods containing three or four seeds. The root, which is the important part, sends out a deep and extensive network of rhizomes, which are grown for three to five years before they are

liquorice sticks

AROMA AND FLAVOUR

When cut, the root is bright yellow and it smells sweet. It tastes strongly of anise, with a rather bitter-sweet flavour.

CULINARY USE

Liquorice is best known as an ingredient in confectionery. It is also used in the making of the famous Irish ale Guinness and to flavour the Italian liqueur sambuco as well as other beers and soft drinks.

sliced liquorice root

Pontefract cakes

harvested. The roots and rhizomes are cleaned, pulped, then boiled and the liquorice extract is then concentrated by evaporation. Today liquorice is cultivated in Russia and Southern Europe.

MEDICINAL AND OTHER USE

The strong smell and distinctive taste of liquorice is often used in medicines to disguise other unpalatable flavours, for example in cough medicines and throat pastilles.

STORAGE

Dried sticks of liquorice are sometimes available: store them in an airtight container in a cool dry place.

sambuco liqueur

53

Star Anise

BOTANICAL NAME: *Illicium verum, syn I. anisatum*

FAMILY NAME: *Magnoliaceae*

FR. *anis de la Chine;* G. *Sternanis;*
SP. *badiana, badián;* IT. *anice stellato*

CULTIVATION

Traditionally the Japanese used to burn the beautifully aromatic bark of the tree as incense. Star anise is the fruit of a small to medium, evergreen tree, native to South-west China and now grown in Indo-China and Japan. Yellow, narcissus-like flowers yield fruits which open out into an eight-pointed star shape. The tree bears fruit after 6 years initially, but then it has a productive life of up to a hundred years. The fruits are harvested before they ripen. When ripe, they are rust red and each point of the star-shaped husk contains an amber-coloured seed. Both the seed and the husk are used for the ground spice.

AROMA AND FLAVOUR

Though star anise could not be more different from anise in appearance, both spices smell and taste very similar, with a distinct liquorice-like aroma and flavour.

CULINARY USE

Star anise is one of the most important spices in Chinese cuisine, and it is the dominant flavour in Chinese five spice powder. More often the whole star or part of it is used whole as in the recipe, right, for Chinese Tea Eggs. Star anise is also used as a flavouring in alcoholic drinks, such as pastis and anisette and in confectionery.

MEDICINAL AND OTHER USE

Star anise is used in cough medicines. It is also added to pet foods. A point, the name given to one section of the

star anise

star anise seeds

ground star anise

star, is often sucked as a breath freshener by the Chinese.

STORAGE

The whole spice has a long shelf life. Buy the ground spice in small quantities and store it in an airtight container, away from strong light.

COOKING TIPS

Star anise goes well with duck or pork. The whole star anise, or part of it, can be used in long-cooked recipes. Try putting a whole star into the body cavity of a duck or chicken with an onion before roasting the bird to add a distinct Oriental-style flavour to the meal.

Chinese Tea Eggs

CH'A YEH TAN

<u>MAKES 6</u>

6 eggs
2 tbsp thick soy sauce
1 tsp salt
1 star anise
2 tbsp China tea
  or 2 tea bags

1 *Cook the eggs in simmering water for 20 minutes, then leave them to cool in the cooking water.*

2 *Gently crack the shells to craze them, without actually removing any of the shell. Place the eggs in a saucepan of cold water. Add the soy sauce, salt, star anise and tea. Bring to the boil, cover and simmer for 1½-2 hours. Check the water level occasionally and top it up with more boiling water, as necessary, to keep the eggs covered. Leave the eggs to cool in the liquid overnight.*

3 *Remove the shells and the surface of the eggs will be crazed with fine lines. Cut the eggs into quarters and serve them with a selection of Chinese dishes, as part of a meal.*

Juniper

BOTANICAL NAME: *Juniperus communis* • FAMILY NAME: *Cupressaceae*

FR. *genièvre;* G. *Wacholder;* SP. *enebro, junipero, nebrini;* IT. *ginepro*

The juniper tree has long had a reputation for being a protector and friend to those in trouble. Old Testament biblical references mention juniper trees as places of refuge, and legend dictates that the baby Jesus was placed into the open branches of a juniper bush when the Holy Family were fleeing from Herod. The soldiers, intent on finding a couple with a baby, passed by Mary and Joseph. Juniper was subsequently dedicated to the Virgin Mary, and in Italy wreaths and branches of the tree are hung in stables and cow sheds. In the Middle Ages juniper branches were hung over doors as protection against witches, and when burned the branches were thought to keep serpents and snakes at bay.

Juniper berries can be ground in a peppermill for use in marinades or as a barbecue seasoning. Otherwise, crush the berries in a mortar using a pestle or by pressing them with the back of a teaspoon in a small cup.

CULTIVATION

The juniper is an evergreen coniferous tree of the cypress family, with sharp, pointed, awl-shaped evergreen leaves. It is a dioecious tree, having male and female counterparts, both of which must be cultivated close together in order that berries are formed. The male flowers are yellow and conical, the female are green and rounded. The berries are little globes, which ripen every two years but at different stages. Wear gloves to avoid being pricked by the spikes and pick only the blue berries which turn inky, blue-black and become slightly wrinkled when dried. The berries are harvested in September or October. The main producers of juniper are Hungary and Southern Europe, especially Italy; it is said that the further south the berries are grown the better their flavour.

AROMA AND FLAVOUR

When bitten, a juniper berry tastes of gin first and then its flavour includes a touch of turpentine. If chewed, gin is the primary flavour, with a slight

juniper berries

gin

crushed juniper berries

bitterness that is not unpleasant. The aroma has the same characteristics: a smell of gin and turpentine.

CULINARY USE

Juniper is used in the production of gin, liqueurs, bitters and Swedish beer. It is a valued seasoning for game birds, venison, duck, rabbit, pork, ham and lamb. It is also widely appreciated as an excellent flavouring in meat pâtés and terrines.

MEDICINAL AND OTHER USE

Juniper is believed to help blood circulation and to restore youthful vigour to the ageing. It is used in the treatment of colic, flatulence and rheumatism, and as an antidote for snake bites. It is a powerful antiseptic and is used in insecticides and perfumes.

Galangal

GREATER GALANGAL

BOTANICAL NAME: *Languas galanga, syn Alpinia galanga*

FAMILY NAME: *Zingiberaceae*

> OTHER NAMES: *galanga, Siamese ginger;* FR. *grand galanga;* G. *galanga;* SP. *galanga;* IT. *galanga;* IND. *laos;* MAL. *lengkuas;* THAI *khaa*

LESSER GALANGAL

BOTANICAL NAME: *Languas officinarum, syn Alpinia officinarum*

FAMILY NAME: *Zingiberaceae*

> OTHER NAMES: *aromatic ginger, Siamese ginger;* FR. *galanga de la Chine, galanga vrai;* G. *Galangawurzel;* SP. *galang;* IT. *galanga;* THAI *krachai*

Fresh greater galangal should be thinly peeled, then sliced.

The spice may be pounded as part of a spice paste. Lesser galangal is more fibrous in texture and is prepared in the same way.

Used in the Middle Ages as a medicine, spice and an aphrodisiac, these members of the ginger family, Zingiberaceae, have only become widely available outside their countries of cultivation as fresh spices over the past few years.

CULTIVATION

The galangals are grown in India and South-east Asia where they are an essential ingredient in many dishes. In addition to greater and lesser galangal, there is another variety known as kaempferia galangal, which is quite different in appearance, looking like a clutch of fingers. Kaempferia galangal is only available in specialist shops.

Greater galangal grows to a height of 1.8 metres/6 feet and it has long, elegant, blade-like leaves. The flowers are green and white with red tips. The root or rhizome is creamy white with brown rings at intervals along its knobbly length and occasionally, when really fresh, it has a few pink sprouts or knobs.

Lesser galangal is native to Southern China and, as its name implies, it is a smaller plant, growing to about half the height of the greater galangal. Although lesser galangal is grown in India and South-east Asia, it is not as well known or widely used as the greater variety.

AROMA AND FLAVOUR

Greater galangal has a pine-like aroma with a corresponding pungent flavour.

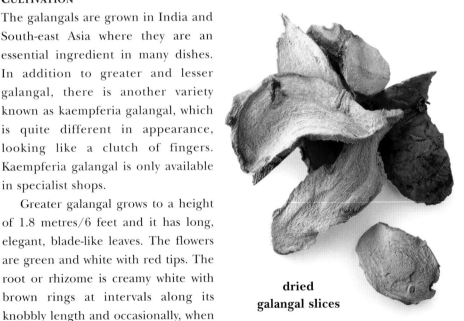

dried galangal slices

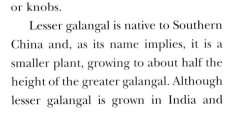

dried galangal (laos powder)

Lesser galangal is distinctly more aromatic with a stronger peppery taste, so when available it is used discreetly. It is well washed and cut into thin slices to add to earthy curries, which can accommodate its pungent aroma and strong taste.

CULINARY USE

Galangal is used in all the cuisines of South-east Asia, particularly in seafood and chicken dishes. It is frequently pounded with onion, garlic, chillies and ginger to make a spice paste. Slices are added to Thai soups with shreds of lemon grass and lime leaves.

**fresh
galangal root**

kaempferia galangal

COOKING TIP

*Use 1 tsp laos powder instead of
4 cm/1½ in of fresh galangal root.*

STORAGE

Wrap the fresh root in a piece of paper and store it in the vegetable compartment of the fridge for up to two weeks. Dried slices and powdered laos are available from specialist shops. The slices are added to curries and stews and removed before serving. Buy small quantities of the powder and store it in an airtight container away from strong light.

MEDICINAL AND OTHER USE

Galangal is used in medicines to treat nausea, flatulence, stomach problems and catarrh; in India it is also recommended as a cure for halitosis. It has anti-bacterial properties and is used in homeopathic medicines.

Bay Leaf

BOTANICAL NAME: *Laurus nobilis* • FAMILY NAME: *Lauraceae*

OTHER NAMES: *bay laurel, Apollo's bay leaf, Indian bay, wreath laurel;* FR. *feuille de laurier, laurier franc;* G. *Lorbeerblatt;* SP. *hoja de laurel;* IT. *foglia d'alloro*

The bay is a tree of the sun under the celestial sign of Leo. Culpeper, the herbalist, regarded bay as a source of protection against 'all the evils of old Satan to the body of man, and they are not a few'. Parkinson, a 17th-century botanist, was full of praise for the virtues of the bay: 'The bay leaves are of a necessary use as any other in the garden or orchard, for they serve both for pleasure and profit, both for ornament and for use, both for honest civil uses and for physic, yea, both for the sick and the sound, both for the living and the dead; ... so that from the cradle to the grave we still have use of it, we still have need of it'.

fresh bay leaves

Bay leaves were fashioned into laurel crowns to be worn by emperors and heroes in ancient Rome as a sign of great honour, and superstition indicated that the bay also gave protection from lightning. Today, the Grand Prix winner is decked with a laurel wreath and the poet of the British Royal Household is still given the title of poet laureate after the laurel wreath awarded to Greek and Roman poets.

CULTIVATION

The bay tree is native to Asia Minor, but spread to all parts of the Mediterranean in ancient times. The flowers, yellow or greenish white, are not very obvious and they produce a dark-purple, one-seeded berry. The true bay tree must not be confused with the cherry laurel, *Prunus laurocerasus*, which bears poisonous leaves, or the Caribbean bay *Pimenta acris*, the leaves of which are used to make bay rum. Bay trees can grow to over

15 metres/50 feet in height, but they are most often pruned into neat bushes. They are often pruned into ornamental shapes or cultivated as standard bushes.

AROMA AND FLAVOUR

The leaves give off a pungent and warm bouquet and flavour when broken and added to a dish. When slightly wilted, they are strongly aromatic, so they should be used sparingly. Bay can be purchased as fresh or dried whole leaves or ground, but the latter rapidly loses its flavour.

CULINARY USE

Bay is always included in a bouquet garni and court bouillon. It is also an essential flavouring ingredient in many classic sauces, such as béchamel, bread sauce and tomato sauce. Bay leaves are used worldwide, in classic and contemporary cuisines, to flavour seafoods, poultry, meat, rice and vegetable dishes. They are added to soups, casseroles, marinades and sautéed foods; threaded on skewers of ingredients to be grilled, or laid in a roasting tin around foods to be baked or roasted. Bay leaves are also added to pickled foods. They are even used in certain sweet dishes, notably custards and creams. Remove bay leaves before serving as they are tough to eat and quite strongly flavoured. You may have noticed bay leaves packed around dried figs: they are there to discourage weevils.

MEDICINAL AND OTHER USE

Medicinally, the properties of the bay leaf and berries are legendary: it has astringent, diuretic

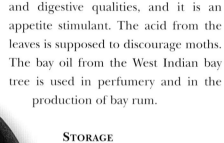

PREPARATION TIP

Bay leaves add a warm pungent flavour to grilled or barbecued kebabs. Push one or two leaves on to each skewer between the chunks of meat.

and digestive qualities, and it is an appetite stimulant. The acid from the leaves is supposed to discourage moths. The bay oil from the West Indian bay tree is used in perfumery and in the production of bay rum.

STORAGE

The leaves should be picked and dried slowly, away from direct sunlight, in order to retain the volatile oils. If left on the branch, the leaves will curl attractively but, if they are to be stored in a jar or container, they should be dried between two sheets of paper to keep them flat. Pack and store away from strong light. The glossy, dark green leaves can be used fresh or dried, but are best after being allowed to wilt for a few days when their bitterness has gone but the leaves still retain their scent.

**dried crushed
bay leaves**

**freeze-dried
bay leaves**

**dried ground
bay leaves**

**dried
bay leaves**

Mango Powder

BOTANICAL NAME: *Mangifera indica* • FAMILY NAME: *Anacardiaceae*

FR. *mangue*; G. *Mango*; SP. *mango, manguey*; IT. *mango*
IN. *amchur, amchoor*

CULTIVATION

The mango tree is a member of the cashew and pistachio family, native to India, where the mango is known as the 'king of fruits'.

The name *amchur* comes from *am*, the Hindu word for mango, and *choor* or *chur*, meaning powder. The unripe mangos are sliced, sun-dried and ground to a powder, then mixed with a little ground turmeric.

mango powder

AROMA AND FLAVOUR

Mango powder has a sweet-and-sour bouquet and flavour, with just a hint of resin.

CULINARY USE

In the high temperatures of the Indian continent, mango powder keeps far

dried mango

better than fresh tamarind or lemons, other typical souring agents. It is used primarily in vegetarian dishes, where it is usually added towards the end of the cooking so that its astringent, yet slightly sweet-sour flavour is still detectable when the food is served. Mango powder is added to soups, marinades, curries and chutneys.

Curry Leaves

BOTANICAL NAME: *Murraya koenigii, syn Chalcas k, Bergara k*
FAMILY NAME: *Rutaceae*

OTHER NAMES: *nim leaf*; FR. *feuille de cari*;
G. *Curryblatt*; SP. *hoja*; IT. *foglia di cari*;
IN. *karipatta, kitha neem*

CULTIVATION

These leaves (in fact they are leaflets) come from a tropical tree of the citrus-rue family, which is native to Southern India and Sri Lanka. The long slender leaflets are dark green on top with a paler underside.

AROMA AND FLAVOUR

The leaves have a strong, warm, curry aroma when bruised or rubbed and they add an aromatic curry flavour to dishes, which cannot be replaced by any other ingredient.

CULINARY USE

A classic way of using curry leaves is by frying mustard seeds in hot ghee, then adding a little asafoetida and several

curry leaves for just a few seconds before stirring them into a plain dhal dish or dhal-based Indian soup. Alternatively, the leaves can be very finely chopped or minced before they are used in curries, added to marinades or omelettes. They are widely used in Madras-style curry powders and pastes, and in shellfish dishes. If the leaves are added whole they should be removed before the dish is served.

STORAGE

The leaves can be bought fresh from Asian shops. They will keep in the vegetable compartment of the refrigerator for up to two weeks or they can be frozen. They are also available vacuum-dried, a process by which the leaves retain their colour and flavour. If the leaves are allowed to dry naturally in the open air, they lose their pungency.

fresh curry leaves

dried curry leaves

Nutmeg and Mace

BOTANICAL NAME: *Myristica fragrans* • FAMILY NAME: *Myristicaceae*

FR. *noix muscade*; G. *Muskatnüsse*; SP. *nuez moscada*;
IT. *noce moscata*

Nutmeg and mace are different parts of the same fruit of the nutmeg tree. These spices have been appreciated since Roman times – the Emperor Henry VI had the streets of Rome fumigated with nutmegs before his coronation. The Portuguese were able to keep the source of nutmeg and mace a close secret for a century, from early in the 16th century until they were driven out of the Spice Islands by the Dutch, who subsequently also jealously guarded the source of their spice treasures. By 1760 there were warehouses in Amsterdam full of these spices, but they were burned in order to keep the price of the spice artificially high. The price of mace in London at that time was 85-90 shillings per pound. So determined were the Dutch to retain their monopoly, that they tried to restrict the growing of nutmeg trees to two islands; however, they had not considered the fruit pigeons that were responsible for the seedlings sprouting on nearby islands.

nutmeg and mace

Pierre Poivre (a French-man who, it is believed, is the Peter Piper in the tongue-twister nursery rhyme beginning with that name) was responsible for trans-porting the precious seedlings to Mauritius, where they flourished. This marked the end of the Dutch monopoly and the decline of their influence in the Spice Islands.

The British East India Company introduced the nutmeg tree to Penang, Singapore, India, Sri Lanka and the West Indies, especially to Grenada. Along with Indonesia, Grenada is the main source of nutmeg and mace.

CULTIVATION

The nutmeg tree is a large evergreen native to the Banda Islands in the Moluccas. It grows to approximately 18 metres/60 feet and produces fruit fifteen to twenty years after planting. Once the tree begins to fruit, it crops for thirty to forty years, bearing 1,500-2,000 fruits per annum. The fruit of the nutmeg tree, which is about the size of an apricot and similar in colour, splits when ripe to reveal brilliant red arils encasing the brown nut. The red arils are the mace, which turns to an orange colour as they dry. The mace is removed from the nut and dried. The nut is also dried until the kernel inside rattles, and this is removed by tapping the end of the nutmeg shell – the kernel can be damaged if the shell is cracked on the side.

It was once fashionable to wear nut-megs on a necklace and to carry a lit-tle grater made from silver or ivory, wood or bone. It is still best to buy the whole nutmeg and grate it as required.

Nutmeg graters produce a fine powder – if you don't have one, use the finest blade on a larger stainless steel grater.

Nutmeg mills are also available, but they are not always very efficient and effective, so select one carefully to ensure it works well. Mills are useful for children – a good one is a lot safer on the fingers than a tiny grater!

AROMA AND FLAVOUR

Mace and nutmeg smell gloriously aromatic, sweet and warm. Both spices have a similar flavour, with the nutmeg being slightly sweeter than the mace.

CULINARY USE

Mace is sold either as whole blades or as the ground spice and it can be used in both forms. Mace is used in savoury dishes, and nutmeg, though used in savoury dishes, is especially complemen-tary to puddings, cakes and drinks. In Malaysia the fleshy outer husk of the nutmeg is crystallized or pickled, then

whole nutmegs

ground nutmeg

whole nutmegs

ground mace

halved or sliced and sold in packs as a delicious snack.

Both spices have well-established roles in classic cuisines. Mace is used to flavour milk-based sauces, such as béchamel, and it is widely used in processed meats, such as sausages and charcuterie. It is also superb when added sparingly to delicate soups and sauces with fish, seafood, particularly potted shrimps, and eggs. Pickles and chutneys may be seasoned with mace. Try adding a little to milk-based puddings, cheesecakes and lemon curd tart.

Nutmeg is delicious with fillings for pasta, especially those using spinach and cheese, it may be added to risotto, tomato sauce or sauces for fish or chicken pies. It is excellent in cheese sauce for a cauliflower cheese or onion sauce to serve with lamb chops and in creamy mashed potatoes.

Nutmeg is a traditional flavouring for cakes, gingerbreads, biscuits and fruit or milk puddings. A little grated or ground nutmeg added to a filling for cherry or apple pie introduces another flavour dimension. For a refreshing end to a meal, try sprinkling a little grated nutmeg and sugar on to slices of well-chilled orange. Mulled alcoholic drinks are enhanced by the addition of a little nutmeg, for example a sprinkling on an egg nog is delicious. It is also a warming addition to hot milk drinks.

MEDICINAL AND OTHER USE

Nutmeg is a narcotic, but not problematic when consumed in the quantities used in domestic recipes. It is astringent, a stimulant and an aphrodisiac; nutmeg oil is used in perfumes and ointments.

Nigella

BOTANICAL NAME: *Nigella sativa* • FAMILY NAME: *Ranunculaceae*

OTHER NAMES: *black caraway, black cumin, wild onion seed;*
FR. *cheveux de Venus, nigelle, poivrette;* G. *Schwarzkümmel;*
SP. *neguilla;* IT. *nigella;* IN. *kalonji*

A plant from the same family as the pretty 'love in a mist' flower. The name nigella comes from the Latin nigellus. *The seeds were used in Roman times and in India for cooking as well as by herbalists.*

nigella seeds

MEDICINAL AND OTHER USE

Used by Indian herbalists and doctors as a stimulant and in treatment of flatulence, indigestion and bowel disorders.

CULTIVATION

Nigella is a herbaceous annual of the buttercup family and it grows to a height of about 0.6 metres/2 feet. It has grey-green wispy leaves and blue-white flowers. The bulk of the crop is grown in India. The seeds are held in a seed head similar to a poppy head: they are triangular in shape, matt black, with two flat sides and the other curved. They are similar to, and often confused with, onion seeds.

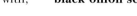

black onion seeds

Bengali five spices (panch phoron)

AROMA AND FLAVOUR

The seeds have little aroma but when rubbed in the fingers they give off a peppery smell; they are sometimes used as a substitute for pepper. Additionally, they have a herb-like taste, similar to oregano or carrots.

CULINARY USE

Nigella is one of the five spices in Bengali five spices (panch phoron). It is widely used in Indian cooking, in dhal and vegetable dishes, pickles and chutneys. The seeds are often scattered on naan bread, where they give a distinctive peppery flavour. In Middle Eastern kitchens the seeds are scattered over breads and cakes, and the seeds are sometimes mixed with sesame seeds for the same purpose.

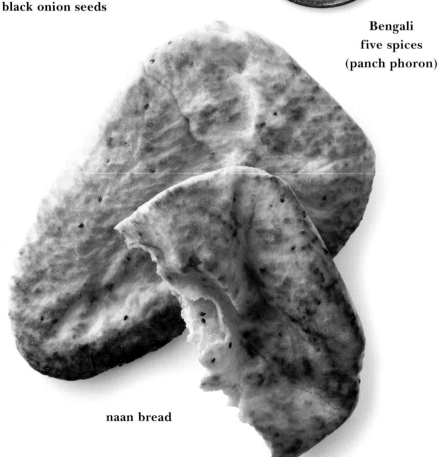

naan bread

Poppy Seeds

BOTANICAL NAME: *Papavera somniferum*

FAMILY NAME: *Papaveraceae*

white poppy seeds

OTHER NAMES: *opium poppy;* FR. *pavot somnifère, oeillette;* G. *Mohn;* SP. *adormidera, amapola;* IT. *papavero;* IN. *kus-kus, khus-khus*

Relics from Ancient Greece have been found which clearly illustrate that people have long been aware of the medicinal and narcotic properties of the poppy. Through Arab traders and the spread of Islam to the East, the opium poppy was introduced to Persia, South-east Asia and India. When used in moderation, opium gave great relief from pain, but soon the trade was exploited as traders and merchants made their fortune from the addiction of countless thousands, bringing suffering and death to those caught in its trap.

black poppy seeds

P*apavera somniferum* means sleep-inducing poppy, referring to the opium in the latex that exudes when the unripe seed pod is cut. Poppy seeds bought for cooking are entirely free from any sinister side effects.

CULTIVATION

The poppy is a tall annual with blue-green stems. The seeds are planted in March and harvested in September. The best-quality blue-grey seeds are grown in Holland; crops are also grown in Poland, Iran, Romania, Russia, Turkey and Argentina.

AROMA AND FLAVOUR

The seeds are sweet smelling and they give off a nutty aroma when cooked.

poppy seed sprouts

The taste is similar to the bouquet, but with a more highly developed, nutty sweetness.

CULINARY USE

The creamy coloured poppy seeds are more common in India, where they are ground and used as a thickening agent in curries and sauces. They are also used in some Indian breads. The dark seeds are also popular as a crunchy topping for Western breads and biscuits, savoury and sweet.

The dark seeds are used extensively as a filling or baking ingredient in German and Eastern European breads, cakes, biscuits and pastries. Delicious pastries and a yeasted poppy seed roll are typical celebration treats baked for Christmas and other festive occasions. They are also sprinkled generously over cooked noodles, or sweetened with honey and made into a dessert dip or sauce.

Dry-fried seeds are an interesting addition to salads and salad dressings, for example in potato, tomato, egg or pasta salads or coleslaw. Both white and black seeds can be sprouted to add to salads, sandwiches and in mixed vegetable dishes.

MEDICINAL AND OTHER USE

Poppy seed oil is used by artists as a drying oil. The blue seeds are used in painkillers, cough mixtures and syrups and as an expectorant. An infusion of the seeds is said to relieve toothache and earache.

STORAGE

If the seeds are to be used in large quantities, for example as a filling in pastries and cakes, it is essential that they are bought from a source which has a high turnover and where they will be fresh. Stale poppy seeds are bitter and rancid in flavour. Delicatessens specializing in Eastern European ingredients usually sell fresh seeds: buy them as you need them. Store seeds in an airtight container in a cool, dark place for no more than a few weeks – they will not keep indefinitely.

Allspice

BOTANICAL NAME: *Pimenta dioica* • FAMILY NAME: *Myrtaceae*

OTHER NAMES: *English spice, Jamaican pepper, pimento;*
FR. *tout-épice, piment poivre de la Jamaïque;* G. *Jamaikapfeffer;*
SP. *pimiento de Jamaica;* IT. *pimento*

The Mayan Indians used allspice to embalm their dead long before the Spaniards arrived in the West Indies. Christopher Columbus is reported to have shown a handful of black peppercorns to natives on the Caribbean islands, which might account for the confusion in name: it is possible that they thought allspice berries and peppercorns (which the Spanish called pimienta) were one and the same spice.

allspice berries

ground allspice

The preservative properties of allspice were valued by 17th-century seafarers for keeping both fish and meat edible on long voyages. The spice is still used extensively in the fishing industry in Scandinavia, where barrels of fish are transported from market to market. At the end of the 19th century, the wood of allspice saplings was much in vogue for making walking sticks and umbrellas; however, legislation was introduced to prevent the young trees from being felled, avoiding the potential decimation of the allspice industry.

CULTIVATION

A member of the myrtle family, the allspice tree is an evergreen indigenous to the West Indies, Central and South America. In the early 19th century saplings were taken to Ceylon and Singapore but they did not flourish. The tree grows to an average height of 9-12 metres/30-40 feet, except in the rain forests of South America where this can be doubled. Avenues of trees are charmingly called 'pimento walks'. Every part of the tree – bark, leaves, white flowers and later the berries – contributes the heady perfume that fills the air in allspice plantations.

The fully developed, but green, berries are harvested between July and September, about three or four months after flowering. The berries change to purple, then brown as they are dried in the sun. Young trees start bearing fruit after five or six years, they are fully productive by their fifteenth year and can thrive for up to a hundred years, so they are a worthwhile investment. Jamaica produces two-thirds of the world's supply of the spice and exports it principally to Germany, USA and the UK.

You may notice an allspice shrub in garden centres called Carolina, Japanese or wild allspice, or strawberry bush; this is an entirely different variety, the *Calycanthus*.

AROMA AND FLAVOUR

Allspice is suitably named for its bouquet and flavour. The spice smells of cloves, nutmeg and cinnamon and some even detect a hint of mace and peppercorns in its aroma. When crushed or ground, allspice has quite a pungent flavour. Ideally, buy the whole spice and grind it when required as the ground spice soon loses its punch. The very best-quality allspice berries come from Jamaica. The round berries have a rough surface because of tiny oil glands; inside, there are two hard, kidney-shaped seeds, but most of the flavour comes from the husk.

CULINARY USE

In Jamaica, a local drink, known as Jamaica dram, is made from allspice and rum. Allspice is also one of the ingredients in Benedictine and Chartreuse. The whole berries are a popular ingredient for mulled wine.

Allspice is widely used in European cooking as an ingredient in sweet recipes and festive baking, including Christmas puddings, cakes and biscuits. The ground or whole spice may be used in preserves and chutneys as well as the Christmas mincemeat.

Many Scandinavian herring dishes are enhanced by the distinctive flavour of allspice, and German recipes often call for allspice.

MEDICINAL AND OTHER USE

The oil from berries and the leaves are used in antiseptics and medicines for flatulence. It is also used in perfumes.

Anise

BOTANICAL NAME: *Pimpinella anisum* • FAMILY NAME: *Umbelliferae*

OTHER NAMES: *aniseed, sweet cumin;*
FR. *anis;* G. *Anis;* SP. *anís;* IT. *anice*

ground anise

anise seeds

Anise is indigenous to the Eastern Mediterranean and coastal countries of the area once referred to as The Levant, and it was well known to the Ancient Egyptians. Its ability to counteract indigestion was recognized by the Romans, who used to serve a special spice cake containing anise after gastronomic orgies.

CULTIVATION

A member of the parsley and carrot family, this feathery plant grows to about 0.6 metres/2 feet in countries as far apart as Southern Russia, North Africa, India and South and Central America. The fruit consists of two united carpels, which are harvested when the fruit begins to ripen and left in stacks until ripening is complete. The seeds are separated from the flower heads by threshing. They are tiny and ovoid, with fine lines marked against a green-grey background.

AROMA AND FLAVOUR

They have a delicately sweet and aromatic bouquet with a distinctive liquorice flavour. The spiciness of the seeds is similar to fennel. The flavour is heightened by dry-frying the seeds. Buy the seeds in small quantities as they soon lose their flavour and, if necessary, grind them finely as required.

CULINARY USE

Anise is used in savoury and sweet cooking, in spicy dishes from India as well as

aniseed balls

anisette

Pernod

lightly flavoured cuisines. This spice flavours fish soups, sauces, breads (particularly rye bread), cakes, biscuits and confectionery. Popular aniseed flavour drinks include French pastis, Pernod and Ricard, a liqueur called anisette, Spanish ojen, Turkish raki, Greek ouzo and Arab arrak.

MEDICINAL AND OTHER USE

Oil from the seeds is used in cough mixtures and lozenges as well as antiseptics. Anise is also used in perfumes and soaps. The seeds are chewed after a meal in India to sweeten the breath. As a simple cure for hiccups, chew a few seeds and wash them down with a glass of water. Dogs find the smell of anise attractive, so it is used to lay a trail in hound trailing.

anise sweets

Pepper

BOTANICAL NAME: *Piper nigrum* • FAMILY NAME: *Piperaceae*

OTHER NAMES: *black pepper, white pepper, green peppercorns;* FR. *poivre (blanc – white, vert – green);* G. *Pfeffer (weisser – white, grüner – green);* SP. *pimienta negra (blanca – white, verde – green);* IT. *pepe (bianco – white, verde – green)*

white peppercorns

five peppercorn mixture

The king of spices, pepper is one of the oldest and most popular spices in the world. It was the search for the source of pepper more than any other spice which led early sailors eastward. At one time, peppercorns were more valuable than gold. The Romans were the first to identify the significance of the prevailing winds and monsoons to sea voyages, and they were able to guarantee supplies of this precious spice from Southern India. They made Alexandria the chief port for trade between Europe and Asia and built huge warehouses to store the spice. One entrance to the city was called Pepper Gate. At the siege of Rome, the King of the Goths demanded a ransom of 3,000 pounds of peppercorns, gold and silver; the Romans reluctantly paid them, but to add insult to injury, the Goths ransacked the city anyway.

By the Middle Ages pepper was considered desirable currency: dowries, taxes and rents were frequently paid in peppercorns. The term 'peppercorn rent', was established in those days to indicate payment in full, which was often expensive due to the scarcity of the spice. Today it means a nominal sum. A Guild of Peppers was set up in London in 1180; similarly, France had *poivriers* and Germany *Pfeffersacke* societies. Its value in the preservation of food and flavouring of tasteless and insipid meat, more than likely in the first stages of decay, kept the demand for pepper high. The race for the Spice Islands began with the great names of Marco Polo, Columbus, Vasco de Gama, Magellan and Drake searching the globe for pepper and the spices that were to make their fortunes.

CULTIVATION

The name pepper comes from the Sanskrit (ancient language of India) word *pippali* meaning berry. It originally referred to the Indian long pepper (*Piper longum*), which looked rather like a catkin and was familiar to the Greeks and Romans but is now difficult to find, even in its native India. *Piper nigrum* is a perennial vine indigenous to the Malabar coast of India, where, it is claimed, the best pepper is still grown. The Hindu colonists are believed to have taken pepper to Java, one of the Indonesian islands, which contributed to its gradual spread throughout the Far East, to Malaysia, Borneo, Sumatra, Sri Lanka, Penang and Singapore. Pepper grows best near the Equator: today it is also grown in Thailand, tropical Africa, the South Sea islands and Brazil.

In the Malaysian state of Sarawak, the vines grow up frames resembling slim wigwams, tapering at the top. In other places, the vines are encouraged to grow around living trees. The vines are pruned to prevent them from growing too high, making harvesting difficult. The vine has leaves that are long, green and pointed. White flowers bloom on the peppercorn 'spikes', which look like slim clusters of redcurrants. The plant starts fruiting after three to five years and continues to do so every third year for up to forty years.

Pickers move from vine to vine on

fresh green peppercorns

tripod-type ladders, hand picking the spikes on which some of the berries are red but the bulk are still green. The peppercorns are then sorted and the stems discarded.

black peppercorns

ground black pepper

coarsely ground
black pepper

green peppercorns
in brine

crushed black pepper

ground white pepper

THE PEPPERS

Black Peppercorns: The green berries are dried on mats in the sun and raked several times a day for a week until they are wrinkled and black. Sometimes, the berries are scalded with boiling water before they are dried.

White Peppercorns: The red and orange berries are packed in sacks and soaked for a week under slowly running water. This process rots the outer husk of the berries so that it can then be removed by rubbing them between the hands over sieves. The husked berries are white peppercorns.

Green Peppercorns: These are occasionally available fresh, still on the long stem. Used particularly in Thai cooking, green peppercorns also complement game and duck dishes, terrines and creamy sauces. Green peppercorns are available pickled in brine or vinegar, or freeze dried. Remember to rinse pickled peppercorns well before using them.

Long Pepper: Though this was popular in Greek and Roman times, it is difficult to find now, even in its indigenous home in India. Part of the *Anacardiaceae* family, this takes the botanical name *Piper longum.*

Cubeb: Grown mostly in the wild, cubeb are the dried unripe fruits of a member of the vine family. They are similar in size to a peppercorn with a distinctive 'tail'. Cubeb can be used as a pepper substitute as it has similar characteristics. Buy it ground in health food and specialist shops.

long pepper

cubeb berries

AROMA AND FLAVOUR

Black peppercorns have a special, earthy, rich aroma and they taste highly pungent with a richness reflected in the aroma. White peppercorns are less earthy and not as pungent or rich as the black spice. The flavour of white pepper is cleaner, less rich and not as complex. Green peppercorns are lighter in flavour than the black spice, but just as hot. They do not smell or taste as complex as the other peppers.

CULINARY USE

Pepper is one of the most versatile spices, used in virtually all savoury cooking. Both black and white pepper is used in cuisines worldwide, at all stages of the cooking process and as a table condiment. Not only does pepper contribute its own special seasoning, it has the capacity to enhance other flavours.

This spice is also used in sweet cookery; black pepper is added to fruit cakes and gingerbreads, sometimes in quite considerable quantities, and it can be served as a light seasoning on fresh fruit. Try grinding pepper on slices of fresh pineapple, fry them in unsalted butter and flambé them with rum for a flavour sensation. Fresh strawberries are excitingly different when topped with a light grinding of black pepper before the ubiquitous dollop of cream is added. Sweet, juicy figs accompanied by soft goats' cheese taste wonderful seasoned with pepper.

White pepper is milder than the black spice and has a distinguishably different flavour. It can be used in pale milk or cream sauces, where specks of black pepper would spoil the appearance; in some instances freshly ground white pepper is more complementary to the flavour of the food, for example with creamy mashed potatoes.

MEDICINAL AND OTHER USE

Pepper has long been recognized as an ingredient for stimulating the appetite as well as being an aid in the relief of nausea. In India it has been used as a medicine since time immemorial for the treatment of anything from paralysis to toothache. East Africans are said to believe that body odour produced after eating substantial amounts of pepper repels mosquitoes.

Szechuan Pepper

BOTANICAL NAME: *Zanthoxylum piperitum, syn Xanthoxylum piperitum*
FAMILY NAME: *Rutaceae*

OTHER NAMES: *anise pepper, fagara, Chinese brown pepper, Japanese pepper;* FR. *poivre anise;* G. *Anispfeffer;* SP. *pimienta de anís;* IT. *pepe d'anis*

Szechuan pepper

This spice is often wrongly assumed to be part of the pepper family when it is the berry of the prickly ash tree. The spice, which is the ground husks of the berries, is common in the Szechuan region of China, and spices from the leaves of the plant are also used in Japan. The ripe seed pods of the tree open out in a similar way to star anise, which is probably why they were named anise pepper.

CULTIVATION

Anise pepper is the fruit of the tree of the prickly ash family. The rust-red berries contain bitter black seeds that are usually removed before the spice is sold.

AROMA AND FLAVOUR

The bouquet is pungent, with a hint of citrus. Dry-frying brings out the flavour, which is pleasantly peppery.

CULINARY USE

Sold whole or ground, Szechuan pepper is much used in Chinese cookery, especially with chicken and duck. It is one of the spices in Chinese five spice powder, and it is used in Japanese seven-flavour seasoning mix. The leaves are dried and ground to make sansho, a Japanese spice (see below).

MEDICINAL AND OTHER USE

The ground bark of the plant is an old-fashioned remedy for toothache in the USA. Both bark and berries are stimulants and they are used in traditional medicines and herbal cures to purify the blood, promote digestion and as an anti-rheumatic.

Pink Peppercorns

BOTANICAL NAME: *Schinus terebinthifolius*
FAMILY NAME: *Piperaceae*

FR. *poivre rose;* G. *blassroter Pfeffer;*
SP. *pimienta rosa;* IT. *pepe rosa*

These are not true peppercorns but they have a pungency associated with that spice and are similar in size to peppercorns.

dried pink peppercorns

CULTIVATION

Native to South America, pink peppercorns are grown in Réunion in the Indian Ocean. They are picked when ripe and dried or pickled in brine.

AROMA AND FLAVOUR

Pink peppercorns do not have a strong aroma until they are crushed, when they give off a faintly sweet-peppery smell. Their flavour is sweet and slightly scented with only a peppery aftertaste.

CULINARY USE

Valued for their appearance and once the subject of a food fashion trend, dried pink peppercorns are frequently mixed with other peppercorns in a clear mill to make an attractive-looking table spice. Pink peppercorns should not be confused with true peppers (black, white and green) for culinary use: they are an interesting seasoning ingredient, but they are not hot pungent seeds to use instead of ordinary pepper. They are popular for seasoning fish and used in Mediterranean cooking.

When they were in vogue and added generously to all sorts of dishes, there were reports of the ill effects they caused when

consumed in quantity. Therefore it is recommended that pink peppercorns be used in small quantities (for example, limit the use to twelve to fifteen peppercorns in any one dish) to avoid any likelihood of adverse reactions to them.

**pink
peppercorns
in brine**

SANSHO

Sometimes confusingly called Japanese pepper. Although it is not a true pepper, this is one of the few spices used in Japanese cooking. It is used mainly to counter fatty flavours, is usually sprinkled on cooked foods and is only available ground.

Salt

CHEMICAL NAME: *Sodium chloride*

FR. *sel de cuisine, gros sel, sel gris;* G. *Kochsalz;*
SP. *sal gema, sal de cocina;* IT. *sale di cucina*

We like salt, we need it and we cannot survive without it. Salt consists of two elements – sodium and chlorine, sodium being an essential trace element for maintaining animal and human life.

fine sea salt

coarse sea salt

black salt

Maldon salt

AROMA AND FLAVOUR

Salt is the universal seasoning ingredient used to bring out the flavour in both sweet and savoury dishes. Salt is odourless but strongly flavoured: without it our meals would be dull and insipid.

CULINARY USE

Salt is used widely in preserving meat, fish and vegetables. An intriguing Chinese recipe envelopes a chicken in hot salt. After one hour the sweet tender juicy chicken is ready, and the salt can be used again.

MEDICINAL AND OTHER USE

A salt water gargle is the traditional source of relief when a cold threatens or for a sore throat.

STORAGE

Store in an airtight container in a cool dry place. Do not keep salt in silver salt cellars or leave a silver spoon in salt. The chlorine in the salt reacts with the silver, causing it to turn green.

table salt

TYPES OF SALT

Rock salt, salt from the earth, comes from underground deposits formed over the millennia by the drying up of inland lakes and seas. Water is pumped into the salt caves and the brine is pumped to the surface. The brine is then boiled and allowed to crystallize.

From this we obtain kitchen salt or cooking salt, which used to be sold as block salt but is now sold as a fairly coarse, refined salt kept free flowing by the addition of magnesium carbonate to prevent it taking in moisture from the air.

Table salt is finer in texture. A few grains of rice used to be added to salt cellars; the rice absorbed moisture from the salt. This tip is still practised in some countries where salt tends to become damp.

Rock salt is the term usually given to the larger crystals produced by the process.

Some believe it to be superior in flavour. The salt is either ground in a salt mill or pounded in a mortar with a pestle.

Sea salt is produced by the evaporation of sea water, either naturally or by artificial means. It is said that there is enough salt in the sea to cover the world's landmass to a depth of over 30 metres/100 feet. Some find that the flavour of sea salt is the best for both cooking and for table use. It is sometimes called bay salt.

English sea salt comes mainly from Maldon in Essex. The characteristic flakes have an excellent 'salty' flavour and can be sprinkled on to bread rolls and savoury biscuits before baking.

Black salt is dark grey and it has a pinkish tinge when ground. It is used as both a seasoning and a spice in Indian cooking. It has a definite tang and there is a hint of smokiness to its flavour.

Pomegranate Seeds

BOTANICAL NAME: *Punica granatum* • FAMILY NAME: *Punicaceae*

FR. *grenade*; G. *Granatapfel*; SP. *granada*; IT. *melagrano*; IN. *anardana, anar*

Romantics would say that the pomegranate was the apple in the garden of Eden; it was certainly known in the gardens of Babylon and mentioned frequently in the Bible. In Turkey, legend has it that a bride can predict the number of children she will have by the number of seeds that spill out of a pomegranate when she drops it on the floor.

CULTIVATION

Pomegranates are grown on small, lush bushes with red flowers, which look rather like those of the hibiscus. Some bushes have thorns. Native to Iran, pomegranates are also grown in Mediterranean countries, South America, the USA (particularly California) and parts of Africa. The bush flourishes in climates that are cool in winter and hot in the summer. The smooth-skinned, golden to red fruit is about the size of a large apple. The plump red seeds are encased in individual compartments, each surrounded by a creamy coloured, bitter membrane and pith. In the old days, a pin was used to spear the encased seeds one by one to avoid eating the bitter pith. The seeds are extracted from the peel, pith and membranes, then dried. When dry, they are small and dark-red to black in colour and slightly sticky.

AROMA AND FLAVOUR

Pomegranate seeds have an astringent smell and sweet-sour taste. Grenadine, a syrup made from the juice of the pomegranate, has a sweet, fresh flavour, while pomegranate syrup, used in Middle Eastern cooking, has an intense concentrated flavour.

CULINARY USE

Crushed pomegranate seeds are sprinkled on the popular Middle Eastern dip, hummus, and they are also used in fruit salads from the region. In Indian cooking, pomegranate seeds are often used as a souring agent.

MEDICINAL AND OTHER USE

Pomegranate seeds are used in gargles, and they are said to ease fevers and assist in counteracting diarrhoea. They are widely used in Indian medicines.

fresh pomegranates

dried pomegranate seeds

fresh pomegranate seeds

grenadine

fresh pomegranate juice

pomegranate syrup

Mahlebi

BOTANICAL NAME: *Prunus mahaleb*

FAMILY NAME: *Rosaceae*

OTHER NAMES: *Mahlab;* FR. *mahaleb;*
G. *Mahaleb;* SP. *mahaleb;* IT. *mahaleb*

mahlebi seeds

mahlebi powder

*Mahlebi is the dried kernel of a small cherry stone. It is an ancient
spice that is used principally in the Middle East and Turkey.*

CULTIVATION

The tree is usually found only in the
Middle East and Turkey. It is decidu-
ous and it grows to a height of about
10 metres/35 feet. The wide, out-
spreading branches bear white flowers
and fruit that are small, oval and green
at first, turning black when they are
picked. The stone is creamy yellow
when powdered.

AROMA AND FLAVOUR

The bouquet is distinctly nutty, with
hints of almond and cherry. The taste
is slightly bitter but not unpleasant.

CULINARY USE

The ground spice is used in breads,
biscuits and pastries from the Middle
East and Turkey. It makes an unusual
addition to pastry for a fruit tart.

STORAGE

Ideally it is best to buy the mahlebi
whole and grind it to a powder in a
mortar, coffee grinder or food processor as required. The powdered version
soon loses its interesting flavour, even
after short periods of storage. Store
the seeds or powder in an airtight
container in a cool drawer or cupboard
away from strong light.

Sumac

BOTANICAL NAME: *Rhus coriaria* • FAMILY NAME: *Anacardiaceae*

FR. *sumac;* G. *Sumach;* SP. *zumaque;* IT. *sommacco*

*The Romans used sumac berries as a souring agent as we would use lemon juice or
vinegar, or tamarind in Eastern cooking. Buy sumac only from a specialist shop selling
Middle Eastern ingredients as some members of the
sumac family (found mostly in the USA) have
poisonous berries.*

CULTIVATION

The sumac bush grows to a modest
3 metres/10 feet and its leaves turn a
vibrant rust-red in the autumn. It grows
wild and is also cultivated around
Southern Italy, Sicily and throughout
the Middle East. It is said that the
higher the altitude at which the bush
grows, the better the quality of the fruit.
The white flowers produce spikes of red
berries, which are picked just before
they ripen, then they are dried and will
keep indefinitely.

ground sumac

AROMA AND FLAVOUR

Although it has little aroma, sumac
has a definite, astringent quality, with
a pleasing sour-fruit flavour.

CULINARY USE

Sumac is widely used in Lebanese,
Syrian, Turkish and Iranian cuisines.
Sometimes the berries are used whole,
with the small brown central seed intact.
They can be ground or cracked, then
soaked for about 15-20 minutes in warm
water and squeezed to release their
astringent juice. This is strained and
usually added to food towards the end
of the cooking process. Ground sumac
is available from specialist Middle
Eastern stores: it may be rubbed on to
fish, chicken, steaks or kebabs before
cooking or over potato, beetroot or
mixed bean salads to give just a hint of
its flavour. The juice can be used in
marinades and salad dressings.

MEDICINAL AND OTHER USE

In the Middle East sumac is used to
make a drink for anyone suffering from
an upset stomach, and to treat fevers
and bowel complaints.

Sesame

BOTANICAL NAME: *Sesamum indicum,*
syn S. orientale • FAMILY NAME: *Pedaliaceae*

FR. *sésame;* G. *Sesam;* SP. *sésamo, ajonjolí;*
IT. *sesamo;* JAP. *goma*

black sesame seeds

halva

The name sesame was listed as sesemt *in about 1500 BC in the* Ebers Papyrus, *a
20-metre/65-feet-long scroll on ancient herbs and spices discovered by the famous German
Egyptologist, Ebers. It is not clear whether sesame originated in Africa or India, but this
valuable crop soon reached China, where 5,000 years ago the Chinese were burning sesame
oil to make soot for their ink-blocks, and both seeds and oil have long been used in cooking.
Slaves from Africa took the sesame seed to America and the West Indies in the belief that
it would bring them luck.*

**sesame
seeds**

**air-dried
sesame seeds**

CULTIVATION

The sesame plant is a tall, tropical herbaceous annual growing to about 1.8 metres/6 feet. It has pink or white foxglove-type flowers and hairy leaves, which are often used in folk medicine to make an eyebath for tired eyes. When ready for harvesting, the stems are cut and hung upside down over mats until the seeds are all disgorged from the pods. The seeds are small, flat and oblate; they may be red, brown, black or yellow. When they are husked they are a creamy colour. Black sesame seeds are available, but the majority are sold as the husked, white type. They are also available ready roasted, when they are a darker beige colour. Sesame grows in many countries: India, China, Burma, Mexico Pakistan, Turkey, Uganda, Sudan and Nigeria; much of each country's crop is consumed at home, except for Sudan and Nigeria, the main exporters.

AROMA AND FLAVOUR

In spite of their high oil content, sesame seeds have little aroma, but when they are dry-fried their nutty aroma is very pronounced and their flavour heightened.

CULINARY USE

Sesame oil is used in margarines and as a cooking medium and a flavouring ingredient. The seeds are ground to an oily, beige-coloured paste known as tahini, which is used in hummus, a Middle Eastern dip. Sometimes the tahini is mixed with lemon juice and garlic and used as a dip with hot pitta bread as a starter or picnic food.

The Chinese are fond of sesame: sesame oil is widely used in Chinese cooking as a flavouring. The seeds are also used, for example sesame prawn toasts are scattered with seeds before they are deep-fried. They are also sprinkled over Chinese toffee apples, pieces of apple fried in a light batter and coated in caramel. Both oil and seeds are used in the cooking of other Far Eastern countries such as Singapore, Malaysia and Indonesia. Gomasio is a Japanese speciality using sesame seeds: a mixture of the ground seeds and salt used as a seasoning.

The seeds are popular scattered on bread, sweet and savoury biscuits, particularly in Greece and Turkey.

MEDICINAL AND OTHER USE

Sesame is used in laxatives, as an emollient and in poultices. Sesame oil, also called gingelly oil, is highly stable and it does not become rancid quickly in hot humid conditions; it is used in lubricants, soap, cosmetics and ointments. The mixture or 'cake' that remains after the pressing of the oil is full of protein and eaten as a subsistence food.

tahini

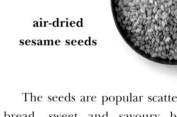

sesame oil

hummus

Tamarind

BOTANICAL NAME: *Tamarindus indica,*
syn T. officinalis • FAMILY NAME: *Leguminosae*

FR. *tamarin;* G. *Tamarinde;* SP. *tamarindo;*
IT. *tamarindo;* IN. *imli, amyli*

tamarind pods

The word tamarind literally means date of India, *which is an apt description. Believed to be native to East Africa, tamarind now grows extensively throughout India, South-east Asia and the West Indies: all areas where its particular sour flavour is used in the diverse cuisines.*

CULTIVATION

A semi-evergreen, tropical tree, the tamarind grows to a magnificent 24 metres/80 feet and it has long, drooping branches. The flowers are yellow, each with a red stripe. The dark brown fruit pods are 15-20 cm/6-8 in long. The sticky pulp surrounding the seeds has a high tartaric acid content, which accounts for its wide use as a souring agent.

AROMA AND FLAVOUR

Tamarind has little smell – perhaps a hint of sweet and sour to its aroma – but its flavour makes up for this, being particularly sour, yet fruity and refreshing, resembling sour prunes.

CULINARY USE

Recipes which have been adapted for Western kitchens may suggest substituting lemon juice for tamarind, but if you know the taste of tamarind, it alone will suffice. Tamarind is readily available in Oriental stores in slices, as a block or as a concentrate. Tamarind is a standard ingredient throughout India and South-east Asia in curries, chutneys, lentil and bean dishes as well as in the famous hot and sour soups. The juice is made into a refreshing drink in both the Middle East and the West Indies. Tamarind is also one of the ingredients in the famous Worcestershire sauce.

PREPARATION TIPS

COMPRESSED BLOCK: Tear off the equivalent of 1 tbsp and soak it in 150 ml/^{1}/$_4$ pint/^{2}/$_3$ cup warm water for 10 minutes. Swirl the tamarind with your fingers so that the pulp is released from the seeds.

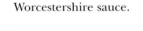

Strain the juice through a nylon sieve: do not use a metal sieve which will react with the acid. Discard the pulp and seeds and use the liquid as required.

TAMARIND SLICES: Soak them in 150 ml/^{1}/$_4$ pint/^{2}/$_3$ cup warm water for 30 minutes to extract their flavour. Squeeze with your fingers, then strain the juice.

TAMARIND CONCENTRATE: Just mix 1 tbsp with 4-6 tbsp warm water and use as required. Once opened, it is best to keep the jar of concentrate in the fridge, with the top firmly secured.

compressed tamarind block

dried tamarind slices

tamarind balls

MEDICINAL AND OTHER USE

Tamarind is used as a laxative and for tummy upsets. It is antiseptic, used in eye baths and for the treatment of ulcers. Over-ripe fruits can be used to clean copper and brass, a common practice in colonial times.

tamarind concentrate

tamarind paste

compressed tamarind

Fenugreek

BOTANICAL NAME: *Trigonella foenum-graecum*

FAMILY NAME: *Leguminosae*

FR. *fenugrec sénegré, trigonelle;* G. *Bockshornklee, Griechisches Heu;* SP. *alholva, fenogreco;* IT. *fieno greco;* IN. *methi*

The botanical name is easily explained: trigonella *refers to the angular seeds and* foenum graecum *translates as 'Greek hay', which explains its use as cattle fodder. Fenugreek was used by the Ancient Egyptians in embalming and for incense. The Romans grew it as fodder for their animals, which is still the practice in India today, with the benefit that it restores nitrogen to the soil and acts as a natural fertilizer.*

dried fenugreek leaves

CULTIVATION

Fenugreek is native to India and Southern Europe, and it grows wild all over North Africa. India, Pakistan, Lebanon, Egypt, France and Argentina all export the crop. The fenugreek plant is an annual, which grows to about 0.6 metres/2 feet with light green leaves, not unlike clover, and white flowers. Between ten and twenty seeds are obtained from each fenugreek pod.

AROMA AND FLAVOUR

Fenugreek is highly aromatic, smelling of curry – the whole plant exudes the characteristic, but mild, curry-powder aroma. The spice has a tangy flavour, rather like burnt sugar, and anyone who has tried old-fashioned or inexpensive curry powder will recognize the smell of fenugreek.

CULINARY USE

Commercially, fenugreek extract is used as a flavouring in imitation maple syrup and in mango chutney. Fenugreek is rich in protein, minerals and vitamins, which makes it an important ingredient in vegetable and dhal dishes eaten in the poorer areas of India. The leaves, called *methi,* are widely used, fresh or dried, in Indian cooking and are often combined with vegetables, such as spinach, potato and yam.

Fenugreek seeds are used in a wide range of home-made or commercial curry powders. The small seeds, which resemble tiny, irregular, beige stones, are extremely hard and difficult to grind at home. Used in spiced fish dishes and vegetable curries.

MEDICINAL AND OTHER USE

Used in the Middle Ages as a cure for baldness, fenugreek is still used in Indonesia as a hair tonic.

Fenugreek is traditionally used to stimulate the metabolism and to help control blood-sugar levels in cases of diabetes. It is also given to assist with stomach and digestive orders, and lowering blood pressure. Having a valuable iron content, fenugreek was also given in cases of anaemia. The powder is sometimes used as a dye.

fresh fenugreek leaves

PREPARATION TIPS

Always dry-fry the seeds before grinding them: a light roast gives a mellow flavour, too dark and the flavour will be bitter. Sometimes the seeds are soaked overnight, when they become gelatinous and easier to combine into curry pastes.

STORAGE
If kept in an airtight container, in a cool, dark place, the whole seeds have a long shelf life. The powder should be bought in small quantities and stored away from strong light as it loses its flavour if stored for long periods.

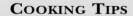

COOKING TIPS

Fenugreek seeds can be sprouted very easily: put 2-3 tbsp in a jar, cover with a double layer of muslin and secure with an elastic band. Rinse with water and drain once or twice a day until the seeds sprout. The sprouts add an intriguing flavour to salads or can be used in a sandwich filling. with avocado, tomato or cheese.

Add ground fenugreek judiciously in cooking because it has a strong penetrating flavour.

fenugreek seeds

fenugreek sprouts

ground fenugreek

fenugreek powder

Vanilla

BOTANICAL NAME: *Vanilla fragrans, syn V. planifolia*
FAMILY NAME: *Orchidaceae*

FR. *vanille;* G. *Vanille;* SP. *vainilla;* IT. *vaniglia*

The name vanilla comes from the Spanish vainilla, *meaning 'little pod'. A drink that combines chocolate and vanilla may seem to be a modern combination, but the Aztecs discovered this combination of exotic flavours centuries before the Spanish first set foot in Mexico in 1520. Vanilla was taken back to Spain and from there it quickly spread throughout Europe, where its magical flavour was much enjoyed by those who could afford to buy it.*

CULTIVATION
Vanilla is the seed pod of a tropical climbing orchid, a native of Mexico and exclusive to the country until the 19th century. Attempts were made to intro-

duce the plant elsewhere but the flowers never produced pods. The flowers open only for one day and are naturally pollinated by the melipona bee and a particular

vanilla pods

long-beaked humming bird, both native to Mexico, which explained the lack of success in propagation elsewhere. The plant was then artifically pollinated, and it now grows principally in Madagascar and the Seychelles, with some crops in Réunion, Mauritius, Indonesia, Puerto Rica, Mexico and the West Indies.

Being vine-like, the plant is encouraged to grow around the trunks of trees, the leaves of which provide the shade in which vanilla thrives. The plant bears fruit after three years and has a productive life of twelve years, after which time the vines are replaced. The unripe pods are harvested when they are 13-20 cm/ 5-8 in long and yellow in colour. At this stage the pod does not have the characteristic smell.

The drying process is somewhat lengthy, and it contributes to the high price of the spice. In Madagascar and Mexico, the pods are blanched briefly in boiling water and then sweated and dried over a period of weeks until they are dark brown and wrinkled, yet supple. The superior pods are coated in a white crystalline efflorescence which is the vanillin, the real vanilla flavour. The pods keep their flavour well.

AROMA AND FLAVOUR

Real vanilla is highly fragrant, with an exotic and memorable aroma. The taste reflects the smell, with a soft, flowery mellowness.

CULINARY USE

One of the finest flavours, used almost exclusively in sweet cookery, vanilla is added to cakes, biscuits, puddings and desserts. It is used to flavour confectionery, and it has a special affinity for chocolate. Vanilla is one of the distinctive ingredients in crème de cacao and Galliano, two popular liqueurs.

MEDICINAL AND OTHER USE

Vanilla is used as a pick-me-up and an antidote to fevers. It is also attributed with aphrodisiac qualities, and it is used in perfume production.

STORAGE

Vanilla pods are usually sold singly or in pairs, packed in a long clear tube. Store one vanilla pod in a jar of sugar (usually caster sugar), allowing three or four weeks for the flavour to permeate the sugar fully, and just top up the jar with more sugar as required. This gloriously fragrant vanilla sugar is marvellous in cakes, biscuits, sweet pies, ice creams and milk puddings. A good-quality pod, with plenty of vanillin crystals, will remain potent for as long as four years.

VANILLA FLAVOURINGS

Natural vanilla flavouring, extract or essence is made by finely chopping the beans or pods and infusing them by dripping alcohol on the pieces. Inferior pods are used; they may not be good enough for selling whole, but their flavour is fine. Madagascar bourbon is one example of a title given to superior vanilla flavouring.

Artificial vanilla essence or flavouring is light years away from the true flavour of vanilla. The flavour is synthesized from wood pulp waste, coal tar or

Galliano

vanilla sugar

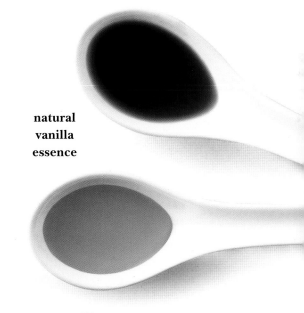

natural vanilla essence

vanilla essence

coumarin, which is banned in many countries. Substantial quantities of the artificial flavouring are sold and used each year. This type of vanilla essence has a harsh flavour with a definite aftertaste. Buy the vanilla pod or natural vanilla flavouring or essence and you will notice the difference in flavour.

Ginger

BOTANICAL NAME: *Zingiber officinale, syn Amoumum officinale*
FAMILY NAME: *Zingiberaceae*

OTHER NAMES: *Jamaican Ginger;* FR. *gingembre;*
G. *Ingwer;* SP. *jengibre;* IT. *zenzero*

Thinly peel or scrape off the skin from a piece of fresh root ginger.

fresh root ginger

The name is believed to come from the Sanskrit (an ancient Indo-Aryan language) singabera, *meaning 'shaped like a horn', evolving to the Greek* zingiberi *and subsequently the Latin* zingiber. *Ginger has a long respected history as a spice. Its origins lie in either India or China, where it was mentioned in 500 BC in the writings of the philospher Confucius. Arab traders from the Orient introduced ginger to Greece and Rome, and it is quite likely that the invading Romans carried it to Britain. The ginger rhizome was easily transported, allowing the Arabs to introduce it to East Africa, and the Portuguese to take it to West Africa in the 13th century. The Spanish expanded the trade by taking ginger to Mexico and the West Indies, especially Jamaica, a country that still claims to produce the best-quality ginger. By the 14th century, ginger was the most common spice after pepper.*

Grate the root, taking care not to graze your fingers at the end!

Peeled ginger can be ground to a paste with garlic, other spices and a little oil to make a smoother mixture.

CULTIVATION

The ginger plant is an upright tropical plant, which is propagated by dividing the rhizomes. It grows to about 0.9 metres/3 feet, with elegant lance-shaped leaves and yellow flowers lightly tinged with purple. Harvesting takes place 9 or 10 months after planting, and in many parts of the world this is still done by hand. Much of the crop is washed, sun dried and then ground to a powder for domestic and commercial use. The largest markets for ground ginger are the UK, Yemen, the USA, Middle East, Singapore and Malaysia. Large crops are grown in India, China, Taiwan, Nigeria, Jamaica and Mauritius; Australia is also now a significant producer.

AROMA AND FLAVOUR

The aroma when you cut into a piece of fresh root ginger has a hint of lemon, with a refreshing sharpness. Jamaica ginger is said to have the finest aroma, with the Kenyan spice being of good

quality too. Other African and Indian gingers have a darker skin and a biting, less pleasant flavour.

CULINARY USE

The essential oil is used in commercial flavourings. Fresh root ginger is extremely popular in a huge variety of stir-fry or curry dishes. Authentically, fresh root ginger is used in a host of dishes from India and Oriental countries. It is incorporated by different techniques: slices may be added to marinades or in cooking, to be discarded on the side of the plate or bowl as the food is eaten. Grated, chopped or crushed ginger is used in pastes or braised dishes. Finely shredded ginger is added to fried and stir-fried dishes, or it may be used raw in salads. Pickled and preserved types are served as appetizers or used in savoury cooking.

All these methods are employed to flavour fish and seafood, poultry, meat, vegetable and noodle dishes. Ginger is also widely appreciated in

Cut thin, peeled, slices into matchstick strips for use in stir-fries or similar dishes. The strips can be cut across to provide coarsely chopped ginger or the spice can be chopped in a food processor.

Bruise the root using the flat blade of a knife for use in dishes where it will be removed or not eaten.

new cooking styles, for example with chicken and game in casseroles.

Ginger is also essential in much Western baking, for example in traditional gingerbreads, cakes, biscuits (such as ginger snaps), French pain d'épice and German Pfefferkuchen. The spice is also important in chutneys, pickles, jams and sweet preserves as well as drinks, such as ginger beer, ginger ale and ginger wine.

MEDICINAL AND OTHER USE

Henry VIII is said to have used ginger as a medicine for its qualities, as outlined by Culpeper, the herbalist, 150 years later: 'Ginger helps digestion, warms the stomach, clears the sight, and is profitable for old men; it heats the joints and is therefore useful against gout'. Ginger has an impressive record in treating all kinds of ailments: it is said to help poor circulation, and to cure flatulence and indigestion; it is taken as a drink for coughs, nausea and influenza. In the East ginger is chewed to ward off evil spirits. It is considered to be a cure for travel sickness. The essential oil is used in perfumery.

TYPES OF GINGER

Fresh Root or Green Ginger: the fresh spice. Look for plump, silvery skinned pieces, which are called a 'hand'. Young ginger has smoother, thin skin firmly clinging to the firm, quite heavy, root. Older ginger has thicker, papery skin, which is buff-coloured or off-white. The root itself is slightly lighter, more fibrous and, by comparison to the young budding ginger, it looks dead. Avoid ginger that is wrinkled, softening or very light in weight. Similarly, reject pieces where cut ends look dehydrated and coarsely fibrous or even slightly mouldy! Fresh, young ginger is usually available only from Oriental stores – buy it when you find it to sample the smooth, juicy and tender texture, and the light, hot, citric flavour.

COOKING TIPS

Use a little crushed ginger in marinades for pork steaks or chops. Try adding a little finely grated fresh or chopped crystallized ginger to fruit puddings using rhubarb, plums or pears, to crumbles, Eve's pudding or pastry pies.

Dried Whole Ginger Root: a traditional pickling spice. It is placed in a muslin bag of spices for flavouring vinegar or other pickle mixtures. The dried root is rarely used where fresh root ginger is readily available.

Ground Ginger: pale sand-colour spice widely used in baking, both domestic and commercial.

Pickled Ginger: a savoury condiment used in Oriental cooking. There are different types: Chinese pickled ginger in sweetened vinegar is light, sweet-sour and quite hot in flavour. It is eaten as an appetizer or used in cooking. Sweet red pickled ginger is artificially coloured and slightly tangy, but mainly sweet as it is candied. Japanese pickled ginger is

more delicate than the Chinese pickles, and there are two different types: one red, one pale, both with traditional savoury roles.

Preserved or Stem Ginger: traditionally packed into the decorative, bulbous Chinese ginger jars, the plump tender young ginger is peeled and preserved in syrup. This is sweet and fairly spicy.

Chopped Candied Ginger: a sweet ingredient. The ginger is preserved in a strong syrup, as for stem ginger, and chopped then packed in a small amount of heavy syrup.

Crystallized Ginger: preserved by cooking in syrup, then drying and rolling in sugar.

pickled ginger

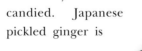

ground ginger

crystallized ginger

stem ginger in syrup

dried root ginger

SPICE MIXTURES

Curry Powders

The name curry is a corruption of the Tamil word karhi. Throughout the days of the Raj, the word evolved as a loose description of any Indian food cooked in a sauce. The early afficionados of richly spiced Indian dishes, the merchants and soldiers who visited India, were keen to introduce the flavours to their home cooking when they returned. Demand for a commercial curry powder developed over decades, and such spice mixtures have slowly become more authentic, better in quality and less crude in terms of flavour. Today there are ready prepared curry spice mixtures for Oriental cuisines as well as Indian cooking in most supermarkets.

Curry powder is a blend of different spices, combined to create seasonings used in different regions. It is not a traditional, authentic ingredient in Indian cooking: in a huge sub-continent like India and in countries throughout the East, individual spices are mixed in particular styles of cooking. Curry powders reflect the availability of the spices and the climate of the region to which they are credited.

Spice blends from the hotter regions contain more fiery chilli flavours; for example, Madras, Mysore and Goa (vindaloo) are all hot, while spice mixtures from cooler, northern climes usually concentrate on warmer and more fragrant flavours.

Achieving the right balance of ingredients for a curry powder is highly personal. The basic recipe with variations can be adapted to suit your taste and the main ingredients for any particular dish.

Curry Powder

MAKES 16 TBSP

6-8 dried red chillies
8 tbsp coriander seeds
4 tbsp cumin seeds
2 tsp fenugreek seeds
2 tsp black mustard seeds
2 tsp black peppercorns
1 tbsp ground turmeric
1 tsp ground ginger

1 Remove the stalks and seeds from chillies unless you like a fiery mixture, in which case leave a few seeds in the pods.

2 Roast or dry-fry the chillies, coriander, cumin, fenugreek, mustard seeds and black peppercorns in a heavy-based pan over a medium heat until they give off a rich aroma. Shake the pan constantly so that the spices are evenly roasted.

3 Grind the roasted spices to a powder in a mortar or coffee grinder, then stir in the ginger and turmeric.

> ### VARIATION
>
> *Dry-fry 4 curry leaves and add them to the ground curry powder mixture; remove from the cooked dish before it is served as the curry leaves are not eaten.*
>
> *For a milder result, halve the number of chillies, then add 1 cinnamon stick, 1 tbsp fennel seeds and 6 cloves to the spices before roasting or dry-frying.*

dried red chillies

black mustard seeds

coriander seeds

black peppercorns

cumin seeds

ground turmeric

fenugreek seeds

ground ginger

Sambaar Powder

Also known as sambar, this classic blend of spices is used extensively in South Indian dishes to flavour vegetable and lentil combinations, braised dishes and spicy broths so typical ofBrahmin cooking. The powder has a pleasing nutty flavour, which comes from dry-roasting the dhal before grinding them. This also gives a smooth, velvet-like thickening to the finished sauce. The dhal are readily available in Asian stores and in some of the larger supermarkets.

<u>MAKES 17 TBSP</u>

8-10 dried red chillies
6 tbsp coriander seeds
2 tbsp cumin seeds
2 tsp black peppercorns
2 tsp fenugreek seeds
2 tsp urad dhal (white split gram beans)
2 tsp channa dhal (yellow split peas)
2 tsp mung dhal (yellow mung beans)
1½ tbsp ground turmeric

1 Discard the stalks and seeds from the chillies. Heat a heavy-based frying pan, add the chillies, coriander, cumin, black peppercorns and fenugreek. Toss all the spices together over a medium heat until they give off a rich aroma, then turn the mixture into a bowl.

2 Repeat the process with the pulses, tossing them over a medium heat continuously until they are toasted but do not allow them to burn.

3 Grind the spices and pulses to a fine powder and then mix in the turmeric.

dried red chillies

coriander seeds

channa dhal

black peppercorns

mung dhal

fenugreek seeds

ground turmeric

urad dhal

cumin seeds

COOK'S TIP

Authentically, spices would usually be prepared and mixed as required, on a daily basis, but the mixture can be made in advance and stored in an airtight jar for 3-4 months, away from strong light, or the spice mixture can be frozen.

Bengali Five Spices

In this spice mix of Bengali origin, also known as panch phoron, equal quantities of the whole spices are simply mixed together, without roasting or grinding. The mixture is used in either of two ways: the mixture may be fried in oil to impart flavour to the oil before adding the main ingredients or fried in ghee and stirred into cooked dhal or vegetable dishes just before they are served.

MAKES 10 TBSP

2 tbsp cumin seeds
2 tbsp fennel seeds
2 tbsp mustard seeds
2 tbsp fenugreek seeds
2 tbsp nigella seeds

1 Mix the spices and store them in an airtight jar away from strong light.

cumin seeds

fennel seeds

mustard seeds

fenugreek seeds

nigella seeds

Sri Lankan Curry Powder

This has quite different characteristics from Indian curry powders. The spices are highly roasted, the coriander, cumin, fennel and fenugreek separately, resulting in a gloriously rich, dark curry powder, which can be used for fish, poultry, meat or vegetable curries.

MAKES 12 TBSP

6 tbsp coriander seeds
3 tbsp cumin seeds
1 tbsp fennel seeds
1 tsp fenugreek seeds
5 cm/2 in piece cinnamon stick
1 tsp cloves
8 green cardamoms
6 dried curry leaves
1-2 tsp chilli powder

1 Dry-fry or roast the coriander, cumin, fennel and fenugreek separately because they turn dark at different stages. Dry-fry or roast the cinnamon stick, cloves and cardamoms together until they give off a spicy aroma.

2 Remove the seeds from the cardamom pods and grind all the ingredients, with curry leaves and chilli powder, to a fine powder.

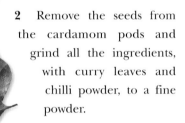
dried curry leaves

coriander seeds

green cardamoms

chilli powder

cinnamon stick

cumin seeds

fenugreek seeds

cloves

Singapore-style Curry Powder

Singapore is a culinary melting pot of different cuisines and cooks who are all extraordinarily keen on their particular type of food, each creating a particular blend of spices. This basic recipe is suitable for poultry and meat dishes.

MAKES 10 TBSP
3-4 dried red chillies
6 tbsp coriander seeds
1 tbsp cumin seeds
1 tbsp fennel seeds
2 tsp black peppercorns
2.5 cm/1 in piece cinnamon stick
4 green cardamoms
6 cloves
2 tsp ground turmeric

1 Unless you like a fiery curry powder, discard the stalks and seeds from the chillies.

2 Dry-fry or roast the chillies with all the remaining spices except the turmeric, stirring continuously, until they give off a rich aroma.

3 Break the cinnamon stick into small pieces and remove the seeds from the cardamom pods. Grind all the spices to a fine powder, then stir in the turmeric.

dried red chillies

coriander seeds

cumin seeds

fennel seeds

black peppercorns

cinnamon stick

green cardamom and cloves

ground turmeric

Singapore Seafood Curry Powder

MAKES 8 TBSP
2-3 dried red chillies
6 tbsp coriander seeds
1 tbsp cumin seeds
2 tbsp fennel seeds
1 tsp fenugreek seeds
1 tsp black peppercorns
2 tsp ground turmeric

1 Prepare as for the Singapore-style curry powder, but add the ground turmeric last.

dried red chillies

coriander seeds

cumin seeds

fennel seeds

ground turmeric

fenugreek seeds

black peppercorns

Seven-seas Curry Powder

This milder blend of spices is much enjoyed in Indonesian and Malaysian cooking, for curries, sambals, casseroles and kebabs. The name is derived from the fact that seven seas, including the Andaman and South China Sea, converge on the shores of Malaysia and the thousands of islands that make up the archipelago of Indonesia.

MAKES 13 TBSP
6-8 white cardamoms
6 tbsp coriander seeds
3 tbsp cumin seeds
1½ tbsp celery seeds
5 cm/2 in piece cinnamon stick
  or cassia
6-8 cloves
1 tbsp chilli powder

1 Bruise the cardamom pods and place them in a heavy-based frying pan with all the other spices except the chilli powder. Dry-fry the mixture, stirring it and shaking the pan continuously, until the spices give off a rich, heady aroma.

2 Remove cardamom seeds from their pods, then grind them with all the other roasted ingredients to a fine powder. Add the chilli powder and mix well.

piece of cassia

white cardamons   **coriander seeds**   **cumin seeds**

celery seeds   **cloves**   **chilli powder**

Tadka

MAKES ENOUGH FOR 1 DISH
2 tbsp ghee
2 tsp black mustard seeds
½ tsp ground asafoetida
about 8 fresh or dried curry leaves

1 Assemble all the ingredients – more curry leaves can be added if liked.

2 Melt the ghee in a frying pan or large saucepan and have a lid ready to cover the pan. When the ghee is hot add the mustard seeds, which will jump when they pop so be ready to cover the pan with a lid.

3 Draw the pan off the heat and add the asafoetida and curry leaves. Stir and then add to a dhal, soup or stew.

black   **ground**
mustard seeds   **asafoetida**

curry leaves   **ghee**

Coriander Baghar

A baghar or tadka is a mixture of spices and flavourings fried in hot ghee or mustard oil to release their flavours. They are then quickly poured over or stirred into Indian dishes of dhal, vegetables, yogurt salads or pulse and vegetable combinations. Traditional regional mixtures are used; for example, garlic and dried red pepper are used in a baghar for lentils in North Indian cooking. The combination of spices below, fried in mustard oil, are also used in North Indian cooking as a topping for dhal; in the south, black mustard seeds, asafoetida and fresh or dried curry leaves are used.

<u>MAKES ENOUGH FOR 1 DISH</u>

4 tbsp mustard oil
3-4 tsp cumin seeds
1 small onion, finely chopped
**4 tbsp finely chopped
  fresh coriander**

1   Assemble all the ingredients. Heat the mustard oil until it is just smoking. Turn off the heat and allow the oil to cool briefly.

2   Reheat the oil and fry the cumin seeds until they are changing colour. Add the onion and cook until it is turning golden.

3   Finally, add the coriander leaves and stir for only a few seconds, then pour the mixture over a dhal, soup or stew.

mustard oil

fresh coriander

chopped onion

cumin seeds

Masalas

Masalas are a blend of spices which can be a dry mixture or a paste. The flavours can be mild and fragrant or more highly spiced. This depends largely on the cook and the dish in which *the masala is to be used. The spices are usually dry-fried before grinding, which greatly enhances the flavour.*

Garam Masala

Garam *means warm or hot and* garam masala *means warm or hot spices.* This is a North Indian spice mix. *Unlike other spice mixtures, garam masala is often sprinkled over a finished dish to enhance the flavours, adding a gentle aroma of roasted spices just before serving. It may also be used in the early stages of cooking to flavour a dish.*

coriander seeds

black peppercorns

cumin seeds

bay leaves

green cardamoms

ground mace

cloves

cinnamon stick

MAKES 16 TBSP

10 green cardamoms
6 tbsp coriander seeds
4 tbsp cumin seeds
10 cloves
5 cm/2 in piece cinnamon stick
1 tbsp black peppercorns
3 dried bay leaves
1 tbsp ground mace

1 Gently warm a dry heavy-based pan before adding the spices.

2 Bruise the cardamom pods and place them in the pan with coriander, cumin, cloves, cinnamon stick, peppercorns and bay leaves. Keep tossing the spices over a gentle heat until they give off a rich aroma.

3 Remove the seeds from the cardamoms and break the cinnamon stick into small pieces. Grind all the spices to a fine powder, then mix in the ground mace.

Kashmiri Masala

This masala is particularly good with prawn and lamb dishes.

MAKES 4¹/₂ TBSP

12 green cardamoms
5 cm/2 in piece
  cinnamon stick
1 tbsp cloves
1 tbsp black peppercorns
1 tbsp black cumin seeds
2 tsp caraway seeds
1 tsp ground nutmeg

cinnamon stick

black peppercorns

cloves

1 Split the cardamom pods and break the cinnamon stick.

2 Warm a heavy-based frying pan and then dry-fry all the spices except the nutmeg, tossing them continuously, until they give off a rich aroma.

3 Remove the cardamom seeds from their pods and grind all the spices to a fine powder. Mix in the nutmeg.

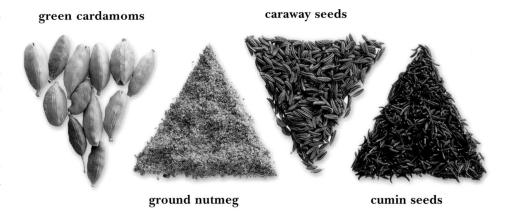

green cardamoms   **caraway seeds**

ground nutmeg   **cumin seeds**

Chat Masala

Chat is an Indian salad snack sold on street stalls or by food hawkers – it might consist of banana, papaya, guavas and chikoo or apples. The following recipe is for the spicy and rather tart mixture used to flavour the salad, which can also be served as a refreshing first course before a main meal. The whole spices and the salt are ground without dry-frying or roasting, and then thoroughly mixed with the other ingredients.

MAKES 2½ TBSP

1 tsp black peppercorns
1 tsp cumin seeds
1 tsp ajowan seeds
1 tsp pomegranate seeds
1 tsp mixed black salt and sea salt,
  or to taste
¼ tsp asafoetida
1 tsp mango powder
½ tsp cayenne pepper, or to taste
½ tsp garam masala (optional)

1 Grind the peppercorns to a powder with the cumin, ajowan, pomegranate seeds and salts.

2 Add the remaining ingredients, adjusting the quantity of cayenne pepper to taste and omitting the garam masala, if preferred, and mix well.

black peppercorns   **cumin seeds**   **ajowan seeds**

pomegranate seeds   **sea salt**   **mango powder**

asafoetida   **cayenne pepper**   **garam masala**

Green Masala

This mild masala paste, rich jewel-green in colour, is tangy with fresh mint and coriander leaves. It makes a wonderful addition to prawn, poultry and vegetable dishes, especially those containing coconut milk, or as an addition to a simple dhal.

MAKES 17 TBSP

1 tsp fenugreek seeds
10 green cardamoms
6 cloves
2 tsp ground turmeric
2 tsp salt
4 cloves garlic, crushed
5 cm/2 in piece fresh root ginger, peeled and finely grated
50 g/2 oz mint leaves
50 g/1 oz coriander leaves
1 small green pepper, seeded and chopped (optional)
50 ml/2 fl oz/¼ cup cider vinegar
120 ml/4 fl oz/½ cup mixed sunflower and sesame oil

1 Soak the fenugreek seeds in water overnight.

2 Next day, bruise the cardamoms and dry-fry them with the cloves until they give off a rich aroma. Grind these roasted spices to a powder and add the turmeric and salt.

3 Drain the fenugreek seeds, place them in a blender or food processor with the garlic, ginger, mint, coriander leaves, green pepper, if using, and the vinegar. Blend the mixture to a purée, then add the salt and ground spices.

coriander leaves

fenugreek seeds

green cardamoms

garlic

mint leaves

cloves

ground turmeric

fresh root ginger

salt   **cider vinegar**

mixed sunflower and sesame oil

green pepper

4 Heat the oil. Add the paste and continue heating until the oil bubbles again, then remove the pan from the heat and allow to cool.

5 Transfer the mixture to a clean jar. Ensure that there is a film of oil floating on the paste to effect an airtight seal, which will act as a preservative and ensure the paste keeps its colour. Store away from strong light, or in the fridge, for 2-3 weeks.

Madrasi Masala

This blend of dry and wet spices is typical of seasonings from South India. The dry spices are roasted and ground before adding garlic, finely grated ginger and vinegar to make a paste, which is then cooked in oil to develop the flavours before being stored in an airtight jar.

MAKES 450 G/1 LB

8 tbsp coriander seeds
4 tbsp cumin seeds
1 tbsp black peppercorns
1 tbsp black mustard seeds
11 tbsp ground turmeric
3-4 tsp chilli powder
1 tbsp salt
8 garlic cloves, crushed
7.5 cm/3 in piece fresh root
  ginger, peeled and finely grated
50 ml/2 fl oz/¼ cup cider vinegar
175 ml/ 6 fl oz/¾ cup sunflower oil

1 Heat a heavy-based frying pan and dry-fry the coriander, cumin and peppercorns briefly; add the mustard seeds, tossing the mixture continuously, until the spices give off a rich aroma. Do not overbrown.

2 Grind the mixture to a fine powder, then add the turmeric, chilli and salt. Add the garlic, ginger and sufficient vinegar to make a paste.

3 Heat the oil and fry the paste, stirring and turning it continuously, until the oil begins to separate from the spicy mixture.

4 Cool the paste and store it in an airtight jar away from light and preferably in a cool place. The paste will keep for about 2-3 weeks.

coriander seeds

**black
peppercorns**

**black mustard
seeds**

cumin seeds

ground turmeric

chilli powder

salt

garlic

fresh root ginger

**sunflower
oil**

**cider
vinegar**

Spice Pastes

Separate mounds of fresh 'wet spices' are available on market stalls throughout South-east Asia. The stall holder simply asks whether a meat, fish or vegetable curry is to be prepared and whether the preference is for a hot spicy curry or something a little milder. He then spoons appropriate quantities of chilli, ginger, galangal, lemon grass and garlic on to a fresh banana leaf, and

folds it in a cone to take home and cook. Perhaps the banana leaf has now been superseded by the inevitable plastic bag! Today we are able to buy ready prepared spice pastes in jars and cans that are of excellent quality, but it is fun to experiment in making up your own paste.

Malaysian Chicken Spice Paste

This fairly fiery paste can be toned down by reducing the number of chillies. Red onions and fresh turmeric give the paste a rich colour. Blachan may appear to be an unusual ingredient, but it adds an unexpected depth of flavour, so do not be tempted to omit it. The candlenuts or macadamia nuts are included to thicken the sauce, and the lemon grass adds its own magic in this classic, basic curry paste.

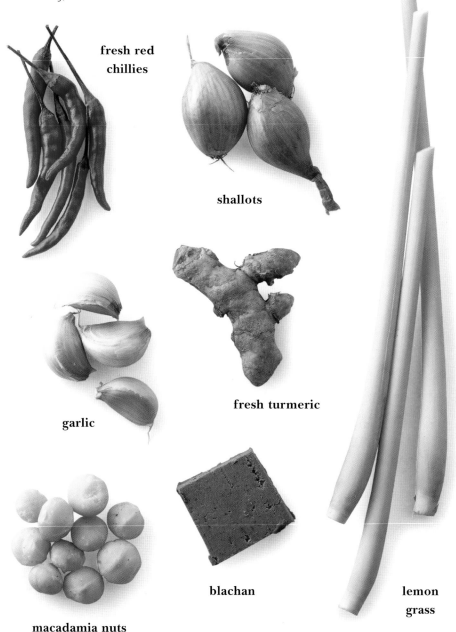

fresh red chillies

shallots

fresh turmeric

garlic

macadamia nuts

blachan

lemon grass

Makes about 350 g/12 oz

6 fresh red chillies, seeded and sliced

3 red Bombay onions or 12 shallots, roughly chopped

4 garlic cloves

2.5 cm/1 in piece fresh turmeric root, peeled and sliced, or 1 tsp ground turmeric

10 candlenuts or macadamia nuts

2.5 cm/1 in cube of blachan, prepared

3 lemon grass stalks

1 Place the chillies, onions or shallots, garlic, turmeric, nuts and blachan in a food processor.

2 Trim the root end from the lemon grass and slice the lower 6 cm/2½ in bulbous section into small pieces.

3 Add the lemon grass to the remaining ingredients and process them to a fine paste. Use the paste at once or store in an airtight glass jar in the fridge for a few days or in a plastic container in the freezer.

> ### COOK'S TIP
> *The top section of the lemon grass can be bruised and added to the curry during cooking, then removed before serving.*

Thai Red Curry Paste

Krueng gaeng phed is the Thai name for this paste, which is used for meat, poultry and vegetable dishes.

MAKES ABOUT 175 G/6 OZ

10 fresh red chillies, seeded and
  sliced, or 1½ tbsp chilli powder
115 g/4 oz dark red onions
  or shallots, sliced
4 garlic cloves
3 lemon grass stalks, lower part
  of stem sliced and bruised
1 cm/½ in piece greater
  galangal, peeled, sliced
  and bruised
4 coriander sprigs, stems only
1-2 tbsp groundnut oil
1 tsp grated magrut or
  dried citrus peel
1 cm/½ in cube of blachan, prepared
1 tbsp coriander seeds
2 tsp cumin seeds
1 tsp salt

1   Pound the chillies or chilli powder, onions or shallots, garlic, bruised lemon grass, galangal and the stems from the coriander sprigs in a mortar to a paste, gradually adding the oil. Alternatively, purée the ingredients in a food processor or blender. Add the grated magrut or dried citrus peel and the blachan.

2   Dry-fry the coriander and cumin seeds, then turn them into a mortar and grind them to a powder. Add the ground spices to the paste with the salt and mix well.

3   Use the paste at once or place in a glass jar. Cover with clear film, and an airtight lid, then store in the fridge. The paste will keep for 3-4 weeks. Alternatively freeze the paste in small plastic containers, making a note of the quantity.

red chillies

groundnut oil

red onion

blachan

garlic

greater galangal

cumin
seeds

lemon grass

salt

green
chillies

citrus peel

Green Curry Paste

Gaeng khiev wan is the green paste, made using the same ingredients as for red curry paste, but with green chillies in place of the red chillies, white onion instead of a red one, and adding the leaves from the coriander to strengthen the colour.

white onion

fresh coriander

coriander seeds

Thai Nam Prik Sauce

This is the most famous of all Thai sauces: it can be served on its own, stirred into a helping of plain cooked rice, or it can be offered as a dip for vegetable crudités, either raw or lightly blanched. Despite the fact that the quantities and proportions vary from cook to cook, the ingredients remain constant.

<u>MAKES 275 G/10 OZ</u>

50 g/2 oz/1 cup dried prawns, soaked in water for 15 minutes and drained

1 cm/½ in cube of blachan, prepared

3-4 cloves garlic, crushed

3-4 fresh red chillies, seeded and sliced

50 g/2 oz peeled cooked prawns (optional)

a few sprigs coriander

8-10 tiny baby aubergines (optional)

3-4 tbsp lemon or lime juice

2 tbsp fish sauce, or to taste

1 tbsp brown sugar, or to taste

1 Pound the soaked prawns, blachan, garlic and chillies together in a mortar. Alternatively, process the ingredients in a food processor or blender. Add the fresh prawns, if using, and the coriander stems and leaves. Pound the ingredients again until combined.

2 Remove the stalks from the aubergines, if using, and gradually pound them into the sauce.

3 Add the lemon or lime juice, fish sauce and sugar to taste. A little water may be added if a thinner sauce is required.

brown sugar

lemon juice

fish sauce

fresh red chillies

dried prawns

blachan

fresh coriander

peeled cooked prawns

garlic

Mus-sa-man Curry Paste

<u>Makes</u> 225 g/8 oz

10 fresh red chillies, seeded
  and sliced, or 1½ tbsp chilli powder
115 g/4 oz dark-red onions or
  shallots, sliced
4 garlic cloves, peeled
3 lemon grass stalks, lower part of
  stem sliced and bruised
1 cm/½ in piece greater galangal,
  peeled sliced and bruised
a little groundnut oil
4 sprigs coriander, stems only
1 tsp grated magrut or
  dried citrus peel
1 cm/½ in cube of blachan,
  prepared
6 green cardamoms
1 tbsp coriander seeds
2 tsp cumin seeds
½ tsp ground cloves
½ tsp ground cinnamon
1 tsp salt

1 Lightly fry the fresh chillies, if using, with the onions or shallots, garlic, bruised lemon grass and galangal in the oil, stirring continuously. This initial frying will enhance the flavours.

2 Turn the mixture into a food processor or blender, add the chilli powder, if using, and process to a smooth paste. Add the stems from the coriander sprigs, the magrut or grapefruit peel and blachan. Process the mixture again until combined.

3 Bruise the cardamoms and dry-fry with the coriander and cumin seeds and salt. Remove the seeds from the cardamoms, discarding the pods, and pound the spices in a mortar. Add the cloves and cinnamon. Process the ground spices with the paste until thoroughly combined. Use as required or store in the fridge for 2-3 weeks.

fresh
red chillies

red
onion

lemon
grass

fresh
coriander

garlic

greater
galangal

blachan

coriander
seeds

cumin
seeds

citrus peel

ground cloves

salt

green
cardamoms

ground
cinnamon

groundnut oil

Sambals

In this context the sambal is an accompaniment that is spooned discreetly on the side of your plate, as others would a little mustard, simply to add a kick to a main course. Additionally the chilli sambal can be used when time is short or fresh chillies are not to hand in both the sambal kecap and the sambal blachan recipes. A ready-made 'chopped chilli' product is now available from most large supermarkets, which reflects our increasing interest in spicy foods.

A sambal can also be a spicy chilli sauce, which may contain a variety of foods from meat balls to cubes of fish, hard-boiled eggs or vegetables and will be found under the recipe for sambal goreng in Indonesian cookbooks.

Chilli Sambal

Sambal ulek, to give this sambal its *Indonesian name, will keep for 4-6 weeks in an airtight jar in the fridge, so it is worth making up a reasonable quantity at a time if you frequently cook Indonesian-style dishes. Use a stainless steel or plastic spoon to measure out the sauce as required. This sauce is fiercely hot, and it will irritate the skin, so should you get any on your fingers, immediately wash them well in soapy water.*

MAKES 450 G/1 LB
450 g/1 lb fresh red chillies, seeded
2 tsp salt

1 Plunge the chillies into a pan of boiling water and cook them for about 5-8 minutes.

2 Drain the chillies and then grind them in a food processor or blender, without making the paste too smooth.

3 Turn the paste into a glass jar, stir in the salt and cover with a piece of grease-proof paper or clear film before screwing on the lid.

4 Store the sambal in the fridge. Spoon it into small dishes to serve as an accompaniment, or use it as suggested in recipes.

fresh red chillies

salt

Sambal Kecap

This Indonesian sauce or sambal can be served as a dip for satays instead of the usual peanut sauce, particularly with beef and chicken, and it is also good with deep-fried chicken.

MAKES 10 TBSP
**1 fresh red chilli, seeded and
  finely chopped
2 garlic cloves, crushed
4 tbsp dark soy sauce
4 tsp lemon juice or 1-1½ tbsp
  tamarind juice
2 tbsp hot water
2 tbsp deep-fried onion
  slices (optional)**

1   Mix the chilli, garlic, soy sauce, lemon or tamarind juice and hot water in a bowl.

2   Stir in the onion slices, if using, and leave to stand for 30 minutes before serving.

dark soy sauce

lemon juice

deep-fried
onion slices

red chilli

garlic

Sambal Blachan

Serve this sambal, which is best made in small quantities, as an accompaniment to rice meals. Vary the amount of chilli and blachan to taste, but it will be hot and pungent nevertheless.

MAKES 2 TBSP
**2-4 fresh red chillies, seeded
salt
1 cm/½ in cube of blachan,
  prepared
juice of ½ lemon or lime**

1   Cut the chillies in half lengthways. Pound them to a paste in a mortar, adding a little salt.

2   Add the blachan and lemon or lime juice to taste.

salt

fresh
red chillies

blachan

lemon
juice

African Spice Mixtures

Highly spiced food is eaten with relish throughout the African continent. The spices were brought by Arab traders and merchants over the centuries from biblical times. Many of the cooks are women, and recipes are passed down through the generations by families meeting and preparing food together for

feasts, festivals and weddings so that culinary knowledge and traditional recipes are kept alive. Of the five following recipes, harissa is the best known and is quite simple to make at home, though it is now available from many supermarkets in small jars, which should be stored in the refrigerator once opened.

Harissa

This chilli-based condiment with a definite kick is widely used in Moroccan, Tunisian and Algerian cooking. It is served neat as a side dish in which to dip pieces of grilled and barbecued meat, stirred into soups and stews or added to the sauce for couscous. Harissa is sometimes added to a purée of skinned and seeded fresh tomatoes and offered as a dip for kebabs or snacks. When added to natural yogurt, harissa is an excellent marinade for pork and chicken.

MAKES 120 ML/4 FL OZ/$\frac{1}{2}$ CUP

12 dried red chillies
1 tbsp coriander seeds
2 tsp cumin seeds
2 garlic cloves
$\frac{1}{2}$ tsp salt
4-6 tbsp olive oil

1 Discard the stems and some of the seeds from the chillies, then soak the chillies in warm water for 30 minutes, until softened.

2 Meanwhile, dry-fry the coriander and cumin seeds to bring out the flavour and grind them to a powder.

3 Pound the garlic with the salt, then add the drained chillies and pound the mixture until it is smooth.

4 Add the spices and gradually pound in the oil, trickling it in and mixing until the sauce is well blended and of a mayonnaise-like consistency.

5 Use the harissa at once or transfer it to an airtight jar. Flood the surface with a little more olive oil to make a seal. Cover closely and store in a cool place or in the fridge for up to 3 weeks.

dried red chillies

VARIATION

For a less pungent sauce, use only 4-6 dried red chillies. Grill and skin 2 red peppers and reserve the seeds, adding them at the end to give texture to the sauce. Purée the peppers until smooth and mix all the ingredients as above.

olive oil

coriander seeds

garlic

cumin seeds

salt

Berbere

This is an Ethiopian blend of spices added to many local dishes, from baked fish dishes to chicken stews. The name is pronounced 'bari-baray'.

MAKES 50 G/2 OZ/SCANT ½ CUP

10 dried red chillies
8 white cardamoms
1 tsp cumin seeds
1 tsp coriander seeds
1 tsp fenugreek seeds
8 cloves
1 tsp allspice berries
2 tsp black peppercorns
1 tsp ajowan seeds
1 tsp ground ginger
½ tsp ground nutmeg
2 tbsp salt

1 Discard the stalk end and some of the seeds from the chillies.

2 Heat a heavy-based frying pan. Bruise the cardamom pods and add them to the pan with the cumin, coriander, fenugreek, cloves, allspice, peppercorns and ajowan seeds. Toast the spices, shaking the pan over a medium heat, until they give off a rich aroma and just begin to turn colour.

3 Remove the seeds from the cardamoms and then grind all the roasted spices to a fine powder. Mix in the ginger, nutmeg and salt.

4 Use at once or transfer to an airtight jar and store away from strong light; alternatively place in an airtight polythene container in the freezer.

dried red chillies   **white cardamoms**   **allspice berries**   **black peppercorns**

cumin seeds   **coriander seeds**   **ajowan seeds**   **ground ginger**

fenugreek seeds   **cloves**   **ground nutmeg**   **salt**

99

Ras el Hanout

Every Moroccan spice merchant has a particular recipe for ras el hanout, which means 'head of the shop'. The mix can contain upwards of twenty different spices, including cinnamon, cardamom, chilli, cumin, coriander, cloves, salt, peppercorns, ginger, nutmeg, turmeric and a sprinkling of dried flowers, plus the occasional ingredient renowned for its aphrodisiac qualities. Nothing is left out or to chance! The spice mixture is always sold whole, then ground by the cook as and when required.

black peppercorns

coriander seeds

cumin seeds

cloves

green cardamoms

ground turmeric

cinnamon stick

ground ginger

salt

nutmegs

dried red chillies

dried flowers

La Kama

La Kama is a Moroccan mixture that is very popular in Tangier – it is altogether simpler than the complex ras el hanout and features a modest five spices. Use to flavour soups and stews – this is especially good with lamb.

MAKES 3 TBSP
2.5 cm/1 in piece
  cinnamon stick
2 tsp black peppercorns
2 tsp ground ginger
2 tsp ground turmeric
¼ tsp ground nutmeg

1 Dry-fry or roast the cinnamon and peppercorns in a heavy-based frying pan to release their flavour.

2 Grind the roasted spices to a powder and mix with the ginger, turmeric and nutmeg.

3 Use at once or store in an airtight jar, away from strong light.

black peppercorns

ground ginger

ground turmeric

ground nutmeg

cinnamon stick

Tsire Powder

This simple spice mixture is used as a coating for kebabs throughout West Africa. The raw meat is dipped first in oil or beaten egg and then in the spice mixture. A little of the mixture is scattered over the cooked meat before serving.

<u>MAKES 4 TBSP</u>

50 g/2 oz/½ cup salted peanuts
1 tsp mixed spice
½-1 tsp chilli powder
salt

1 Grind the peanuts to a coarse powder in a mortar, blender or food processor, then add the ground mixed spice, chilli powder and a little salt.

2 Use at once or transfer to an airtight container and store in a cool place for up to 6 weeks.

chilli powder

ground mixed spice

salt

salted peanuts

COOK'S TIP

Mixed spice is a ready ground, commercial spice mixture, sometimes called pudding spice, that contains allspice, cinnamon, cloves, ginger and nutmeg.

Barbecue Spice Mixtures

Barbecuing is perhaps the most primitive yet delicious method of cooking whereby pieces of meat, poultry or fish are rendered even more delicious with the addition of an aromatic blend of *spices and herbs. These are either rubbed into the flesh a short time before cooking or converted into a marinade. Dry spice mixtures will keep for several months in a cool, dark place.*

Barbecue Spice Mixture

MAKES ABOUT 4 TBSP

2 tsp celery seeds
1 tsp paprika
1 tsp ground nutmeg
1 tsp chilli powder
1 tsp garlic powder
1 tsp onion salt
2 tsp dried marjoram
1 tsp salt
1-2 tsp soft light brown sugar
1 tsp freshly ground
  black pepper

1 Grind the celery seeds to a powder, then add to the remaining ingredients. Use the spice mixture immediately or transfer it to an airtight jar and store in a cool place.

celery seeds

paprika

ground nutmeg

chilli powder

garlic powder

onion salt

dried marjoram

salt

soft light brown sugar

ground black pepper

COOK'S TIP

For a marinade, simply add this mixture to a glass of red or white wine with a few slices of onion and stir in 4 tbsp garlic-flavoured oil.

Juniper Barbecue Spice

This pungent blend of spices is perfect for duck breasts, beef, venison and ostrich steaks. For a marinade, add this mixture to a small glass of gin along with 1-2 chopped shallots and a couple of rosemary sprigs.

MAKES 4 TBSP
2 tbsp juniper berries
1 tsp black peppercorns
½ tsp salt
1 tsp ground allspice
1 tbsp soft dark brown sugar

juniper berries

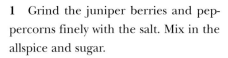

salt

1 Grind the juniper berries and peppercorns finely with the salt. Mix in the allspice and sugar.

2 Rub the spice mixture on to meats before cooking them on the barbecue.

black peppercorns

ground allspice

dark brown sugar

Old-fashioned Philadelphia Spice Powder

Use this as a seasoning for a pork joint or rub it on to steaks or chops. Do this well ahead of roasting or barbecuing the meat to allow the flavours to develop.

MAKES 2-3 TBSP
8 cloves
1 tsp chilli powder
½ tsp ground nutmeg
¼ tsp ground mace
1 tsp dried basil
1 tsp dried thyme
2 dried bay leaves
salt

1 Grind the cloves to a coarse powder, then add the other ingredients and continue grinding until fine.

2 Use at once or store in an airtight container, away from strong light.

cloves   **chilli powder**

ground nutmeg   **ground mace**   **bay leaves**

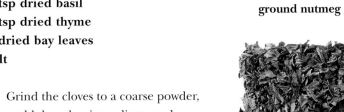

dried basil   **dried thyme**   **salt**

Cajun Spice Mix

The name Cajun evolved from the corruption of 'Acadian', the French settlers who left Canada after the English took over in 1755. They eventually settled in Louisiana, where the exchange of cooking techniques and dishes between the Creoles and the French began. This spice mixture can be used as a seasoning for the famous jambalaya and gumbo, as well as for fish steaks, chicken or meat. If you plan to make up the mixture in advance, prepare the dry spice ingredients and store them in an airtight container. When the mixture is required, chop the onion and garlic in a food processor and add to the spice mixture.

MAKES ABOUT 10 TBSP

1 tsp black peppercorns
1 tsp cumin seeds
1 tsp white mustard seeds
2 tsp paprika
1 tsp chilli powder or
  cayenne pepper
1 tsp dried oregano
2 tsp dried thyme
1 tsp salt
2 garlic cloves
1 onion, sliced

1 Dry-fry or roast the peppercorns, cumin and mustard seeds over a medium heat to release their flavours.

2 Grind the roasted spices to a fine powder, then add the paprika, chilli or cayenne, oregano, thyme and salt and grind again.

3 If it is to be used immediately, add the spices to the finely chopped garlic and onion in a blender or food processor and process until well combined.

garlic

dried oregano

white mustard seeds

salt

black peppercorns

chilli powder

onion

cumin seeds

paprika

dried thyme

Chinese Five Spice Powder

The aroma of this spice always seems to dominate Chinese supermarkets. The mixture is made up of equal quantities of Szechuan pepper, cinnamon or cassia, cloves, fennel seeds and star anise. Use in chicken, pork and red-cooked meat dishes with soy sauce and, of course, to season Chinese spareribs. Grind all the ingredients to a fine powder and store in an airtight container.

Szechuan pepper

cassia

cloves

fennel seeds

star anise

Chinese spiced salt

CHINESE SPICED SALT

A magical accompaniment to crisp-skinned barbecued or roast chicken: the cooked chicken is dipped into the seasoning before it is eaten. Thoroughly mix 1 tbsp of salt and ½ tsp five spice powder. Divide it among four small shallow dishes.

VARIATION

To make salt and cinnamon mix, toast the salt in a heavy-based frying pan until it is just beginning to turn in colour, then remove it from heat and stir in 1 tsp ground cinnamon and a pinch of Chinese five spice powder. Use as above.

Chinese five spice powder

salt

Chinese Roasted Salt and Pepper

This seasoning is best made up as required. It is particularly good as a dip for Szechuan duck, which is first steamed and then deep fried to obtain a really crisp skin. The pieces of duck are dipped in the roasted salt and pepper mixture and eaten with steamed flower rolls. This mixture is also delicious with deep-fried chicken, prawns and roasted meats, especially pork.

SERVES 4-6
2 tbsp salt
2 tsp freshly ground black pepper

1 Heat the salt and pepper in a heavy-based frying pan over a medium heat, shaking the pan continuously until the pepper aroma is evident. Leave to cool.

ground black pepper

salt

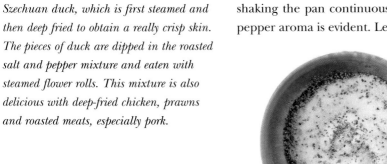

Sweet Spice Mixtures

Pickling Spice

This typically British mixture can be bought ready-mixed, but keen cooks enjoy experimenting with different flavours. Sometimes the spices are crushed before they are added to the mixture; for other recipes, the spices are tied into a muslin bag, which can be removed after cooking. In some recipes, the bag of spices may be boiled with the vinegar, then allowed to infuse. The spices are then discarded and the flavoured vinegar is used in the pickle.

allspice berries

white peppercorns

coriander seeds

dried red chillies

cloves

mustard seeds

cinnamon stick

dried bay leaves

dried root ginger

MAKES 8 TBSP
1 tbsp coriander seeds
1 tbsp mustard seeds
1 tbsp black or white peppercorns
1 tbsp cloves
1 tbsp allspice berries
3-4 dried red chillies
2.5 cm/1 in piece dried root ginger
2.5 cm/1 in piece cinnamon stick (optional)
3 dried bay leaves (optional)

1 Mix all the spices. Tie them in a piece of muslin and use as directed in a recipe.

2 Alternatively, place the spices in a stainless steel or enamelled saucepan and pour in vinegar. Heat gently until boiling, allow to cool, then strain the vinegar and discard the spices.

3 To make cold spice vinegar, add the spices to a jar or bottle of vinegar and leave to infuse for 1-2 days. Strain and use as required; the spices may be discarded or used to flavour another bottle of vinegar.

Apple Pie Spice

This spice mixture is a perfect flavouring combination for the universally popular apple pie. Some cooks prefer to leave the cloves whole. Use in stewed fruit, fruit sauces and fruit pies filled with plums, pears or rhubarb as well as apples.

MAKES 4-5 TSP
1 tsp ground or whole cloves
1 tbsp ground cinnamon
½-1 tsp ground nutmeg

1 Mix the spices and use at once or store in an airtight container away from strong light.

ground cloves

ground cinnamon

ground nutmeg

Mixed Spice or Pudding Spice

This is another typically British spice mix, which can be bought ready ground. It is used in a variety of cakes and puddings, such as fruit cake, gingerbread and Christmas pudding. Make it up or buy it in small quantities as the mixture soon loses its rich flavour. Allspice, cinnamon, cloves, nutmeg and ginger are the usual blend of spices, but some cooks like to add a few cardamom and coriander seeds.

<u>MAKES 2 TBSP</u>
1 tsp allspice berries
2.5 cm/1 in cinnamon stick
1 tsp cloves
1 tsp ground nutmeg
1 tsp ground ginger

1 Grind the allspice, cinnamon and cloves to a fine powder and mix well with the nutmeg and ginger. Use at once or store in an airtight jar away from strong light.

allspice berries

ground nutmeg

cloves

cinnamon stick

ground ginger

Quatre Epices

As the name indicates, this is a blend of four spices; it is a favourite seasoning for French charcuterie and Arabian cooking. The proportions can be varied to suit the food or dish. Equivalent quantities of allspice and cinnamon can be substituted for white pepper and ginger respectively.

<u>MAKES 5 TBSP</u>
3 tbsp ground white pepper
1 tbsp grated nutmeg
1 tsp ground cloves
1 tbsp ground ginger

1 Mix all the spices and use at once or store in an airtight jar away from strong light.

white pepper

ground nutmeg

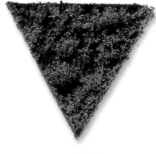

ground cloves

ground ginger

Flavoured Aromatic Oils

Few gifts give more pleasure than those that are hand-made to suit the recipient. Aromatic spiced oils are a perfect example: they give the impression that hours have been spent in their preparation when they are, in truth, quick and simple to make. Plan ahead and collect attractive corked wine bottles if you do not want to invest in bought bottles. If you can afford to buy bottles, you will find a wide selection available from mail order catalogues as well as high street stores. The bottles must be pristine clean and cork stoppers are preferable. Wash them well and clean them with a proprietary sterilizing solution if necessary (look for wine-making sterilizing agents or solutions

for cleaning babies' bottles), leave upside down on the draining rack to dry completely.

There are no hard and fast rules on the type of oil or the spices to use, except that they should be complementary. For instance, extra virgin olive oil is an ideal oil for Mediterranean spices and herbs; groundnut oil goes well with the Oriental flavours of lemon grass and ginger; nut oils, like walnut and hazelnut, are wonderful flavoured with coriander seeds and cinnamon sticks for adding to salad dressings to serve with pasta. Remember to label the bottles so that there is no possible doubt about the flavour of the oil!

Ginger, Garlic and Shallot Oil

Often referred to as the 'trinity' of flavours used in Oriental recipes, this is ideal for fish, shellfish and chicken. For 475 ml/16 fl oz/2 cups oil, peel and lightly bruise a 6 cm/2½ in piece of fresh root ginger and place in a clean bottle with the oil, 2 garlic cloves (left whole) and 3 small peeled shallots. Cover tightly and leave in a cool dark place for 2 weeks. Taste the oil and then strain it into a clean bottle if the flavours are strong enough. If the flavour is not sufficiently pronounced, leave the oil for another week before using. Label clearly and store.

garlic

shallots

fresh ginger

Garlic and Spice Aromatic Oil

Almost fill a clean bottle with best virgin olive oil. For 600 ml/1 pint/ 2½ cups oil, peel and halve a large garlic clove, then add it to the bottle with 3 whole red chillies, 1 tsp coriander seeds, 3 allspice berries, 6 black peppercorns, 4 juniper berries and 2 bay leaves. Cover tightly and leave in a cool dark place for 2 weeks. If the flavour is not sufficiently pronounced, leave the oil for another week before using. Label clearly and store or wrap decoratively as a gift.

juniper berries

fresh bay leaves

allspice berries

dried red chillies

coriander seeds

black peppercorns

Lemon Grass and Lime Leaf Oil

Almost fill a clean bottle with ground-nut oil. Trim and discard the root end from a lemon grass stalk. Lightly bruise the bulbous end and cut the stem into lengths to fit in the bottle. Tear 3-4 lime leaves into pieces to release more flavour. Slip the pieces of lemon grass into the bottle with the lime leaves. Cover tightly and leave in a cool dark place for 2 weeks. Label and store. If the flavour is not sufficiently pronounced, leave the oil for another week before using.

kaffir lime leaves

lemon grass

cinnamon sticks

Cinnamon- and Coriander-Spiced Nut Oil

Almost fill a clean bottle with walnut or hazelnut oil. Add a cinnamon stick and 2 tsp coriander seeds. Seal and leave in a cool dark place for 2 weeks. Taste the oil and then strain it into a clean bottle if it is sufficiently well flavoured. Label and store.

Alternatively, omit the coriander seeds and add a long piece of pared lemon or orange rind. Use to make dressings and mayonnaise to serve with fish and poultry dishes.

coriander seeds

Spiced Vinegars

Vinegar is an essential ingredient in every kitchen, and flavoured vinegars add another dimension in the preparation of dressings, mayonnaise, marinades, sauces and preserves. Use white or red wine vinegar, sherry or cider vinegar as a medium for a huge range of spice flavours. Malt vinegar is best left as a condiment for British fish and chips or for pickling and preserving.

Flavoured vinegar can be made in two ways: where strong flavours are used and/or required, for example with garlic or fresh ginger, the vinegar is heated to extract the maximum flavour. When using milder spices, such as fennel, celery or dill seeds, steep them in the cold vinegar for up to a fortnight before tasting to check on the flavour.

Garlic Vinegar

Crush 3-4 garlic cloves and pound them in a mortar, then place in a stainless steel or glass mixing bowl. Meanwhile, heat about 250 ml/8 fl oz/1 cup white wine or cider vinegar until just boiling and pour it over the garlic. Leave to cool. Then add a further 250 ml/8 fl oz/1 cup cold vinegar. Pour into a clean jar, cover tightly and leave for 2 weeks, or less for a milder flavour. Shake the jar occasionally. Strain the vinegar into a clean bottle, adding two or three unpeeled garlic cloves to the vinegar for identification. The liquid must completely fill the bottle. Cover tightly and label, then store in a cool dark place.

garlic

Gingered Vinegar

Follow the instructions for garlic vinegar, using rice wine vinegar and ginger instead of garlic. Use a 5 cm/ 2 in piece of fresh root ginger for every 600 ml/1 pint/ 2½ cups vinegar. Use in Oriental recipes, such as sweet and sour or Szechuan-style dishes.

fresh ginger

Fennel Seed Vinegar

Select a clean preserving jar, not a narrow-topped bottle. Place 2 tbsp fennel seeds in the jar for every 600 ml/1 pint/2½ cups white wine vinegar. Cover and leave in a cool dark place for 2-3 weeks, shaking the jar from time to time, until the flavour is as intense as you require. Strain the vinegar into clean bottles, label and store in a cool place away from direct sunlight. Use the vinegar in salad dressings and to sharpen herb sauces.

celery seeds

fennel seeds

VARIATION

This spiced vinegar can be made with other seeds, try celery or dill.

dill seeds

Chilli Vinegar

Use a clean preserving jar. Place 25 g/1 oz (about 8) dried red chillies in the jar. Heat 600 ml/1 pint/2½ cups red wine or sherry vinegar until just boiling, then pour it into the jar. Cool, cover tightly and allow to infuse for 2 weeks, shaking the jar occasionally. Taste for flavour and strain when sufficiently strong, pouring the vinegar into a clean bottle. Make sure that the bottle is full to the top. Cover tightly, label and store. Use to pep up soups and sauces or to deglaze a pan after cooking venison or beef steaks.

**dried
red chillies**

Chilli Ho Ho

An old colonial-style vinegar to add pep and character to rather dull soups, sauces and stews. Fill a clean bottle – a pretty wine bottle will do – with lots of small red chillies. Top up with sherry vinegar. Cover tightly or seal with a cork and leave for 2 weeks, shaking occasionally. Use a few drops at a time and top up with more of the sherry vinegar to keep the ho ho going for months. Label and store in a cool dark place. The ho ho can also be made with sherry, gin or vodka instead of sherry vinegar.

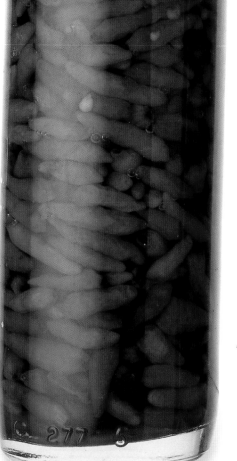

**small
red chillies**

Spiced Drinks

Cardamom, cinnamon, cloves, ginger and nutmeg flavours all have an affinity with hot or cold drinks, alcoholic or otherwise. In India tea is sometimes flavoured with cardamoms, cinnamon and cloves.

Coffee may have originated from either the Yemen or Ethiopia where it is mentioned in records from the 6th century. As tastes became more sophisticated and coffee became an international drink, different ways of serving it were devised.

Cardamom Tea

In India, this tea may be served with very sweet sweetmeats or savoury snacks. If you wish to drink it black, then reduce the quantity of tea by half or it will be too strong to be enjoyable.

SERVES 4

8 green cardamoms
1.2 litres/2 pints/5 cups cold water
4 tsp orange pekoe tea or
  4 tea bags
small strip of pared orange rind
sugar and freshly boiled milk,
  to serve

green cardamoms

VARIATION

Use 1 cinnamon stick instead of the cardamoms.

---

1 Split the cardamom pods. Boil the water and cardamoms in a large saucepan, then reduce the heat and simmer for 3-4 minutes. Remove from heat and allow to infuse for 10 minutes.

2 Just before serving, warm a teapot, add the tea and the orange rind. Bring the infused liquid to the boil and pour it into the teapot. Brew for 2-3 minutes.

3 Serve the tea with sugar and freshly boiled milk for a traditional flavour.

cloves

Grace's Easy Iced Lemon Tea

An ideal container is the plastic container in which you buy orange juice. Wash it well and fill with hot, not boiling, water and 1 tsp bicarbonate of soda to render it free of flavour. Rinse well before using.

1 Place all the ingredients in a clean container. Cover tightly and place in the fridge overnight (at least) for the flavours to infuse.

2 Strain into glasses and serve decorated with cucumber, lemon or orange slices and some more mint leaves.

SERVES 6

1.75 litres/3 pints/7½ cups
  cold water
8-10 cloves
1 cinnamon stick
3-4 Earl Grey or Lapsang
  Souchong tea bags
juice of 2 lemons, strained
6 tbsp sugar or to taste
6-8 mint leaves
DECORATION
cucumber, lemon or orange slices
mint leaves

cinnamon stick

Spiced Tea

This tea, masala chah or chai, is a delicious drink to round off an Indian meal. Traditionally it would be served with milk and plenty of sugar, but many people find it more refreshing when served black.

SERVES 4

**1.2 litres/2 pints/5 cups
  cold water
1 cinnamon stick
4 green cardamoms
3 cloves
2 tsp orange pekoe tea or
  2 tea bags
sugar to taste (optional)**

cinnamon stick

Masala for Tea

In Bombay, masala chai is always offered to guests as a welcoming drink. The masala mixture is ground and stored in an airtight jar until required.

MAKES 6 TBSP

**12 green cardamoms
1 tbsp black peppercorns
6 cloves
2 tbsp ground ginger**

1 Split the cardamoms and scrape out the tiny black seeds. Grind them with the peppercorns and cloves to a fine powder: a coffee grinder is ideal for this. Then mix well with the ground ginger.

cloves

1 Boil the water with the cinnamon stick, cardamoms and cloves. Draw off the heat and allow to infuse for about 10 minutes.

2 Add the tea or tea bags and sugar, if used, and bring to the boil again, then simmer gently for 3-4 minutes.

3 Taste the tea and strain it into a warmed teapot or jug, then serve it at once. Float one or two cardamoms in each cup, if you like.

green cardamoms

2 Use at once or store in an airtight jar away from strong light. Add ½ tsp to a pot of freshly made tea.

**black
peppercorns**

cloves

Café Brûlot

This flaming mixture of coffee, spice and brandy is a speciality of the southern states of the USA. A fondue pot is ideal for making the coffee at the table: when the spice and brandy mixture is warm, it is ignited before strong black coffee is added. It is often performed with great panache in restaurants, when the waiter pours the coffee from a ladle down a long strip of orange rind into the pan.

SERVES 4–6

**pared rind of 1 orange,
in one long strip**
**pared rind of 1 lemon,
in one long strip**
4 sugar lumps
6 cloves
1 cinnamon stick
**175 ml/6 fl oz/¾ cup
brandy**
**3-4 tbsp curaçao or
orange liqueur**
**475 ml/16 fl oz/2 cups
strong black coffee**

1 Assemble all the ingredients. Place the orange and lemon rind in a pan. Add the sugar, cloves, cinnamon, brandy and curaçao or orange liqueur. Heat until the sugar dissolves, stirring continuously.

2 Have the coffee ready; ignite the brandy mixture, then slowly add the coffee in a thin stream. Serve at once with a cinnamon stick and orange rind garnish, if you like.

cloves

**cinnamon
sticks**

Southern Iced Spiced Coffee

Another classic coffee from the southern states of the USA. This one is served chilled and makes a refreshing summer-time drink.

SERVES 4

**1 litre/1¾ pints/4 cups freshly
made strong black coffee**
4 cinnamon sticks
6 cloves
3-4 tbsp sugar, or to taste
**4 tbsp Tia Maria or
coffee liqueur**
plenty of ice cubes

1 Pour the coffee into a large bowl. Add the cinnamon sticks, cloves and sugar to taste. Stir well and leave for at least an hour to infuse.

2 Strain the coffee into a large jug, then add the liqueur and ice cubes. Serve in chilled glasses.

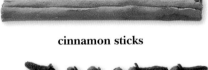

cinnamon sticks

cloves

Mocha on a Cloud

Vanilla is used to flavour this coffee and chocolate combination. Add a cinnamon stick to each glass to stir the cream.

SERVES 6

1.2 litres/2 pints/5 cups milk
1 vanilla pod or 2-3 drops
  natural vanilla essence
600ml/1 pint/2½ cups freshly
  made strong black coffee
sugar to taste
3 tbsp vanilla sugar
115 g/4 oz dark plain chocolate
150 ml/¼ pint/⅔ cup whipping
  cream, whipped
6 cinnamon sticks and ground
  nutmeg, to serve

1 Pour 750 ml/1¼ pints/3 cups milk into a saucepan. Add the vanilla pod, if using, and place the pan over a low heat until hot, but not boiling. Set aside to infuse for 10 minutes, then remove the vanilla pod.

2 Mix the coffee with the remaining milk in a large heatproof jug. Add sugar to taste but do not make the mixture too sweet as the hot milk will also be sweetened.

3 Return the saucepan of milk to the heat and add the vanilla sugar with the vanilla essence, if using. Bring to the boil, then reduce the heat. Break the chocolate into squares and add them to the milk. Heat gently, whisking until the chocolate has melted.

4 Pour the chocolate milk into the jug and whisk until frothy.

5 Serve in tall mugs or glasses, topped with whipped cream, a cinnamon stick and a sprinkling of nutmeg.

vanilla sugar

natural
vanilla essence

vanilla pods

**ground
cinnamon**

ground nutmeg

Mulled Wine

Cinnamon, cloves, ginger and nutmeg add spice to this winter warmer.

SERVES 6-8

1 cinnamon stick
8 cloves
few pinches each of ground
** ginger and nutmeg**
1 orange, sliced
1 lemon, sliced
2 tbsp dark brown sugar
750 ml/1¼ pints/3 cups red wine
** (1 bottle)**
4 tbsp brandy
120 ml/4 fl oz/½ cup water

VARIATION

To make a lemon- and sherry-flavoured Bishop, replace the orange with a lemon and use sherry instead of port. Prepare in the same way. Add the strained juice of another lemon, if required.

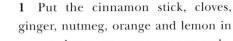

cloves

1 Put the cinnamon stick, cloves, ginger, nutmeg, orange and lemon in a large saucepan or casserole. Add the sugar, wine, brandy and water.

2 Place over a low heat and stir to dissolve the sugar. Do not overheat or allow to boil because this evaporates the alcohol. Heat gently until required, then ladle into cups or heat-proof glasses.

The Bishop

A clove-studded orange is used to impart a warm, spicy flavour to this festive drink.

SERVES 8

1 orange
12 cloves
12 allspice berries, ground
750 ml/1¼ pints/3 cups port
3-4 tbsp sugar, or to taste

1 Preheat the oven to 160°C/325°F/gas 3. Stud the orange with the cloves and wrap loosely in foil. Bake for 45 minutes.

2 Cut the baked orange into quarters and place them in a saucepan. Add the allspice, port and sugar to taste. Heat gently until warm, without allowing the port to boil. Serve in warmed glasses with a slice of clove-studded orange, to decorate.

allspice berries

Jamaican Rum Punch

Ground allspice, mace and cinnamon sticks are used to flavour this cider-based punch.

SERVES 8-10
10 allspice berries
1 blade of mace
2 cinnamon sticks
1.2 litres/2 pints/5 cups
  sweet cider
3 tbsp dark Jamaican rum
3 tbsp brandy, or to taste

1   Place the allspice, mace and cinnamon in a saucepan with the cider. Heat the mixture very gently for 20-30 minutes, without boiling.

2   Add the rum and brandy. Serve hot, in warmed glasses.

allspice berries

cinnamon sticks

**ground
black pepper**

Tequila Maria

In Mexico, this spicy drink might be decorated with exotic bouganvillea or hibiscus flowers.

SERVES 2
½ tsp freshly grated horseradish
  or 2 tsp horseradish
generous pinch of freshly ground
  black pepper
generous pinch of celery salt
175ml/6 fl oz/¾ cup tomato juice
50ml/2 fl oz/¼ cup tequila
dash of Worcestershire sauce
dash of Tabasco sauce
juice of 1 lime
pinch of dried oregano
a few ice cubes
plenty of crushed ice
2 lime slices, to decorate

1   Mix all the ingredients in a large jug. Add a few ice cubes and mix again. Taste for seasoning.

2   Half fill two glasses with crushed ice. Pour in the tequila Maria and serve, decorated with lime slices.

**fresh
horseradish**

Tabasco sauce

SPICES IN THE HOME

Spices for Decoration and Fragrant Gifts

Today we associate spices mainly with cooking, but at one time spices played a much larger role in the home – their fragrance was used to scent the air, and it was thought that they had antiseptic qualities and could both prevent disease and ward off insects. Spice bags were carried around or hung from a belt, and fragrant bowls and boxes of pot pourri were used to scent the air. Included here are some traditional ideas for using spices in the home: clove-scented pomanders, festive spiced gingerbread biscuits and pot pourri, and, to make as gifts for keen cooks, spice baskets, cinnamon bundles and chilli ropes.

Pomanders

Pomanders are delightful Christmas gifts. Make them three or four weeks before Christmas so that they have time to mature. Attach long ribbons so that they can be hung in the wardrobe or on a door knob, where they last for ages.

MAKES 1 POMANDER
**1 thin-skinned orange
300-400 cloves
1 tsp ground cinnamon
1 tsp ground orris root
ribbon or velvet cord**

ground cinnamon

1   Wash and dry the chosen fruit. Use a skewer to puncture the skin of the fruit all over in an attractive pattern. This will make it easier to push in the cloves, which should completely cover the surface of the fruit.

2   Place the cinnamon and orris root in a plastic bag and toss the orange in the mixture until well coated. Place the orange in a flat basket lined with foil and leave it for 3-4 weeks to dry out and harden. Turn the fruit occasionally. If you make a number of pomanders, it is important to prevent the fruits from touching each other while they are drying out as they may turn mouldy. Tie a length of ribbon or velvet cord around the fruit.

cloves

VARIATIONS

Lemons and limes can also be made into pomanders. Tie a ribbon around the fruits, leaving a length to tie them by. Puncture and stud with cloves as described left. Leave one or two segments without cloves, or cover the whole fruit if you prefer.

Kumquats or mandarin oranges, studded with cloves and prepared as for a pomander, may be added to a wreath made from fir cones, bay leaves and cranberries threaded on to wire.

Gingerbread Tree Decorations

These biscuits are traditionally made at Christmas time in Scandinavia. Ginger and cinnamon are always used to spice the mixture, but ½ tsp ground cloves may also be added. Decorate the biscuits with silver and gold dragees if you like. Stick them to the icing while it is still soft.

Makes about 30-40
225 g/8 oz/2 cups plain flour
1 tsp baking powder
2 tsp ground ginger
1 tsp ground cinnamon
50 g/2 oz/4 tbsp butter or
  margarine
50 g/2 oz/4 tbsp soft light
  brown sugar
2 tbsp golden syrup
DECORATION
115 g/4 oz/1 cup icing sugar,
  sifted

1 Preheat the oven to 180°C/350°F/ gas 4. Grease two baking trays. Sift the flour, baking powder, ginger and cinnamon into a bowl.

2 Melt the butter or margarine, sugar and syrup together in a saucepan over a gentle heat. Add the melted mixture to the dry ingredients and mix to a dough.

3 Gather the dough into one piece and knead it on a lightly floured surface until it is smooth. If the dough is too soft to roll, allow it to rest for a few minutes.

4 Roll out the dough and cut out Christmas shapes – stars, Christmas trees and angels using the appropriate cutters. Use a skewer to make a hole in each biscuit for the ribbon to be threaded through after cooking. Place on the trays and bake for 10-12 minutes, or until lightly brown and firm.

5 While the biscuits are still warm, make sure that the holes are big enough for ribbons to be threaded through them. Transfer to a wire rack to cool.

6 Place the icing sugar in a bowl and mix in a little water, adding it from a teaspoon and beating to make a thick glacé icing. Put the icing in a small paper piping bag and use to decorate the biscuits.

7 When the icing has dried, thread ribbons through the biscuits. Tie the biscuits on to the Christmas tree or a garland decoration.

COOK'S TIP
Eat the biscuits on the same day as they are hung. For longer keeping, each biscuit may be carefully wrapped in clear film, sealed with freezer tape on the back.

123

Pot Pourri

Summer and Spice

Mix 1 litre/1³/₄ pints/4 cups dried rose petals with 250 ml/8 fl oz/1 cup mixed rosemary, lemon thyme and lavender flowers. Add the very finely grated rind of 1 lemon and 1 orange. Leave for about 24 hours, then add 2 tsp lightly crushed cloves and 1 tsp crushed allspice berries. Add 1 tbsp ground orris root to fix the perfume. Lightly toss the mixture daily for a week, then transfer to bowls or boxes.

dried rose petals

dried rose leaves

allspice berries

dried lavender

dried citrus rind

dried rosebuds

cloves

dried rosemary

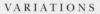

dried rosebuds

Cottage Garden Mix

Combine a mixture of rose petals, orange blossom, lavender and honeysuckle. Spread the petals on a wooden tray and leave to dry in a warm, dry place, turning occasionally, for several days. Add 1 tsp ground cinnamon, 6 lightly crushed cloves and 1 tbsp ground orris root to each 1.2 litres/2 pints/5 cups petals. Add 1-2 drops rose perfume oil and 2 tsp brandy and transfer to bowls or boxes.

Spice Baskets

These make useful and interesting gifts. Choose small baskets, line them with pretty patterned fabric, tissue paper or a banana leaf. Fill with a collection of spices. If you like, pick a theme for each basket, for example pack spices for Thai cooking, seasoning mixtures for Indian cooking or spice mixtures to mull warming drinks. Or just make a selection from the following:

cinnamon sticks tied in a bundle
   with ribbon or raffia
whole nutmegs
cardamoms packed in a
   cellophane or muslin bag
coriander seeds and cumin seeds in
   packed muslin 'purses'
vanilla pods
a few lemon grass stalks and lime
   leaves
a bundle of fresh red and
   green chillies
dried pomegranates

dried red chillies

KITCHEN DEVIL

To make a dried chilli rope, thread red chillies on to a long piece of fine string and hang them in a cool airy place. They should retain their rich colour and can be used when quite dry.

CINNAMON BUNDLES

Tie 3 cinnamon sticks and a piece of dried orange peel together with a tartan ribbon.

small
green chillies

Cooking with Spices

SOUPS AND STARTERS

Hot and Sour Prawn Soup

How hot this soup is depends upon the type of chilli used. Try tiny Thai chillies if you really want to go for the burn.

SERVES 6

225 g/8 oz raw prawns,
 in shells
2 lemon grass stalks
1.5 litres/2½ pints/6¼ cups
 vegetable stock
4 kaffir lime leaves
2 slices peeled fresh
 root ginger
4 tbsp Thai fish sauce
4 tbsp fresh lime juice
2 garlic cloves, crushed
6 spring onions, chopped
1 fresh red chilli, seeded and cut
 into thin strips
115 g/4 oz/generous 1½ cups
 oyster mushrooms, sliced
fresh coriander sprigs,
 to garnish

1 Peel the prawns and set them aside. Put the shells in a large saucepan.

COOK'S TIP

It is important that the prawns are only heated through and not overcooked, or they will become tough.

2 Lightly crush the lemon grass and add the stalks to the pan with the stock, lime leaves and ginger. Bring to the boil, lower the heat and simmer for 20 minutes.

3 Strain the stock into a clean pan, discarding the prawn shells and aromatics. Add the fish sauce, lime juice, garlic, spring onions, chilli and mushrooms. Bring to the boil, lower the heat and simmer for 5 minutes. Add the peeled prawns and cook for 1 minute to heat through. Garnish with the coriander sprigs and serve.

Provençal Fish Soup with Rouille

Although many of the tiny rock fish traditionally used in this recipe are not available away from the Mediterranean, this version is still full of Provençal flavours and is served with an authentic chilli-spiked rouille.

SERVES 4-6

2 tbsp olive oil
1 leek, sliced
2 celery sticks, chopped
1 onion, chopped
2 garlic cloves, chopped
4 ripe tomatoes, chopped
1 tbsp tomato purée
150 ml/¼ pint/⅔ cup dry white wine
1 bay leaf
1 tsp saffron strands
1 kg/2¼ lb mixed fish fillets and prepared shellfish
fish trimmings, bones and heads
salt and ground black pepper
croûtons and grated Gruyère cheese, to serve
ROUILLE
1 slice of white bread, crusts removed
1 red pepper, cored, seeded and quartered
1-2 fresh red chillies, seeded and chopped
2 garlic cloves, crushed
olive oil (optional)

1 Make the rouille. Soak the bread in 2-3 tbsp cold water for 10 minutes. Meanwhile, grill the red pepper quarters, skin side up, until the skin is charred and blistered. Put into a polythene bag and leave until cool enough to handle. Peel off the skin. Drain the bread and squeeze out the excess moisture.

2 Roughly chop the pepper quarters and place in a blender or food processor with the bread, chillies and garlic. Process to a fairly coarse paste, adding a little olive oil, if necessary. Scrape the rouille into a small bowl and set it aside.

3 Heat the olive oil in a large saucepan. Add the leek, celery, onion and garlic. Cook gently for 10 minutes until soft. Add the tomatoes, tomato purée, wine, bay leaf, saffron, any shellfish and the fish trimmings. Bring to the boil, lower the heat, cover and simmer for 30 minutes.

4 Strain through a colander pressing out the liquid. Cut the fish fillets into large chunks and add to the strained soup. Cover and simmer for about 5-10 minutes until the fish is cooked.

5 Strain through a colander into a clean pan. Put half the cooked fish into a blender or food processor with about 300 ml/½ pint/1¼ cups of the soup. Process for just long enough to blend, while retaining some texture.

6 Stir all the fish back into the remaining soup. Add salt and pepper to taste. Reheat gently. Serve the soup with the rouille, croûtons and cheese.

Butternut Squash Soup with Curried Horseradish Cream

The combination of cream, curry powder and horseradish makes a wonderful topping for this beautiful golden soup.

SERVES 6

1 butternut squash
1 cooking apple
25 g/1 oz/2 tbsp butter
1 onion, finely chopped
1-2 tsp curry powder
900 ml/1½ pints/3¾ cups chicken
** or vegetable stock**
1 tsp chopped fresh sage
150 ml/¼ pint/⅔ cup apple juice
salt and ground black pepper
curry powder, to garnish
CURRIED HORSERADISH CREAM
4 tbsp double cream
2 tsp horseradish sauce
½ tsp curry powder

1 Peel the squash, remove the seeds and chop the flesh. Peel, core and chop the apple.

2 Heat the butter in a large saucepan. Add the onion and cook, stirring occasionally, for 5 minutes until soft. Stir in the curry powder. Cook to bring out the flavour, stirring constantly, for 2 minutes.

3 Add the stock, squash, apple and sage. Bring to the boil, lower the heat, cover and simmer for 20 minutes until the squash and apple are soft.

4 Meanwhile, make the horseradish cream. Whip the cream in a bowl until stiff, then stir in the horseradish sauce and curry powder. Cover and chill until required.

5 Purée the soup in a blender or food processor. Return to the clean pan and add the apple juice, with salt and pepper to taste. Reheat gently, without allowing the soup to boil.

6 Serve the soup in individual bowls, topping each portion with a spoonful of horseradish cream and a dusting of curry powder. Garnish with a few lime shreds, if you like.

Spiced Lentil Soup

A subtle blend of spices takes this warming soup to new heights. Serve it with crusty bread for a satisfying lunch.

SERVES 6

2 onions, finely chopped
2 garlic cloves, crushed
4 tomatoes, roughly chopped
½ tsp ground turmeric
1 tsp ground cumin
6 cardamoms
½ cinnamon stick
225 g/8 oz/1 cup red lentils
400 g/14 oz can coconut milk
1 tbsp fresh lime juice
salt and ground black pepper
cumin seeds, to garnish

1 Put the onions, garlic, tomatoes, turmeric, cumin, cardamoms, cinnamon and lentils into a saucepan with 900 ml/1½ pints/3¾ cups water. Bring to the boil, lower the heat, cover and simmer gently for 20 minutes or until the lentils are soft.

2 Remove the cardamoms and cinnamon stick, then purée the mixture in a blender or food processor. Press the soup through a sieve, then return it to the clean pan.

3 Reserve a little of the coconut milk for the garnish and add the remainder to the pan with the lime juice. Stir well. Season with salt and pepper. Reheat the soup gently without boiling. Swirl in the reserved coconut milk, garnish with cumin seeds and serve.

> **COOK'S TIP**
>
> *If the tomatoes do not have much flavour, stir in a little tomato purée or use a small can of tomatoes.*

Crab Spring Rolls and Dipping Sauce

Chilli and grated ginger add a hint of heat to these sensational treats. Serve them as a starter or with other Chinese dishes.

SERVES 4-6

1 tbsp groundnut oil

1 tsp sesame oil

1 garlic clove, crushed

1 fresh red chilli, seeded and finely sliced

450 g/1 lb pack fresh stir-fry vegetables

2.5 cm/1 in piece of fresh root ginger, grated

1 tbsp dry sherry or rice wine

1 tbsp soy sauce

350 g/12 oz fresh dressed crabmeat (brown and white meat)

12 spring roll wrappers

1 small egg, beaten

oil, for deep-frying

salt and ground black pepper

lime wedges and fresh coriander, to garnish

1 quantity Indonesian sambal kecap, for dipping

1 Heat a wok briefly, then add the groundnut and sesame oils. When hot, stir-fry the crushed garlic and chilli for 1 minute. Add the vegetables and ginger and stir-fry for 1 minute more, then drizzle over the sherry or rice wine and soy sauce. Allow the mixture to bubble up for 1 minute.

2 Using a slotted spoon, transfer the vegetables to a dish. Set aside until cool, then stir in the crab meat and season with salt and pepper.

COOK'S TIP

Spring roll wrappers are available in many supermarkets as well as Oriental grocers. If you are unable to find them, use filo pastry instead. Keep the wrappers – and the filled rolls – covered with clear film, as they will rapidly dry out if exposed to the air.

3 Soften the spring roll wrappers, following the directions on the packet. Place some of the filling on a wrapper, fold over the front edge and the sides and roll up neatly, sealing the edges with a little beaten egg. Repeat with the remaining wrappers and filling.

4 Heat the oil in the wok and fry the spring rolls in batches, turning several times, until brown and crisp. Remove with a slotted spoon, drain on kitchen paper and keep hot while frying the remainder. Serve at once, garnished with lime wedges and coriander with the dipping sauce.

Chick-pea and Coriander Cakes with Tahini

These spicy little cakes are equally good served hot or cold. For a more substantial snack, tuck them into pockets of pitta bread with salad.

SERVES 4

2 x 425 g/15 oz cans chick-peas
2 garlic cloves, crushed
1 bunch spring onions (white parts only), chopped
2 tsp ground cumin
2 tsp ground coriander
1 fresh green chilli, seeded and finely chopped
2 tbsp chopped fresh coriander
1 small egg, beaten
2 tbsp plain flour
seasoned flour, for shaping
oil, for shallow frying
salt and ground black pepper
lemon wedges and fresh coriander, to garnish

TAHINI AND LEMON DIP
2 tbsp tahini
juice of 1 lemon
2 garlic cloves, crushed

1   Drain the chick-peas thoroughly. Tip them into a blender or food processor and process until smooth. Add the garlic, spring onions, cumin and ground coriander. Process again until well mixed.

2   Scrape the mixture into a bowl and stir in the chilli, fresh coriander, egg and flour. Mix well and season with salt and pepper. If the mixture is very soft add a little more flour. Chill for about 30 minutes to firm the mixture.

3   Make the dip. Mix the tahini, lemon juice and garlic in a bowl, adding a little water if the sauce is too thick. Set aside.

4   Using floured hands, shape the chick-pea mixture into 12 cakes. Heat the oil in a frying pan and fry the cakes in batches for about 1 minute on each side, until crisp and golden. Drain on kitchen paper and serve with the dip and lemon and coriander garnish.

VARIATION

Another quick and easy sauce is made by mixing Greek yogurt with a little chopped chilli and fresh mint.

Spiced Dolmades

These dolmades contain sumac, a spice with a sharp lemon flavour. It is available from specialist food shops.

MAKES 20

**20 vacuum-packed vine leaves
 in brine
90 g/3½ oz/½ cup long grain rice
3 tbsp olive oil
1 small onion, finely chopped
50 g/2 oz/⅔ cup pine nuts
3 tbsp raisins
2 tbsp chopped fresh mint
½ tsp ground cinnamon
½ tsp ground allspice
2 tsp ground sumac
2 tsp lemon juice
2 tbsp tomato purée
salt and ground black pepper
lemon slices and fresh mint sprigs,
 to garnish**

1 Rinse the vine leaves well under cold running water, then drain. Bring a saucepan of lightly salted water to the boil. Add the rice, lower the heat, cover and simmer for 10-12 minutes, until almost cooked. Drain.

2 Heat 2 tbsp of the olive oil in a frying pan, add the onion and cook until soft. Stir in the pine nuts and cook until lightly browned, then add the raisins, mint, cinnamon, allspice and sumac, with salt and pepper to taste. Stir in the rice and mix well. Leave to cool.

VARIATION

Fresh vine leaves may be used but must be blanched in boiling water first to make them pliable.

3 Line a saucepan with any damaged vine leaves. Trim the stalks from the remaining leaves and lay them flat. Place a little filling on each. Fold the sides over and roll up each leaf neatly. Place the dolmades side by side in the leaf-lined pan, so that they fit tightly.

4 Mix 300 ml/½ pint/1¼ cups water with the lemon juice and tomato purée in a bowl. Add the remaining olive oil. Pour over the dolmades and place a heatproof plate on top to keep them in place.

5 Cover the pan and simmer the dolmades for 1 hour until all the liquid has been absorbed and the leaves are tender. Transfer to a platter, garnish with lemon slices and mint and serve hot or cold.

Marinated Feta Cheese with Capers

Marinating cubes of feta cheese with herbs and spices gives a marvellous flavour. Serve on toast or with salad.

SERVES 6

**350 g/12 oz/2 cups feta cheese
2 garlic cloves
½ tsp mixed peppercorns
8 coriander seeds
1 bay leaf
1-2 tbsp drained capers
fresh oregano or thyme sprigs
olive oil, to cover
hot toast, to serve**

1 Cut the feta cheese into cubes. Thickly slice the garlic. Mix the peppercorns and coriander seeds in a mortar and crush lightly with a pestle.

2 Pack the feta cubes into a large preserving jar with the bay leaf, interspersing layers of cheese with garlic, crushed peppercorns and coriander, capers and the fresh oregano or thyme sprigs.

3 Pour in enough olive oil to cover the cheese. Close tightly and leave to marinate for two weeks in the fridge.

4 Lift out the feta cubes and serve on hot toast, sprinkled with a little of the oil from the jar.

VARIATION

Add stoned black or green olives to the feta cheese in the marinade.

Spicy Potato Wedges with Chilli Dip

For a healthy snack with superb flavour, try these dry-roasted potato wedges. The crisp spice crust makes them irresistible, especially when served with a chilli dip.

SERVES 2

2 baking potatoes,
  about 225 g/8 oz each
2 tbsp olive oil
2 garlic cloves, crushed
1 tsp ground allspice
1 tsp ground coriander
1 tbsp paprika
salt and ground black pepper
DIP
1 tbsp olive oil
1 small onion, finely chopped
1 garlic clove, crushed
200 g/7 oz can chopped tomatoes
1 fresh red chilli, seeded and
  finely chopped
1 tbsp balsamic vinegar
1 tbsp chopped fresh coriander,
  plus extra to garnish

1 Preheat the oven to 200°C/400°F/ gas 6. Cut the potatoes in half, then into 8 wedges.

2 Place the wedges in a saucepan of cold water. Bring to the boil, then lower the heat and simmer gently for 10 minutes or until the potatoes have softened slightly. Drain well and pat dry on kitchen paper.

3 Mix the olive oil, garlic, allspice, coriander and paprika in a roasting tin. Add salt and pepper to taste. Add the potatoes to the pan and shake to coat them thoroughly. Roast for 20 minutes, turning the potato wedges occasionally, or until they are browned, crisp and fully cooked.

4 Meanwhile, make the chilli dip. Heat the oil in a saucepan, add the onion and garlic and cook for 5-10 minutes until soft. Add the tomatoes, with their juice. Stir in the chilli and vinegar. Cook gently for 10 minutes until the mixture has reduced and thickened, then check the seasoning. Stir in the fresh coriander and serve hot, with potato wedges. Garnish with salt and fresh coriander.

COOK'S TIP

To save time, parboil the potatoes and toss them with the spices in advance, but make sure that the potato wedges are perfectly dry and completely covered in the mixture.

Baby Onions and Mushrooms à la Grecque

There are many variations of this classic dish, but they always contain coriander seeds.

SERVES 4

2 carrots

375 g/12 oz baby onions

4 tbsp olive oil

120 ml/4 fl oz/½ cup dry white wine

1 tsp coriander seeds, lightly crushed

2 bay leaves

pinch of cayenne pepper

1 garlic clove, crushed

375 g/12 oz button mushrooms

3 tomatoes, peeled, seeded and quartered

salt and ground black pepper

3 tbsp chopped fresh parsley, to garnish

1 Peel the carrots and cut them into small dice. Peel the baby onions and trim the tops and roots.

2 Heat 3 tbsp of the olive oil in a deep frying pan. Add the carrots and onions and cook, stirring occasionally, for about 20 minutes until the vegetables have browned lightly and are beginning to soften.

3 Add the white wine, coriander seeds, bay leaves, cayenne, garlic, button mushrooms and tomatoes, with salt and pepper to taste. Cook, uncovered, for 20-30 minutes until the vegetables are soft and the sauce has thickened.

COOK'S TIP

Don't trim too much from either the top or root end of the onions: if you do, the centres will pop out during cooking.

4 Transfer to a serving dish and leave to cool. Cover and chill until needed. Before serving, pour over the remaining olive oil and sprinkle with the parsley. Serve with crusty bread.

VARIATION

This treatment is ideal for a single vegetable or a combination. Try leeks, fennel or artichokes, with or without baby onions.

Turkey, Juniper and Peppercorn Terrine

This is an ideal dish for entertaining, as it can be made several days in advance. If you prefer, arrange some of the pancetta and pistachios as a layer in the middle of the terrine.

SERVES 10-12

225 g/8 oz chicken livers, trimmed

450 g/1 lb minced turkey

450 g/1 lb minced pork

225 g/8 oz cubetti pancetta

50 g/2 oz/½ cup shelled pistachio nuts, roughly chopped

1 tsp salt

½ tsp ground mace

2 garlic cloves, crushed

1 tsp drained green peppercorns in brine

1 tsp juniper berries

120 ml/4 fl oz/½ cup dry white wine

2 tbsp gin

finely grated rind of 1 orange

8 large vacuum-packed vine leaves in brine

oil, for greasing

1   Chop the chicken livers finely. Put them in a bowl and add the turkey, pork, pancetta, pistachio nuts, salt, mace and garlic. Mix well.

2   Lightly crush the peppercorns and juniper berries and add them to the mixture. Stir in the white wine, gin and orange rind. Cover and chill overnight to allow the flavours to mingle.

3   Preheat the oven to 160°C/325°F/ gas 3. Rinse the vine leaves under cold running water. Drain them thoroughly. Lightly oil a 1.2 litre/2 pint/5 cup pâté terrine or loaf tin. Line the terrine or tin with the leaves, letting the ends hang over the sides. Pack the mixture into the terrine or tin and fold the leaves over to enclose the filling. Brush lightly with oil.

4   Cover the terrine with its lid or with foil. Place it in a roasting tin and pour in boiling water to come halfway up the sides of the terrine. Bake for 1¾ hours, checking the level of the water occasionally, so that the roasting tin does not dry out.

5   Leave the terrine to cool, then pour off the surface juices. Cover with clear film, then foil and place weights on top. Chill overnight. Serve at room temperature with a pickle or chutney such as spiced kumquats or red pepper and chilli jelly.

Baba Ganoush with Lebanese Flatbread

Baba Ganoush is a delectable aubergine dip from the Middle East. Tahini – a sesame seed paste with cumin – is the main flavouring, giving a subtle hint of spice.

SERVES 6

2 small aubergines
1 garlic clove, crushed
4 tbsp tahini
25 g/1 oz/¼ cup ground almonds
juice of ½ lemon
½ tsp ground cumin
2 tbsp fresh mint leaves
2 tbsp olive oil
salt and ground black pepper
LEBANESE FLATBREAD
4 pitta breads
3 tbsp toasted sesame seeds
3 tbsp fresh thyme leaves
3 tbsp poppy seeds
150 ml/¼ pint/⅔ cup olive oil

1 Start by making the Lebanese flatbread. Split the pitta breads through the middle and carefully open them out. Mix the sesame seeds, chopped thyme and poppy seeds in a mortar. Crush them lightly with a pestle to release the flavour.

2 Stir in the olive oil. Spread the mixture lightly over the cut sides of the pitta bread. Grill until golden brown and crisp. When cool, break into rough pieces and set aside.

3 Grill the aubergine, turning them frequently, until the skin is blackened and blistered. Remove the peel, chop the flesh roughly and leave to drain in a colander.

COOK'S TIP

It may be easier to split the pitta breads if they are warmed slightly, either under the grill or in the oven.

4 Squeeze out as much liquid from the aubergine as possible. Place the flesh in a blender or food processor. Add the garlic, tahini, ground almonds, lemon juice and cumin, with salt to taste and process to a smooth paste. Roughly chop half the mint and stir into the dip.

5 Spoon into a bowl, scatter the remaining leaves on top and drizzle with olive oil. Serve with the Lebanese flatbread.

FISH AND SEAFOOD

Mussels and Clams with Lemon Grass and Coconut Cream

Lemon grass has an incomparable flavour and is widely used in Thai cookery, especially with seafood. If you have difficulty obtaining the clams for this recipe, use a few extra mussels instead.

SERVES 6

1.75 kg/4-4½ lb mussels
450 g/1 lb baby clams
120 ml/4 fl oz/½ cup dry
 white wine
1 bunch spring onions, chopped
2 lemon grass stalks, chopped
6 kaffir lime leaves, chopped
2 tsp Thai green curry paste
200 ml/7 fl oz coconut cream
2 tbsp chopped fresh coriander
salt and ground black pepper
garlic chives, to garnish

1 Clean the mussels by pulling off the beards, scrubbing the shells well and removing any barnacles. Discard any mussels that are broken or which do not close when tapped sharply. Wash the clams.

2 Put the wine in a large saucepan with the spring onions, lemon grass, lime leaves and curry paste. Simmer until the wine has almost evaporated.

> ### COOK'S TIP
>
> *Buy a few extra mussels in case there are any which have to be discarded.*

3 Add the mussels and clams to the pan, cover tightly and steam the shellfish over a high heat for 5-6 minutes, until they open.

4 Using a slotted spoon, transfer the mussels and clams to a heated serving bowl and keep hot. Discard any shellfish that remain closed. Strain the cooking liquid into a clean pan and simmer to reduce to about 250 ml/8 fl oz/1 cup.

5 Stir in the coconut cream and coriander, with salt and pepper to taste. Heat through. Pour the sauce over the mussels and clams and serve, garnished with garlic chives.

Sardines in Escabeche

This spicy marinade is widely used in Spain and Portugal as a traditional means of preserving fish, poultry or game. It is good with fried fish.

SERVES 2-4

16 sardines, cleaned
seasoned flour
2 tbsp olive oil
roasted red onion, green pepper and tomatoes, to garnish
MARINADE
6 tbsp olive oil
1 onion, sliced
1 garlic clove, crushed
3-4 bay leaves
2 cloves
1 dried red chilli
1 tsp paprika
120 ml/4 fl oz/½ cup wine or sherry vinegar
120 ml/4 fl oz/½ cup white wine
salt and ground black pepper

1   Cut the heads off the sardines and split each of them along the belly. Turn them over so that the backbone is uppermost. Press down along the backbone to loosen it, then carefully lift out the backbone and as many remaining bones as possible.

2   Close the sardines up again and dust them with seasoned flour. Heat the olive oil in a frying pan and fry the sardines for 2-3 minutes on each side. Remove the fish from the pan and allow to cool, then place in a single layer in a large shallow dish.

VARIATION

White fish can be prepared in this way, but the method is particularly successful with oily fish such as herrings or sprats.

3   To make the marinade, add the olive oil to the oil remaining in the frying pan. Fry the onion and garlic gently for 5-10 minutes until soft. Add the bay leaves, cloves, chilli and paprika, with pepper to taste. Fry, stirring, for another 1-2 minutes.

4   Stir in the vinegar, wine and a little salt. Allow to bubble up then pour over the sardines. When cool, cover and chill overnight or for up to three days. Serve, garnished with onion, pepper and tomatoes.

Cajun Blackened Fish with Papaya Salsa

This is an excellent way of cooking fish, leaving it moist in the middle and crisp and spicy on the outside.

SERVES 4

1 quantity cajun spice, without the onion and garlic
4 x 225-275 g/8-10 oz skinned fish fillets such as snapper or bream
50 g/2 oz/¼ cup butter, melted
PAPAYA SALSA
1 papaya
½ small red onion, diced
1 fresh red chilli, seeded and finely chopped
3 tbsp chopped fresh coriander
grated rind and juice of 1 lime
salt
lime and coriander, to garnish

1 Start by making the salsa. Cut the papaya in half and scoop out the seeds. Remove the skin, cut the flesh into small dice and place it in a bowl. Add the onion, chilli, coriander, lime rind and juice, with salt to taste. Mix well and set aside.

> ### COOK'S TIP
>
> *Cooking fish in this way can be a smoky affair, so make sure the kitchen is well ventilated or use an extractor fan.*

2 Preheat a heavy-based frying pan over a medium heat for approximately 10 minutes. Spread the cajun spice on a plate. Brush the fish fillets with melted butter then dip them in the spices until well coated.

3 Place the fish in the hot pan and cook for 1-2 minutes on each side until blackened. Serve at once with the papaya salsa. Garnish with lime and coriander.

Caribbean Fish Steaks

West Indian cooks love spices and use them to good effect. This quick and easy recipe is a typical example of how chillies, cayenne and allspice can add an exotic accent to a tomato sauce for fish.

SERVES 4

3 tbsp oil
6 shallots, finely chopped
1 garlic clove, crushed
1 fresh green chilli, seeded and finely chopped
400 g/14 oz can chopped tomatoes
2 bay leaves
¼ tsp cayenne pepper
1 tsp crushed allspice
juice of 2 limes
4 cod steaks
1 tsp brown muscovado sugar
2 tsp angostura bitters
salt

1 Heat the oil in a frying pan. Add the shallots and cook for 5 minutes until soft. Add the garlic and chilli and cook for 2 minutes, then stir in the tomatoes, bay leaves, cayenne pepper, allspice and lime juice, with a little salt to taste.

> ### VARIATION
>
> *Almost any robust fish steaks or fillets can be cooked in this way. Try haddock or swordfish. The sauce is also good over grilled pork chops.*

2 Cook gently for 15 minutes, then add the cod steaks and baste with the tomato sauce. Cover and cook for 10 minutes or until the steaks are cooked. Transfer the steaks to a warmed dish and keep hot. Stir the sugar and angostura bitters into the sauce, simmer for 2 minutes then pour over the fish. Serve with steamed okra or green beans.

Crabcakes with Ginger and Wasabi

Wasabi – a Japanese horseradish mustard – is available as a powder or a paste. It is very hot so should be used sparingly.

SERVES 6

450 g/1 lb fresh dressed crab meat (brown and white meat)
4 spring onions, finely chopped
2.5 cm/1 in piece of fresh root ginger, grated
2 tbsp chopped fresh coriander
2 tbsp mayonnaise
½-1 tsp wasabi paste
1 tbsp sesame oil
50-115 g/2-4 oz/1-2 cups fresh breadcrumbs
salt and ground black pepper
oil, for frying

DIPPING SAUCE

1 tsp wasabi paste
6 tbsp soy sauce

1 Make the dipping sauce by mixing the wasabi and soy sauce in a small bowl. Set aside.

2 Mix the crab meat, spring onions, ginger, coriander, mayonnaise, wasabi paste and sesame oil in a bowl. Stir in a little salt and pepper and enough breadcrumbs to make a mixture that is firm enough to form patties, but is not too stiff.

3 Chill for 30 minutes then form the mixture into 12 cakes. Heat a shallow layer of oil in a frying pan and fry the crabcakes for 3-4 minutes on each side, until browned. Serve with lettuce leaves and kaffir lime slices, accompanied by the dipping sauce, garnished with chilli and spring onion slices.

COOK'S TIP

Fresh crabmeat will have the best flavour, but if it is not available, use frozen or canned crabmeat.

Stir-fried Five Spice Squid with Black Bean Sauce

Squid is perfect for stir-frying as it should be cooked quickly. The spicy sauce makes the ideal accompaniment.

SERVES 6

450 g/1 lb small cleaned squid
3 tbsp oil
2.5 cm/1 in piece fresh root
  ginger, grated
1 garlic clove, crushed
8 spring onions, cut diagonally into
  2.5 cm/1 in lengths
1 red pepper, seeded and cut
  into strips
1 fresh green chilli, seeded and
  thinly sliced
6 mushrooms, sliced
1 tsp five spice powder
2 tbsp black bean sauce
2 tbsp soy sauce
1 tsp granulated sugar
1 tbsp rice wine or dry sherry

COOK'S TIP

As with all stir-fried dishes, it is important to have all the ingredients ready before you start to cook.

1 Rinse the squid and pull away the outer skin. Dry on kitchen paper. Slit the squid open and score the outside into diamonds with a sharp knife. Cut the squid into strips.

2 Heat a wok briefly and add the oil. When it is hot, stir-fry the squid quickly. Remove the squid strips from the wok with a slotted spoon and set aside. Add the ginger, garlic, spring onions, red pepper, chilli and mushrooms to the oil remaining in the wok and stir-fry for 2 minutes.

3 Return the squid to the wok and stir in the five spice powder. Stir in the black bean sauce, soy sauce, sugar and rice wine or sherry. Bring to the boil and cook, stirring, for 1 minute.

Cod and Prawn Green Coconut Curry

If you have a jar of green masala in the store-cupboard, this curry takes just minutes to make!

SERVES 4

675 g/1½ lb cod fillets, skinned
6 tbsp green masala
175 ml/6 fl oz/¾ cup canned coconut milk or 200 ml/7 fl oz/ scant 1 cup coconut cream
175 g/6 oz peeled prawns, raw or cooked
fresh coriander, to garnish
basmati rice, to serve

1   Cut the skinned cod fillets into 4 cm/1½ in pieces.

2   Put the green masala and coconut milk or cream into a frying pan. Heat to simmering and simmer gently for 5 minutes, stirring occasionally.

VARIATION

Any firm fish, such as monkfish, can be used instead of cod. Whole fish steaks can be cooked in the sauce, but allow an extra 5 minutes' cooking time and baste them with the sauce from time to time.

3   Add the cod and prawns (if raw) and cook for 5 minutes. If using cooked prawns, then add them and heat through. Garnish with coriander and serve at once with rice.

Piri-piri Prawns with Aïoli

Piri-piri is a Portuguese hot pepper sauce. The name literally means small chilli.

SERVES 4

1 fresh red chilli, seeded and finely chopped
½ tsp paprika
½ tsp ground coriander
1 garlic clove, crushed
juice of ½ lime
2 tbsp olive oil
20 large raw prawns in shells, heads removed and deveined
salt and ground black pepper
AÏOLI
150 ml/¼ pint/⅔ cup mayonnaise
2 garlic cloves, crushed
1 tsp Dijon mustard

1   Make the aïoli. Mix the mayonnaise, garlic and mustard in a small bowl and set aside.

VARIATION

The piri-piri marinade can be used for all types of fish. It is also very good with chicken, although this will need to be marinated for longer.

2   Mix the chilli, paprika, coriander, garlic, lime juice and olive oil in a bowl. Add salt and pepper to taste. Place the prawns in a dish. Add the spice mixture and mix well. Cover and leave in a cool place for 30 minutes.

3   Thread the prawns on to skewers and grill or barbecue, basting and turning frequently, for 6-8 minutes until pink. Serve with the aïoli, garnished with two or three extra chillies, if you like.

Marrakesh Monkfish with Chermoula

Chermoula is a Moroccan spice mixture, which is used as a marinade for meat, poultry and fish.

SERVES 4

1 small red onion, finely chopped
2 garlic cloves, crushed
1 fresh red chilli, seeded and
  finely chopped
2 tbsp chopped fresh coriander
1 tbsp chopped fresh mint
1 tsp ground cumin
1 tsp paprika
generous pinch of
  saffron strands
4 tbsp olive oil
juice of 1 lemon
salt
675 g/1½ lb monkfish fillets,
  skinned
salad and pitta bread, to serve

1 To make the chermoula, mix the onion, garlic, chilli, coriander, mint, cumin, paprika, saffron, olive oil, lemon juice and salt in a bowl.

2 Cut the monkfish into cubes. Add them to the spice mixture in the bowl. Mix well to coat, cover and leave in a cool place for 1 hour.

COOK'S TIP

If you use bamboo or wooden skewers, soak them in cold water for about 30 minutes before draining and threading them. This helps to prevent the skewers from scorching.

3 Thread the monkfish on to skewers and place on a rack over a grill pan. Spoon over a little of the marinade.

4 Grill the monkfish skewers, close to the heat, for about 3 minutes on each side, until cooked through and lightly browned. Serve with salad and warm pitta bread.

Salmon Marinated with Thai Spices

This recipe takes a suggestion from the Scandinavian cooks and transforms it with Thai spices.

<u>SERVES 4-6</u>

tail piece of 1 salmon, about 675 g/1½ lb, cleaned and prepared (see Cook's tip)

4 tsp coarse sea salt

4 tsp granulated sugar

2.5 cm/1 in piece fresh root ginger, grated

2 lemon grass stalks, coarse outer leaves removed, thinly sliced

4 kaffir lime leaves, finely chopped or shredded

grated rind of 1 lime

1 fresh red chilli, seeded and finely chopped

1 tsp black peppercorns, coarsely crushed

2 tbsp chopped fresh coriander

coriander and kaffir limes, to garnish

CORIANDER AND LIME DRESSING

150 ml/¼ pint/⅔ cup mayonnaise

juice of ½ lime

2 tsp chopped fresh coriander

1 Remove all the bones from the salmon (a pair of tweezers is the best tool). In a bowl, mix together the salt, sugar, ginger, lemon grass, lime leaves, lime rind, chilli, peppercorns and coriander.

2 Place one quarter of the spice mixture in a shallow dish. Place one salmon fillet, skin down, on top of the spices. Spread two-thirds of the remaining mixture over the flesh then place the remaining fillet on top, flesh side down. Sprinkle the rest of the spice mixture over the fish.

COOK'S TIP

Ask your fishmonger to scale the fish, split it lengthways and remove it from the backbone in two matching fillets.

3 Cover the fish with foil, then place a board on top. Add some weights, such as clean cans of fruit. Chill for 2-5 days, turning the fish daily in the spicy brine.

4 Make the dressing by mixing the mayonnaise, lime juice and chopped coriander in a bowl.

5 Scrape the spices off the fish. Slice it as thinly as possible. Serve with the lime dressing, garnished with coriander and wedges of kaffir limes.

POULTRY AND GAME

Moroccan Harissa-spiced Roast Chicken

The spices and fruit in this stuffing give the chicken an unusual flavour and help to keep it moist.

SERVES 4-5

1.5 kg/3-3½ lb chicken
2-4 tbsp garlic and spice
  aromatic oil
a few bay leaves
2 tsp clear honey
2 tsp tomato purée
4 tbsp lemon juice
150 ml/¼ pint/⅔ cup
  chicken stock
½-1 tsp harissa

STUFFING
25 g/1 oz/2 tbsp butter
1 onion, chopped
1 garlic clove, crushed
1½ tsp ground cinnamon
½ tsp ground cumin
225 g/8 oz/1⅓ cups dried fruit,
  soaked for several hours or
  overnight in water to cover
25 g/1 oz/¼ cup blanched
  almonds, finely chopped
salt and ground black pepper

COOK'S TIP

If you do not particularly like mixed dried fruit, use a single variety such as apricots instead.

---

1 Make the stuffing. Melt the butter in a saucepan. Add the onion and garlic and cook gently for 5 minutes until soft. Add the ground cinnamon and cumin and cook, stirring, for 2 minutes.

2 Drain the dried fruit, chop it roughly and add to the stuffing with the almonds. Season with salt and pepper and cook for 2 minutes more. Tip into a bowl and leave to cool.

3 Preheat the oven to 200°C/400°F/ gas 6. Stuff the neck of the chicken with the fruit mixture, reserving any excess. Brush the garlic and spice oil over the chicken. Place the chicken in a roasting tin, tuck in the bay leaves and roast for 1-1¼ hours, basting occasionally with the juices, until cooked.

4 Transfer the chicken to a carving board. Pour off any excess fat from the roasting tin. Stir the honey, tomato purée, lemon juice, stock and harissa into the juices in the roasting tin. Add salt to taste. Bring to the boil, lower the heat and simmer for 2 minutes, stirring frequently. Meanwhile, reheat any excess stuffing. Carve the chicken, pour the sauce into a small bowl and serve with the stuffing and chicken.

Fragrant Chicken Curry with Thai Spices

This is perfect for a party as the chicken and sauce can be prepared in advance and combined at the last minute.

SERVES 4

3 tbsp oil
1 onion, roughly chopped
2 garlic cloves, crushed
1 tbsp Thai red curry paste
115 g/4 oz creamed coconut
  dissolved in 900 ml/1½ pints/
  3¾ cups boiling water
2 lemon grass stalks,
  roughly chopped
6 kaffir lime leaves, chopped
150 ml/¼ pint/⅔ cup Greek-style
  yogurt
2 tbsp apricot jam
1 cooked chicken, about 1.5 kg/
  3-3½ lb
2 tbsp chopped fresh coriander
salt and ground black pepper
kaffir limes leaves, shredded
  coconut and fresh coriander,
  to garnish
boiled rice, to serve

1 Heat the oil in a saucepan. Add the onion and garlic and fry over a low heat for 5-10 minutes until soft. Stir in the curry paste. Cook, stirring, for 2-3 minutes. Stir in the diluted creamed coconut then add the lemon grass, lime leaves, yogurt and apricot jam. Stir well. Cover and simmer for 30 minutes.

2 Process the sauce in a blender or food processor, then strain it back into a clean pan, pressing as much of the puréed mixture as possible through the sieve.

3 Remove the skin from the chicken, slice the meat off the bones and cut it into bite-size pieces. Add the chicken to the sauce.

4 Bring the sauce back to simmering point. Stir in the fresh coriander and season with salt and pepper. Serve with rice, garnished with extra lime leaves, shredded coconut and coriander.

COOK'S TIP

If you prefer the sauce a little thicker, stir in a little more creamed coconut after adding the chicken.

Turkey Sosaties with a Curried Apricot Sauce

This is a South African way of cooking meat or poultry in a delicious sweet and sour sauce spiced with curry powder.

SERVES 4

1 tbsp oil
1 onion, finely chopped
1 garlic clove, crushed
2 bay leaves
juice of 1 lemon
2 tbsp curry powder
4 tbsp apricot jam
4 tbsp apple juice
salt
675 g/1½ lb turkey fillet
4 tbsp crème fraîche

1 Heat the oil in a saucepan. Add the onion, garlic and bay leaves and cook over a low heat for 10 minutes until the onions are soft. Add the lemon juice, curry powder, apricot jam and apple juice, with salt to taste. Cook gently for 5 minutes. Leave to cool.

VARIATION

This marinade is traditionally used with lamb, but is equally good with cubes of steak or pork fillet or chicken.

2 Cut the turkey into 2 cm/³⁄₄ in cubes and add to the marinade. Mix well, cover and leave in a cool place and marinate for at least 2 hours or overnight in the fridge. Thread the turkey on to skewers, allowing the marinade to run back into the bowl. Grill or barbecue the sosaties for 6-8 minutes, turning several times, until cooked.

3 Meanwhile, transfer the marinade to a pan and simmer for 2 minutes. Stir in the crème fraîche and serve with the sosaties.

Spicy Indonesian Chicken Satay

This spicy marinade quickly gives an exotic flavour to tender chicken breasts. The satays can be cooked on a barbecue or under the grill.

SERVES 4

4 skinless, boneless chicken breasts, about 175 g/6 oz each
1 quantity sambal kecap, with the deep-fried onions separate

1 Cut the chicken breasts into 2.5 cm/1 in cubes and place in a bowl with the sambal kecap. Mix thoroughly. Cover and leave in a cool place to marinate for at least 1 hour. Soak 8 bamboo skewers in cold water for 30 minutes.

2 Tip the chicken and marinade into a sieve placed over a saucepan and leave to drain for a few minutes. Set the sieve aside.

3 Add 2 tbsp hot water to the marinade and bring to the boil. Lower the heat and simmer for 2 minutes, then pour into a bowl and leave to cool. When cool, add the deep-fried onions.

4 Drain the skewers, thread them with the chicken and grill or barbecue for about 10 minutes, turning regularly until the chicken is golden brown and cooked through. Serve with the sambal kecap as a dip.

Roast Rabbit
with Three Mustards

In France rabbit and mustard are a popular combination. In this recipe each of the three different mustards adds a distinctive flavour to the dish.

SERVES 4

1 tbsp Dijon mustard
1 tbsp tarragon mustard
1 tbsp wholegrain mustard
1.5 kg/3-3½ lb rabbit portions
1 large carrot, sliced
1 onion, sliced
2 tbsp fresh chopped tarragon
120 ml/4 fl oz/½ cup dry
  white wine
150 ml/¼ pint/⅔ cup
  double cream
salt and ground black pepper
fresh tarragon, to garnish

VARIATION

If the three different mustards are not available, use one or two varieties, increasing the quantities accordingly. The flavour will not be quite as interesting, but the dish will still taste good!

1 Preheat the oven to 200°C/400°F/ gas 6. Mix the mustards in a bowl and spread over the rabbit. Put the carrot and onion slices in a roasting tin and scatter the tarragon over. Pour in 120 ml/4 fl oz/½ cup of water, then arrange the meat on top.

2 Roast for 25-30 minutes, basting frequently with the juices, until the rabbit is tender. Remove the rabbit to a heated serving dish and keep hot. Using a slotted spoon, remove the carrot and onion slices from the roasting tin and discard.

3 Place the roasting tin on the hob and add the white wine. Boil to reduce by about two-thirds. Stir in the cream and allow to bubble up for a few minutes. Season with salt and pepper then pour over the rabbit and serve, garnished with fresh tarragon.

Venison in Guinness with Horseradish and Mustard Dumplings

Mustard, juniper berries and bay leaves combine with lean dark venison to create a casserole with a rich flavour and wonderful aroma.

SERVES 6

1 tbsp olive oil

675 g/1½ lb stewing venison, cut into cubes

3 onions, sliced

2 garlic cloves, crushed

1 tbsp plain flour

1 tsp mustard powder

6 juniper berries, lightly crushed

2 bay leaves

400 ml/14 fl oz/1⅔ cups Guinness

2 tsp soft light brown sugar

2 tbsp balsamic vinegar

salt and ground black pepper

DUMPLINGS

175 g/6 oz/1½ cups self-raising flour

1 tsp mustard powder

75 g/3 oz/generous ½ cup shredded beef suet

2 tsp horseradish sauce

1 Preheat the oven to 180°C/350°F/gas 4. Heat the oil in a flameproof casserole. Fry the meat, a few pieces at a time, until browned. As each batch browns, remove it to a plate. Add the onions, with a little more oil, if necessary. Cook, stirring, for 5 minutes until soft. Add the garlic, then return the venison to the pan.

2 Mix the flour and mustard in a small bowl, sprinkle over the venison and stir well until the flour has been absorbed. Add the juniper berries and bay leaves and gradually stir in the Guinness, sugar and vinegar. Pour over enough water to cover the meat. Season with salt and pepper and bring to simmering point.

3 Cover and transfer the casserole to cook in the oven for 2-2½ hours, until the venison is tender. Stir the casserole occasionally and add a little more water, if necessary.

4 About 20 minutes before the end of the cooking time, make the dumplings. Sift the flour and mustard into a bowl. Season with salt and pepper and mix in the suet. Stir in the horseradish sauce and enough water to make a soft dough. With floured hands, form into six dumplings. Place these gently on top of the venison. Return the casserole to the oven and cook for 15 minutes more, until the dumplings are well risen and cooked. Serve at once.

Spiced Grilled Poussins

The cumin and coriander coating on the poussins keeps them moist during grilling as well as giving them a delicious and unusual flavour.

SERVES 4

2 garlic cloves, roughly chopped
1 tsp ground cumin
1 tsp ground coriander
pinch of cayenne pepper
½ small onion, chopped
4 tbsp olive oil
½ tsp salt
2 poussins
lemon wedges, to garnish

1 Combine the garlic, cumin, coriander, cayenne pepper, onion, olive oil and salt in a blender or food processor. Process to make a paste that will spread smoothly.

VARIATION

Chicken portions and quail can also be cooked in this way.

2 Cut the poussins in half lengthways. Place them skin-side up in a shallow dish and spread with the spice paste. Cover and leave to marinate in a cool place for 2 hours.

3 Grill or barbecue the poussins for 15-20 minutes, turning frequently, until cooked and lightly charred on the outside. Serve immediately, garnished with lemon wedges.

Chicken with 40 Cloves of Garlic

This recipe is not as alarming as it sounds. Long slow cooking makes the garlic soft and fragrant and the delicious flavour permeates the chicken.

SERVES 4-6

½ lemon
fresh rosemary sprigs
1.5-1.75 kg/3-4½ lb chicken
4 or 5 heads of garlic
4 tbsp olive oil
salt and ground black pepper
steamed broad beans and spring
  onions, to serve

1 Preheat the oven to 190°C/375°F/gas 5. Place the lemon half and the rosemary sprigs in the chicken. Separate 3 or 4 of the garlic heads into cloves and remove the papery husks, but do not peel. Slice the top off the other garlic head.

COOK'S TIP

Make sure that each guest receives an equal portion of garlic. The idea is to mash the garlic into the pan juices to make an aromatic sauce.

2 Heat the oil in a large flameproof casserole. Add the chicken, turning it in the hot oil to coat the skin completely. Season with salt and pepper and add all the garlic.

3 Cover the casserole with a sheet of foil, then the lid, to seal in the steam and the flavour. Cook for 1-1¼ hours until the chicken is cooked. Serve the chicken with the garlic, accompanied by steamed broad beans and spring onions.

Mediterranean Duck with Harissa and Saffron

Harissa is a fiery chilli sauce from North Africa. Mixed with cinnamon, saffron and preserved lemon, it gives this colourful casserole an unforgettable flavour.

SERVES 4

1 tbsp olive oil
1.75 kg/4-4½ lb duck, quartered
1 large onion, thinly sliced
1 garlic clove, crushed
½ tsp ground cumin
400 ml/14 fl oz/1⅔ cups duck or
  chicken stock
juice of ½ lemon
1-2 tsp harissa
1 cinnamon stick
1 tsp saffron strands
50 g/2 oz/⅓ cup black olives
50 g/2 oz/⅓ cup green olives
peel of 1 preserved lemon, rinsed,
  drained and cut into
  fine strips
2-3 lemon slices
2 tbsp chopped fresh coriander
salt and ground black pepper
coriander sprigs, to garnish

1 Heat the oil in a flameproof casserole. Add the duck quarters and cook until browned all over. Remove with a slotted spoon and set aside. Add the onion and garlic to the oil remaining in the casserole and cook for 5 minutes until soft. Add the cumin and cook, stirring, for 2 minutes.

2 Pour in the stock and lemon juice, then add the harissa, cinnamon and saffron. Bring to the boil. Return the duck to the casserole and add the olives, preserved lemon peel and lemon slices. Season with salt and pepper.

3 Lower the heat, partially cover the casserole and simmer gently for 45 minutes until the duck is cooked through. Discard the cinnamon stick. Stir in the chopped coriander and garnish with the coriander sprigs.

Tea-smoked Duck Breasts

Smoking spiced duck breasts over fragrant tea leaves gives them a slightly smoky flavour, which is not too overpowering.

SERVES 2-4

2 duck breasts

4 tbsp seven seas curry powder or Singapore-style curry powder

1 tbsp soy sauce

115 g/4 oz/½ cup long grain rice

115 g/4 oz/½ cup granulated sugar

2 tbsp Earl Grey tea leaves

stir-fried bok choy, to serve

VARIATION

Whole chicken and duck, chicken portions, quail, other game or fish steaks can be smoked in the same way. Fish does not need to be steamed first. A whole bird will take about 1 hour.

1 Pat the duck breasts dry with kitchen paper. Rub the curry powder all over the meat. Pour water into a wok to the depth of 5-7.5 cm/2-3 in.

2 Place the duck on a steaming rack over the water. Cover the wok and steam the duck breasts for 20-30 minutes, depending on the thickness of the meat. Remove the duck and sprinkle with soy sauce. Set aside.

3 Wash and dry the wok and line with two sheets of foil. Mix together the raw rice, sugar and tea. Spread the mixture in the bottom of the lined wok. Place the duck breasts on the steaming rack above the tea mixture. Put the lid on and seal the rim with damp kitchen paper.

4 Place the wok over a medium heat. As soon as you can smell that it has started smoking leave it, undisturbed, for 10-15 minutes. Remove from the heat, and leave, covered, for 15 minutes more. Discard the rice. Cut the duck breasts into thin slices and serve warm or cold with bok choy.

BEEF, LAMB AND PORK

Beef Teryaki

Mirin, which is used in this ginger and garlic marinade, is a sweetened sake, widely used in Japanese cooking. However, it is difficult to find outside Japanese grocers, so a medium-sweet sherry can be used instead.

SERVES 4

1 tbsp oil

4 tbsp soy sauce

2 tbsp mirin or medium sherry

1 tsp soft light brown sugar

1 tbsp ginger juice (see
  Cook's tip)

1 garlic clove, crushed

675-900 g/1½-2 lb rump steak,
  about 2.5 cm/1 in thick, in one
  piece if possible

sansho pepper

1 daikon radish (mooli), peeled,
  2 tbsp wasabi paste and fresh
  coriander sprigs, to garnish

1   Mix the oil, soy sauce, mirin or sherry, sugar, ginger juice and garlic in a large shallow dish. Add the steak and turn to coat both sides. Leave in a cool place to marinate for at least 4 hours, turning from time to time.

2   Preheat a grill, ridged cast iron grill pan or barbecue and grill the steak for 3-5 minutes on each side. Season with sansho pepper.

3   To prepare the Japanese-style garnish, grate the daikon radish and squeeze out as much liquid as possible. Place a little pile of grated daikon, a dessertspoonful of wasabi paste, and a coriander sprig on each of four plates.

4   With a sharp knife, slice the steak into thin diagonal slices and arrange on the plates with the garnish.

> COOK'S TIP
>
> *To make ginger juice, peel and grate a knob of root ginger and squeeze out the liquid.*

Black Bean Chilli con Carne

Two chillies add plenty of fire to this Tex-Mex classic.

SERVES 6

225 g/8 oz/1¼ cups dried black beans
500 g/1¼ lb braising steak
2 tbsp oil
2 onions, chopped
1 garlic clove, crushed
1 fresh green chilli, seeded and finely chopped
1 tbsp paprika
2 tsp ground cumin
2 tsp ground coriander
400 g/14 oz can chopped tomatoes
300 ml/½ pint/1¼ cups beef stock
1 dried red chilli, crumbled
1 tsp hot pepper sauce
1 fresh red pepper, seeded and chopped
2 tbsp fresh coriander leaves
salt
plain boiled rice, to serve

1   Put the beans in a saucepan. Add water to cover, bring to the boil and boil vigorously for 10-15 minutes. Drain, tip into a clean bowl, cover with cold water and leave to soak for about 8 hours or overnight.

2   Preheat the oven to 150°C/300°F/ gas 2. Cut the beef into very small dice. Heat the oil in a large flameproof casserole. Add the onion, garlic and green chilli and cook them gently for 5 minutes until soft. Using a slotted spoon transfer the mixture to a plate.

3   Increase the heat and brown the meat, then stir in the paprika, cumin and ground coriander.

4   Add the tomatoes, stock, dried chilli and hot pepper sauce. Drain the beans and add them to the casserole, with enough water to cover. Bring to simmering point, cover and cook in the oven for 2 hours. Stir the casserole occasionally and add extra water, if necessary, to prevent it from drying out.

5   Season with salt and add the red pepper. Return to the oven and cook for 30 minutes more, until the meat and beans are tender. Scatter over the coriander and serve with rice.

Wild Boar Chops with Romesco Sauce

Romesco is a fiery Spanish sauce that takes its name from the small dried red peppers used for making it in Catalonia. It is often served cold as a dip for vegetables, but it is equally delicious served hot with grilled meat and fish.

SERVES 4

4 wild boar loin chops, about 175 g/6 oz each

olive oil, for shallow frying

braised Savoy cabbage, to serve

ROMESCO SAUCE

3 dried red chillies

150 ml/¼ pint/⅔ cup olive oil

1 slice white bread, crusts removed

3 garlic cloves, chopped

3 tomatoes, peeled, seeded and roughly chopped

25 g/1 oz/¼ cup ground almonds

4 tbsp balsamic vinegar

4 tbsp red wine vinegar

salt and ground black pepper

VARIATION

Wild boar is increasingly available in good butchers and large supermarkets. However, if you can't find it, thick pork loin chops can be used instead and are equally delicious with this spicy sauce.

1 To make the romesco sauce, slit the chillies and remove the seeds, then leave the chillies to soak in warm water for about 30 minutes until soft. Drain the chillies, dry them on kitchen paper, then chop finely.

2 Heat 3 tbsp of the olive oil in a frying pan and fry the bread until golden on both sides. Lift out with a slotted spoon and drain on kitchen paper, then crumble into a blender or food processor.

3 Add the garlic to the oil remaining in the frying pan and cook gently for 2-3 minutes until softened, then leave to cool for a few minutes.

4 Add the chillies, tomatoes and ground almonds to the fried bread in the food processor. Tip in the garlic, with the oil in which it was cooked. Blend to a paste.

5 With the motor running, gradually add the remaining olive oil and then the balsamic and red wine vinegars. When the sauce is smooth, scrape it into a bowl and stir in salt and pepper to taste. Cover and chill for 2 hours.

6 Season the boar chops with pepper. Heat the olive oil in a heavy-based frying pan and fry the chops for about 15 minutes on each side, until golden brown and cooked through.

7 When the chops are almost cooked, place the romesco sauce in a saucepan and heat it gently. If it is too thick, stir in a little boiling water. Serve with the wild boar chops, accompanied by braised Savoy cabbage.

COOK'S TIP

Remember to wash your hands, the knife and the chopping board thoroughly after preparing the chillies.

Roast Lamb with Apricot, Cinnamon and Cumin Stuffing

Cinnamon and cumin make perfect partners for apricots in the bulgur wheat stuffing in this easy-to-carve joint.

SERVES 6-8

75 g/3 oz/½ cup bulgur wheat
2 tbsp olive oil
1 small onion, finely chopped
1 garlic clove, crushed
1 tsp ground cinnamon
1 tsp ground cumin
175 g/6 oz/¾ cup ready-to-eat
  dried apricots, chopped
50 g/2 oz/⅔ cup pine nuts
1 boned shoulder of lamb, about
  1.75 kg/4-4½ lb
120 ml/4 fl oz/½ cup red wine
120 ml/4 fl oz/½ cup lamb stock
salt and ground black pepper
mint sprigs, to garnish

1 Place the bulgur wheat in a bowl and add warm water to cover. Leave to soak for 1 hour, then drain thoroughly.

2 Heat the oil in a saucepan. Add the onion and crushed garlic and cook for 5 minutes until soft. Stir in the cinnamon, cumin, apricots and pine nuts, with salt and pepper to taste. Leave to cool. Preheat the oven to 180°C/350°F/gas 4.

3 Open out the shoulder of lamb and spread the stuffing over. Roll up firmly and tie tightly with string. Place in a roasting tin. Roast for 1 hour, then pour the red wine and stock into the roasting tin. Roast for 30 minutes more. Transfer the joint to a heated plate, cover with tented foil and allow the meat to rest for 15-20 minutes before carving.

4 Meanwhile, skim the surface fat from the wine-flavoured stock in the roasting tin. Place the tin over a high heat and allow the gravy to bubble for a few minutes, stirring occasionally to incorporate any sediment. Carve the lamb neatly, arrange the slices on a serving platter and pour over the gravy. Serve at once, garnished with mint.

Green Peppercorn and Cinnamon Crusted Lamb

Racks of lamb are perfect for serving at a dinner parties. This version has a spiced crumb coating.

SERVES 6

50 g/2 oz ciabatta bread
1 tbsp drained green
  peppercorns in brine,
  lightly crushed
1 tbsp ground cinnamon
1 garlic clove, crushed
½ tsp salt
25 g/1 oz/2 tbsp butter, melted
2 tsp Dijon mustard
2 racks of lamb, trimmed
4 tbsp red wine
400 ml/14 fl oz/1⅔ cups lamb stock
1 tbsp balsamic vinegar
fresh vegetables, to serve

VARIATION

The spicy crumbs also make a tasty coating for chicken pieces, fish or chops.

1 Preheat the oven to 220°C/425°F/ gas 7. Break the ciabatta into pieces, spread out on a baking sheet and bake for 10 minutes or until pale golden. Process in a blender or food processor to make crumbs.

2 Tip the crumbs into a bowl and add the green peppercorns, cinnamon, garlic and salt. Stir in the melted butter. Spread the mustard over the lamb. Press the crumb mixture on to the mustard to make a thin even crust. Put the racks in a roasting tin and roast for 30 minutes, covering the ends with foil if they start to over-brown.

3 Remove the lamb to a carving dish and keep hot under tented foil. Skim the fat off the juices in the roasting tin. Stir in the wine, stock and vinegar. Bring to the boil, stirring in any sediment, then lower the heat and simmer for about 10 minutes until reduced to a rich gravy. Carve the lamb and serve with the gravy and vegetables.

Lamb Tagine

Combining meat, dried fruit and spices is typical of Middle Eastern cooking. This type of casserole takes its name from the earthenware pot (tagine) in which it is traditionally cooked.

SERVES 4-6

115 g/4 oz/½ cup dried apricots
2 tbsp olive oil
1 large onion, chopped
1 kg/2¼ lb boneless shoulder of lamb, cubed
1 tsp ground cumin
1 tsp ground coriander
1 tsp ground cinnamon
grated rind and juice of ½ orange
1 tsp saffron strands
1 tbsp ground almonds
about 300 ml/½ pint/1¼ cups lamb or chicken stock
1 tbsp sesame seeds
salt and ground black pepper
fresh parsley, to garnish
couscous, to serve

COOK'S TIP

If you do not have time to soak the apricots use the ready-to-eat variety and add extra stock to replace the soaking liquid.

1 Cut the apricots in half and put in a bowl with 150 ml/¼ pint/²⁄₃ cup water. Leave to soak overnight.

2 Preheat the oven to 180°C/350°F/gas 4. Heat the olive oil in a flame-proof casserole. Add the onion and cook gently for 10 minutes until soft and golden.

3 Stir in the lamb. Add the cumin, coriander and cinnamon, with salt and pepper to taste. Stir to coat the lamb cubes in the spices. Cook, stirring, for 5 minutes.

4 Add the apricots and their soaking liquid. Stir in the orange rind and juice, saffron, ground almonds and enough stock to cover. Cover the casserole and cook in the oven for about 1-1½ hours, until the meat is tender, stirring occasionally and adding extra stock, if necessary.

5 Heat a heavy-based frying pan, add the sesame seeds and dry-fry, shaking the pan, until golden. Sprinkle the seame seeds over the meat, garnish with parsley and serve with couscous.

Turkish Kebabs with Tomato and Olive Salsa

The mix of aromatic spices, garlic and lemon give these kebabs a wonderful flavour – a fiery salsa makes the perfect accompaniment.

SERVES 4

2 garlic cloves, crushed
4 tbsp lemon juice
2 tbsp olive oil
1 dried red chilli, crushed
1 tsp ground cumin
1 tsp ground coriander
500 g/1¼ lb lean lamb,
  cut into 4 cm/1½ in cubes
8 bay leaves
salt and ground black pepper
TOMATO AND OLIVE SALSA
175 g/6 oz/1½ cups mixed pitted
  green and black olives,
  roughly chopped
1 small red onion, finely chopped
4 plum tomatoes, peeled and finely
  chopped
1 fresh red chilli, seeded and
  finely chopped
2 tbsp olive oil

1 Mix the garlic, lemon juice, olive oil, chilli, cumin and coriander in a large shallow dish. Add the lamb cubes, with salt and pepper to taste. Mix well. Cover and marinate in a cool place for 2 hours.

2 Make the salsa. Put the olives, onion, tomatoes, chilli and olive oil in a bowl. Stir in salt and pepper to taste. Mix well, cover and set aside.

3 Remove the lamb from the marinade and divide the cubes among four skewers, adding the bay leaves at intervals. Grill over a barbecue, on a ridged iron grill pan or under a hot grill, turning occasionally, for 10 minutes, until the lamb is browned and crisp on the outside and pink and juicy inside. Serve with the salsa.

Veal Escalopes with Ruby Grapefruit and Ginger

The ginger and pink peppercorns give the grapefruit sauce a subtle spiciness without being overpowering.

SERVES 4

4 veal escalopes
25 g/1 oz/2 tbsp butter
1 tbsp olive oil
juice of 1 large ruby grapefruit
150 ml/¼ pint/⅔ cup chicken stock
2 tsp grated fresh root ginger
1 tsp pink peppercorns, drained and lightly crushed
15 g/½ oz/1 tbsp cold butter
salt
GARNISH
1 ruby grapefruit
oil, for shallow frying

1 Start by making the garnish. Wash and dry the grapefruit, then pare off thin strips of rind, using a citrus zester. Scrape off any pith that remains attached to the strips. Cut the grapefruit in half. Squeeze the juice from half the grapefruit into a small bowl, add the strips of pared rind and leave to macerate for 1 hour. Cut the other half grapefruit into wedges and reserve.

2 Drain the strips of rind and pat them dry with kitchen paper. Heat oil to a depth of 1 cm/½ in in a small saucepan and add the strips. As soon as they are brown strain the strips through a sieve into a bowl. Discard the oil in the bowl.

3 Place the veal escalopes between two sheets of greaseproof paper and beat them with a rolling pin until they are about 3 mm/⅛ in thick. If the escalopes are very large, cut them into neat pieces.

4 Melt the butter and the oil in a heavy-based frying pan. Fry the veal, in batches if necessary, for 1 minute on each side. Remove the escalopes to a heated dish and keep hot.

5 Add the grapefruit juice, stock and grated ginger to the pan. Allow to boil until reduced by half. Strain the sauce into a saucepan, add the peppercorns and heat through. Whisk in the butter and season with salt. Pour the sauce over the veal, then garnish with fried grapefruit rind and reserved wedges.

Tsire Koftas with Avocado and Melon Salsa

Tsire powder makes a lovely crunchy coating for the meat on these kebabs.

SERVES 4-6

675 g/1½ lb lean minced lamb
2 tbsp Greek-style yogurt
1 small onion, finely chopped
1 garlic clove, crushed
¼ tsp chilli powder
1 egg, beaten
double quantity tsire powder
salt and ground black pepper
mint leaves, to garnish

VARIATION

Use minced beef in place of lamb.

SALSA
1 ripe avocado
juice of 1 lime
225 g/8 oz melon, peeled, seeded and cut into small dice
4 spring onions, very finely chopped
1 fresh red chilli, seeded and finely chopped

1   Make the salsa. Cut the avocado in half, remove the stone and peel off the skin. Dice the flesh finely and toss it with the lime juice in a bowl. Add the melon, spring onions and chilli, with salt and pepper to taste. Cover closely and leave to stand for 30 minutes.

2   Put the minced lamb in a food processor with the yogurt, onion, garlic and chilli powder. Add a little salt and pepper and process until smooth.

3   Divide the lamb mixture into 12 portions and shape each one into a sausage shape. Push a pre-soaked bamboo skewer into each kofta and press the meat on to the stick.

4   Dip each kofta in egg, then roll it in the tsire powder. Cook over a barbecue or under a hot grill for 10 minutes, turning occasionally until cooked. Serve with the avocado and melon salsa, garnished with mint leaves.

Paprika Pork with Fennel and Caraway

Fennel always tastes very good with pork, and combined with caraway seeds adds an aromatic flavour to this Middle European dish.

SERVES 4

1 tbsp olive oil
4 boneless pork steaks
1 large onion, thinly sliced
400 g/14 oz can chopped tomatoes
1 tsp fennel seeds, lightly crushed
½ tsp caraway seeds, lightly
  crushed
1 tbsp paprika
2 tbsp soured cream
salt and ground black pepper
paprika, to garnish
buttered noodles and poppy seeds,
  to serve

COOK'S TIP

Always buy good quality paprika and replace it regularly as it loses its distinctive flavour very quickly.

1 Heat the oil in a large frying pan. Add the pork steaks and brown on both sides. Lift out the steaks and put them on a plate.

2 Add the onion to the oil remaining in the pan. Cook for 10 minutes, until soft and golden. Stir in the tomatoes, fennel, caraway seeds and paprika.

3 Return the pork to the pan and simmer gently for 20-30 minutes until tender. Season with salt and pepper. Lightly swirl in the soured cream and sprinkle with a little paprika. Serve with noodles, tossed in butter and sprinkled with poppy seeds.

Baked Maple Ribs

The only way to eat these spicy ribs is with your fingers. So provide plenty of paper napkins!

SERVES 6

2 tbsp oil

1 onion, cut into thin wedges

1 garlic clove, crushed

100 ml/3½ fl oz/scant ½ cup maple syrup

1 tbsp soy sauce

1 tbsp tomato ketchup

1 tbsp Worcestershire sauce

1 tsp ground ginger

1 tsp paprika

1 tsp mustard powder

1 tbsp red wine vinegar

1 tsp Tabasco sauce

1 kg/2¼ lb pork spare ribs

1 Preheat the oven to 200°C/400°F/ gas 6. Heat the oil in a saucepan, add the onion and garlic and cook for about 5 minutes until soft.

2 Add the maple syrup, soy sauce, tomato ketchup, Worcestershire sauce, ginger, paprika, mustard powder, wine vinegar and Tabasco sauce. Bring to the boil, lower the heat and simmer for 2 minutes.

3 Place the ribs in a roasting tin, pour over the sauce and turn the ribs to coat them completely. Cover the tin with foil and bake the ribs for 45 minutes. Remove the foil and bake for 15 minutes more, basting occasionally. The ribs should be sticky and tender.

COOK'S TIP

Make sure you use real maple syrup and not maple-flavoured syrup for this recipe.

Jerk Pork

This is a Jamaican way of spicing meat or poultry before roasting in the oven or over a fire.

SERVES 4

1 tbsp oil

2 onions, finely chopped

2 fresh red chillies, seeded and finely chopped

1 garlic clove, crushed

2.5 cm/1 in piece of fresh root ginger, grated

1 tsp dried thyme

1 tsp ground allspice

1 tsp hot pepper sauce

2 tbsp rum

grated rind and juice of 1 lime

salt and ground black pepper

4 pork chops

fresh thyme, small red chillies and lime wedges, to garnish

1 Heat the oil in a frying pan. Add the onions and cook for 10 minutes until soft. Add the chillies, garlic, ginger, thyme and allspice and fry for 2 more minutes. Stir in the hot pepper sauce, rum, lime rind and juice.

VARIATION

Chicken joints or a whole chicken can also be coated with this delicious spicy paste before roasting.

2 Simmer until the mixture forms a dark paste. Season with salt and pepper and leave to cool. Rub the paste over the chops. Put them in a shallow dish, cover and chill overnight.

3 Preheat the oven to 190°C/375°F/ gas 5. Place the chops on a rack in a roasting tin and roast for 30 minutes until fully cooked. Serve at once, garnished with fresh thyme, chillies and lime wedges.

VEGETABLES AND SALADS

Vegetable Korma

The blending of spices is an ancient art in India. Here the aim is to produce a subtle, aromatic curry rather than an assault on the senses.

SERVES 4

50 g/2 oz/¼ cup butter

2 onions, sliced

2 garlic cloves, crushed

2.5 cm/1 in piece fresh root ginger, grated

1 tsp ground cumin

1 tbsp ground coriander

6 cardamoms

5 cm/2 in cinnamon stick

1 tsp ground turmeric

1 fresh red chilli, seeded and finely chopped

1 potato, peeled and cut into 2.5 cm/1 in cubes

1 small aubergine

115 g/4 oz/1½ cups mushrooms, thickly sliced

115 g/4 oz/1 cup French beans, cut into 2.5 cm/1 in lengths

4 tbsp natural yogurt

150 ml/¼ pint/⅔ cup double cream

1 tsp garam masala

salt and ground black pepper

fresh coriander sprigs, to garnish

poppadums, to serve

1 Melt the butter in a heavy-based saucepan. Add the onions and cook for 5 minutes until soft. Add the garlic and ginger and cook for 2 minutes, then stir in the cumin, coriander, cardamoms, cinnamon stick, turmeric and chilli. Cook, stirring for 30 seconds.

2 Add the potato, aubergine and mushrooms and about 175 ml/6 fl oz/ ¾ cup water. Cover the pan, bring to the boil, then lower the heat and simmer for 15 minutes. Add the beans and cook, uncovered, for 5 minutes.

VARIATION

Any combination of vegetables can be used for this korma, including carrots, cauliflower, broccoli, peas and chick-peas.

3 With a slotted spoon, remove the vegetables to a warmed serving dish and keep hot. Allow the cooking liquid to bubble up until it reduces a little. Season with salt and pepper, then stir in the yogurt, cream and garam masala. Pour the sauce over the vegetables and garnish with coriander. Serve with poppadums.

Dhal with Tadka

Boost your pulse rate with this delectable dish of red lentils with a spicy topping.

SERVES 4

50 g/2 oz/¼ cup butter

2 tsp black mustard seeds

1 onion, finely chopped

2 garlic cloves, finely chopped

1 tsp ground turmeric

1 tsp ground cumin

2 fresh green chillies, seeded and finely chopped

225 g/8 oz/1 cup red lentils

300 ml/½ pint/1¼ cups canned coconut milk

1 quantity tadka or coriander baghar

fresh coriander, to garnish

1 Melt the butter in a large heavy-based saucepan. Add the mustard seeds. When they start to pop, add the onion and garlic and cook for 5-10 minutes until soft.

2 Stir in the turmeric, cumin and chillies and cook for 2 minutes. Stir in the lentils, 1 litre/1¾ pints/4 cups water and coconut milk. Bring to the boil, then cover and simmer for 40 minutes, adding water if needed. The lentils should be soft and should have absorbed most of the liquid.

3 Prepare the tadka or baghar and pour immediately over the lentil (dhal) mixture. Garnish with coriander leaves and serve at once, with naan bread to mop up the sauce.

VARIATION

This dish is excellent made with moong dhal, the yellow split mung bean that is widely used in Indian cookery.

Glazed Sweet Potatoes with Ginger and Allspice

Fried sweet potatoes acquire a candied coating when cooked with ginger, syrup and allspice. Cayenne cuts through the sweetness.

SERVES 4

900 g/2 lb sweet potatoes

50 g/2oz /¼ cup butter

3 tbsp oil

2 garlic cloves, crushed

2 pieces of stem ginger, finely chopped

2 tsp ground allspice

1 tbsp syrup from ginger jar

salt and cayenne pepper

2 tsp chopped fresh thyme, plus a few sprigs to garnish

1 Peel the sweet potatoes and cut into 1 cm/½ in cubes. Melt the butter with the oil in a large frying pan. Add the sweet potato cubes and fry, stirring frequently, for about 10 minutes until they are just soft.

COOK'S TIP

Some sweet potatoes have white flesh and some have yellow. Although they taste similar, the yellow-fleshed variety look particularly colourful and attractive.

2 Stir in the garlic, ginger and all-spice. Cook, stirring, for 5 minutes more. Stir in the ginger syrup, salt, a generous pinch of cayenne pepper and the fresh thyme. Stir for 1-2 minutes more, then serve scattered with thyme sprigs.

Roasted Root Vegetables with Whole Spice Seeds

Roast these vegetables alongside a joint or whole chicken and they virtually look after themselves.

SERVES 4

3 parsnips, peeled

3 potatoes, peeled

3 carrots, peeled

3 sweet potatoes, peeled

4 tbsp olive oil

8 shallots, peeled

2 garlic cloves, sliced

2 tsp white mustard seeds

2 tsp coriander seeds, lightly crushed

1 tsp cumin seeds

2 bay leaves

salt and ground black pepper

1 Preheat the oven to 190°C/375°F/ gas 5. Bring a saucepan of lightly salted water to the boil. Cut the parsnips, potatoes, carrots and sweet potatoes into chunks. Add them to the pan and bring the water back to the boil. Boil for 2 minutes, then drain the vegetables thoroughly.

2 Pour the olive oil into a large heavy roasting tin and place over a moderate heat. Add the vegetables, shallots and garlic. Fry, tossing the vegetables over the heat until they are pale golden at the edges.

3 Add the mustard seeds, coriander seeds, cumin seeds and bay leaves. Cook for 1 minute, then season with salt and pepper. Transfer the roasting tin to the oven and roast for 45 minutes, turning occasionally, until the vegetables are crisp and golden and cooked through.

VARIATION

Vary the selection of vegetables according to what is available. Try using swede or pumpkin instead of, or as well as, the vegetables suggested.

Mexican Tortilla Parcels

Seeded green chillies add just a flicker of fire to the spicy filling in these parcels – perfect as a starter or snack.

SERVES 4

675 g/1½ lb tomatoes
4 tbsp sunflower oil
1 large onion, finely sliced
1 garlic clove, crushed
2 tsp cumin seeds
2 fresh green chillies, seeded
  and chopped
2 tbsp tomato purée
1 vegetable stock cube
200 g/7 oz can sweetcorn, drained
1 tbsp chopped fresh coriander
115 g/4 oz/1 cup grated
  Cheddar cheese
8 wheatflour tortillas
coriander leaves, shredded lettuce
  and soured cream, to serve

1 Peel the tomatoes: place them in a heatproof bowl, add boiling water to cover and leave for 1 minute. Lift out with a slotted spoon and plunge into a bowl of cold water. Leave for 1 minute, then drain. Slip the skins off the tomatoes and chop the flesh.

2 Heat half the oil in a frying pan and fry the onion with the garlic and cumin seeds for 5 minutes, until the onion softens. Add the chillies and tomatoes, then stir in the tomato purée. Crumble the stock cube over, stir well and cook gently for 5 minutes, until the chilli is soft but the tomato has not completely broken down. Stir in the sweetcorn and fresh coriander and heat gently to warm through. Keep warm.

3 Sprinkle grated cheese in the middle of each tortilla. Spoon some tomato mixture over the cheese. Fold over one edge of the tortilla then the sides and finally the remaining edge, to enclose the filling completely.

4 Heat the remaining oil in a separate frying pan and fry the filled tortillas for 1-2 minutes on each side until golden and crisp. Serve with coriander, shredded lettuce and soured cream.

COOK'S TIP

Mexican wheatflour tortillas are available in most supermarkets. They are very useful to keep in the cupboard as a wrapping for a variety of meat, chicken and vegetable mixtures.

Vegetable Couscous with Saffron and Harissa

A North African favourite, this spicy dish makes an excellent meal for vegetarians.

SERVES 4

3 tbsp olive oil
1 onion, chopped
2 garlic cloves, crushed
1 tsp ground cumin
1 tsp paprika
400 g/14 oz can chopped tomatoes
300 ml/½ pint/1¼ cups
  vegetable stock
1 cinnamon stick
generous pinch of
  saffron strands
4 baby aubergines, quartered
8 baby courgettes, trimmed
8 baby carrots
225 g/8 oz/1⅓ cups couscous
425 g/15 oz can chick-peas,
  drained
175 g/6 oz/¾ cup prunes
3 tbsp chopped fresh parsley
3 tbsp chopped fresh coriander
2-3 tsp harissa
salt

1 Heat the olive oil in a large saucepan. Add the onions and garlic and cook gently for 5 minutes until soft. Add the cumin and paprika and cook, stirring, for 1 minute.

2 Add the tomatoes, stock, cinnamon stick, saffron, aubergines, courgettes and carrots. Season with salt. Bring to the boil, cover, lower the heat and cook for 20 minutes until the vegetables are just tender.

3 Line a steamer, metal sieve or colander with a double thickness of muslin. Soak the couscous according to the instructions on the packet. Add the chick-peas and prunes to the vegetables and cook for 5 minutes. Fork the couscous to break up any lumps and spread it in the prepared steamer. Place on top of the vegetables, cover, and cook for 5 minutes until the couscous is hot.

4 Stir the parsley and coriander into the vegetables. Heap the couscous on to a warmed serving plate. Using a slotted spoon, arrange the vegetables on top. Spoon over a little sauce and toss gently to combine. Stir the harissa into the remaining sauce and serve separately.

Orange and Red Onion Salad with Cumin

Cumin and mint give this refreshing salad a Middle Eastern flavour. Choose small seedless oranges if you can.

SERVES 6

6 oranges

2 red onions

1 tbsp cumin seeds

1 tsp coarsely ground black pepper

1 tbsp chopped fresh mint

6 tbsp olive oil

salt

TO SERVE

fresh mint sprigs

black olives

1 Slice the oranges thinly, working over a bowl to catch any juice. Then, holding each orange slice in turn over the bowl, cut round with scissors to remove the peel and pith. Slice the onions thinly and separate the rings.

COOK'S TIP

It is important to let the salad stand for 2 hours, so that the flavours develop and the onion softens slightly. However, do not leave the salad for much longer than this before serving.

2 Arrange the orange and onion slices in layers in a shallow dish, sprinkling each layer with cumin seeds, black pepper, mint, olive oil and salt to taste. Pour over the orange juice left over from slicing the oranges.

3 Leave the salad to marinate in a cool place for about 2 hours. Just before serving, scatter the salad with the mint sprigs and black olives.

Spanish Salad with Capers and Olives

Make this refreshing salad in the summer when tomatoes are sweet and full of flavour.

SERVES 4

4 tomatoes

½ cucumber

1 bunch spring onions

1 bunch purslane or watercress, washed

8 pimiento-stuffed olives

2 tbsp drained capers

DRESSING

2 tbsp red wine vinegar

1 tsp paprika

½ tsp ground cumin

1 garlic clove, crushed

5 tbsp olive oil

salt and ground black pepper

1 Peel the tomatoes by placing them in a heatproof bowl. Then add boiling water to cover and leave for 1 minute. Lift out the tomatoes using a slotted spoon and plunge them into a bowl of cold water. Leave for 1 minute, then drain. Slip the skins off the tomatoes and dice the flesh finely. Place in a salad bowl.

2 Peel the cucumber, dice it finely and add it to the tomatoes. Trim and chop half the spring onions, add them to the salad bowl and mix lightly.

3 Break the purslane or watercress into small sprigs. Add to the tomato mixture, with the olives and capers. Make the dressing. Mix the wine vinegar, paprika, cumin and garlic in a bowl. Whisk in the oil and add salt and pepper to taste. Pour over the salad and toss lightly. Serve with the remaining spring onions.

COOK'S TIP

Serve this salad as soon as possible after adding the dressing.

Gado Gado

The peanut sauce on this traditional Indonesian salad owes its flavour to galangal, an aromatic rhizome that resembles ginger.

SERVES 4

250 g/9 oz white cabbage, shredded

4 carrots, cut into matchsticks

4 celery sticks, cut into matchsticks

250 g/9 oz/4 cups beansprouts

½ cucumber, cut into matchsticks

fried onion, salted peanuts and sliced chilli, to garnish

PEANUT SAUCE

1 tbsp oil

1 small onion, finely chopped

1 garlic clove, crushed

1 small piece galangal, peeled and grated

1 tsp ground cumin

¼ tsp chilli powder

1 tsp tamarind paste or lime juice

4 tbsp crunchy peanut butter

1 tsp soft light brown sugar

1 Steam the cabbage, carrots and celery for 3-4 minutes until just tender. Leave to cool. Spread out the beansprouts on a large serving dish. Arrange the cabbage, carrots, celery and cucumber on top.

2 Make the sauce. Heat the oil in a saucepan, add the onion and garlic and cook gently for 5 minutes until soft. Stir in the galangal, cumin and chilli powder and cook for 1 minute more. Add the tamarind paste or lime juice, peanut butter and sugar. Mix well.

COOK'S TIPS

As long as the sauce remains the same, the vegetables can be altered at the whim of the cook and to reflect the contents of the vegetable rack or chiller. Pour the sauce over the salad and toss lightly or serve it in a separate bowl.

3 Heat gently, stirring occasionally and adding a little hot water, if necessary, to make a coating sauce. Spoon a little of the sauce over the vegetables and garnish with fried onions, peanuts and sliced chilli. Serve the rest of the sauce separately.

Sesame Duck and Noodle Salad

This salad is complete in itself and makes a lovely summer lunch. The marinade is a marvellous blend of spices.

SERVES 4

2 duck breasts

1 tbsp oil

150 g/5 oz sugarsnap peas

2 carrots, cut into 7.5 cm/3 in sticks

225 g/8 oz medium egg noodles

6 spring onions, sliced

salt

2 tbsp coriander leaves, to garnish

MARINADE

1 tbsp sesame oil

1 tsp ground coriander

1 tsp five spice powder

DRESSING

1 tbsp garlic vinegar

1 tsp soft light brown sugar

1 tsp soy sauce

1 tbsp toasted sesame seeds
  (see Cook's tip)

3 tbsp sunflower oil

2 tbsp sesame oil

ground black pepper

1   Slice the duck breasts thinly across and place them in a shallow dish. Mix all the ingredients for the marinade, pour over the duck and mix well to coat thoroughly. Cover and leave in a cool place for 30 minutes.

2   Heat the oil in a frying pan, add the slices of duck breast and stir-fry for 3-4 minutes until cooked. Set aside.

3   Bring a saucepan of lightly salted water to the boil. Place the sugarsnap peas and carrots in a steamer that will fit on top of the pan. When the water boils, add the noodles. Place the steamer on top and steam the vegetables, while cooking the noodles for the time suggested on the packet. Set the steamed vegetables aside. Drain the noodles, refresh them under cold running water and drain again. Place them in a large serving bowl.

4   Make the dressing. Mix the vinegar, sugar, soy sauce and sesame seeds in a bowl. Add a generous grinding of black pepper, then whisk in the oils.

5   Pour the dressing over the noodles and mix well. Add the sugarsnap peas, carrots, spring onions and duck slices and toss to mix. Scatter the coriander leaves over and serve.

> COOK'S TIP
>
> *To toast the sesame seeds, place them in a dry heavy-based frying pan and heat gently, stirring frequently until they are lightly browned.*

PIZZA, PASTA AND GRAINS

Chilli, Tomato and Olive Pasta

The sauce for this pasta packs a punch, thanks to the robust flavours of red chillies, anchovies and capers.

SERVES 4

3 tbsp olive oil
2 garlic cloves, crushed
2 fresh red chillies, seeded and chopped
6 drained canned anchovy fillets
675 g/1½ lb ripe tomatoes, peeled, seeded and chopped
2 tbsp sun-dried tomato purée
2 tbsp drained capers
115 g/4 oz/1 cup pitted black olives, roughly chopped
350 g/12 oz/3 cups penne
salt and ground black pepper
chopped fresh basil, to garnish

1 Heat the oil in a saucepan and gently fry the garlic and chilli for 2-3 minutes. Add the anchovies, mashing them with a fork, then stir in the tomatoes, sun-dried tomato purée, capers and olives. Add salt and pepper to taste. Simmer gently, uncovered, for 20 minutes, stirring occasionally.

2 Meanwhile, bring a large pan of lightly salted water to the boil and cook the penne according to the instructions on the packet, or until *al dente*. Drain and immediately stir into the sauce. Mix thoroughly, tip into a heated serving dish, garnish with basil and serve at once.

> COOK'S TIP
>
> *If ripe well-flavoured tomatoes are not available, use two 400 g/14 oz cans chopped tomatoes.*

Spaghettini with Garlic and Olive Oil

It is essential to use a good quality virgin olive oil and a brightly coloured fresh red chilli for this simply delicious pasta sauce.

SERVES 4

350 g/12 oz spaghettini
5 tbsp virgin olive oil
3 garlic cloves, finely chopped
1 fresh red chilli, seeded and chopped
75 g/3 oz/1½ cups drained sun-dried tomatoes in oil, chopped
2 tbsp chopped fresh parsley
salt and ground black pepper
freshly grated Parmesan cheese, to serve

1 Bring a large saucepan of lightly salted water to the boil. Add the pasta and cook according to the instructions on the packet, or until *al dente*. Towards the end of the cooking time, heat the oil in a second large pan. Add the garlic and chilli and cook gently for 2-3 minutes. Stir in the sun-dried tomatoes and remove from the heat.

> COOK'S TIP
>
> *Save the oil from the jar of sun-dried tomatoes for adding to salad dressings.*

2 Drain the pasta thoroughly and add to the hot oil. Return to the heat and cook for 2-3 minutes, tossing the pasta to coat the strands in the sauce. Season with salt and pepper, stir in the parsley and transfer to a warmed serving bowl. Scatter with grated Parmesan cheese and serve.

Pastitsio

Macaroni in a cheese sauce is layered with cinnamon and cumin-spiced minced beef to make a Greek version of lasagne.

SERVES 4-6

225 g/8 oz/2 cups macaroni
2 tbsp olive oil
1 large onion, finely chopped
2 garlic cloves, crushed
450 g/1 lb minced steak
300 ml/½ pint/1¼ cups beef stock
2 tsp tomato purée
1 tsp ground cinnamon
1 tsp ground cumin
1 tbsp chopped fresh mint
50 g/2 oz/¼ cup butter
40 g/1½ oz/⅓ cup plain flour
120 ml/4 fl oz/½ cup milk
120 ml/4 fl oz/½ cup natural yogurt
175 g/6 oz/1½ cups grated
 Kefalotiri cheese
salt and ground black pepper

1 Bring a saucepan of lightly salted water to the boil. Add the macaroni and cook for 8 minutes, or according to the instructions on the packet, until *al dente*. Drain, rinse under cold water and drain again. Set aside. Preheat the oven to 190°C/375°F/gas 5.

2 Heat the oil in a frying pan, add the onion and garlic and cook for about 8-10 minutes until soft. Add the minced steak and stir until browned. Stir in the stock, tomato purée, cinnamon, cumin and mint, with salt and pepper to taste. Cook gently for 10-15 minutes until the sauce is thick and flavoursome.

3 Melt the butter in a saucepan. Stir in the flour and cook for 1 minute. Remove the pan from the heat and gradually stir in the milk and yogurt. Return the pan to the heat and cook gently for 5 minutes. Stir in half the cheese and season with salt and pepper. Stir the macaroni into the cheese sauce.

> COOK'S TIP
>
> *If Kefalotiri cheese is unavailable, use a well flavoured Cheddar cheese or similar.*

4 Spread half the macaroni mixture over the base of a large gratin dish. Cover with the meat sauce and top with the remaining macaroni. Sprinkle the remaining cheese over the top and bake for 45 minutes or until golden brown on top.

Hot Pepperoni Pizza

There is nothing more mouth-watering than a freshly baked pizza, especially when the topping includes pepperoni and red chillies.

SERVES 4

225 g/8 oz/2 cups strong white bread flour

2 tsp easy-blend dried yeast

1 tsp sugar

½ tsp salt

1 tbsp olive oil

175 ml/6 fl oz/¾ cup mixed hand-hot milk and water

TOPPING

400 g/14 oz can chopped tomatoes, well drained

2 garlic cloves, crushed

1 tsp dried oregano

225 g/8 oz mozzarella cheese, coarsely grated

2 dried red chillies, crumbled

225 g/8 oz pepperoni, sliced

2 tbsp drained capers

fresh oregano, to garnish

1 Sift the flour into a bowl. Stir in the yeast, sugar and salt. Make a well in the centre. Stir the olive oil into the milk and water, then stir the mixture into the flour. Mix to a soft dough.

2 Knead the dough on a lightly floured surface for 5-10 minutes until it is smooth and elastic. Return it to the clean, lightly oiled, bowl and cover with clear film. Leave in a warm place for about 30 minutes or until the dough has doubled in bulk.

3 Preheat the oven to 220°C/425°F/gas 7. Turn the dough out on to a lightly floured surface and knead lightly for 1 minute. Divide it in half and roll each piece out to a 25 cm/10 in circle. Place on lightly oiled pizza trays or baking sheets. To make the topping, mix the drained tomatoes, garlic and oregano in a bowl.

COOK'S TIP

If time is short, use ready-made pizza bases or scone bases.

4 Spread half the mixture over each round, leaving a margin around the edge. Set half the mozzarella aside. Divide the rest between the pizzas. Bake for 7-10 minutes until the dough rim on each pizza is pale golden.

5 Sprinkle the crumbled chillies over the pizzas, then arrange the pepperoni slices and capers on top. Sprinkle with the remaining mozzarella, then return the pizzas to the oven and bake for 7-10 minutes more. Scatter over the oregano and serve at once.

Singapore Noodles

Dried mushrooms add an intense flavour to this lightly curried dish. Use Oriental mushrooms if possible.

SERVES 4

20 g/¾ oz/⅓ cup dried Chinese mushrooms
225 g/8 oz fine egg noodles
2 tsp sesame oil
3 tbsp groundnut oil
2 garlic cloves, crushed
1 small onion, chopped
1 fresh green chilli, seeded and thinly sliced
2 tsp curry powder
115 g/4 oz green beans, topped, tailed and halved
115 g/4 oz/1 cup Chinese leaves, thinly shredded
4 spring onions, sliced
2 tbsp soy sauce
115 g/4 oz cooked prawns, peeled and deveined
salt

1 Place the mushrooms in a bowl. Cover with warm water and soak for 30 minutes. Drain, reserving 2 tbsp of the soaking water, then slice.

2 Bring a saucepan of lightly salted water to the boil and cook the noodles according to the directions on the packet. Drain, tip into a bowl and toss with the sesame oil.

VARIATION

Ring the changes with the vegetables used in this dish. Try mangetouts, broccoli, peppers or baby sweetcorn. The prawns can be omitted or substituted with ham or chicken.

3 Heat a wok and add the groundnut oil. When it is hot, stir-fry the garlic, onion and chilli for 3 minutes. Stir in the curry powder and cook for 1 minute. Add the mushrooms, green beans, Chinese leaves and spring onions. Stir-fry for 3-4 minutes until the vegetables are crisp-tender.

4 Add the noodles, soy sauce, reserved mushroom soaking water and prawns. Toss over the heat for 2-3 minutes until the noodles and prawns are heated through.

Jambalaya

This popular Cajun dish has something in common with paella, but is distinguished by the addition of fiery spices.

SERVES 4

2 tbsp oil

225 g/8 oz boneless skinless chicken, cubed

225 g/8 oz chorizo sausage, cut into chunks

3 celery sticks, chopped

1 red pepper, seeded and chopped

1 green pepper, seeded and chopped

1 quantity Cajun spice mix, including onion and garlic

250 g/9 oz/generous 1 cup long grain rice

200 g/7 oz can chopped tomatoes

600 ml/1 pint/2½ cups chicken stock

celery leaves, to garnish

1 Heat the oil in a large heavy-based frying pan. Fry the chicken and chorizo sausage until lightly browned. Remove from the pan with a slotted spoon and set aside. Add the celery and red and green pepper and fry for 2-3 minutes. Return the chicken and sausage to the pan.

VARIATION

Raw tiger prawns can be added with the rice. Alternatively, duck and ham may be used instead of chicken and sausage.

2 Stir in the Cajun spice mix and cook, stirring, for 2-3 minutes more. Stir in the rice and add the tomatoes and stock. Bring to the boil and stir.

3 Turn the heat to low, cover the pan and simmer gently for 15-20 minutes until the rice is tender and the liquid has been absorbed. Garnish and serve.

COOK'S TIP

This dish is very hot. If a milder result is preferred, use less chilli powder in the Cajun spice mix.

Thai Fried Rice

This recipe uses jasmine rice which is sometimes known as Thai fragrant rice.

SERVES 4

50 g/2 oz/½ cup coconut
  milk powder
375 g/12 oz/1⅓ cups jasmine rice
2 tbsp groundnut oil
2 garlic cloves, chopped
1 small onion, finely chopped
2.5 cm/1 in piece fresh root
  ginger, grated
225 g/8 oz boneless, skinless
  chicken breasts, cut into
  1 cm/½ in dice
1 red pepper, seeded and diced
115 g/4 oz drained canned
  sweetcorn kernels
1 tsp chilli oil
1 tbsp hot curry powder
salt
2 eggs, beaten
spring onion shreds, to garnish

1 In a saucepan, whisk the coconut milk powder into 475 ml/16 fl oz/ 2 cups water. Add the rice, bring to the boil and stir once. Lower the heat to a gentle simmer, cover and cook for 10 minutes or until the rice is tender and the liquid has been absorbed. Spread the rice on a baking sheet and leave until completely cold.

2 Heat the oil in a wok, add the garlic, onion and ginger and stir-fry for 2 minutes. Push the vegetables to the sides of the wok, add the chicken to the centre and stir-fry for 2 minutes. Add the rice and stir-fry over a high heat for 3 minutes more.

3 Stir in the pepper, sweetcorn, chilli oil, curry powder and season with salt. Toss over the heat for 1 minute. Stir in the beaten egg and cook for 1 minute more. Garnish with chopped spring onion and serve.

COOK'S TIPS

It is important that the rice is completely cold before it is fried and the oil should be very hot, or the rice will absorb too much oil. Add some sliced baby corn cobs along with the rice, if you like.

Pilau Rice with Whole Spices

This fragrant rice dish makes a perfect accompaniment to any Indian meal.

SERVES 4-6

generous pinch of
  saffron strands
600 ml/1 pint/2½ cups hot
  chicken stock
50 g/2 oz/¼ cup butter
1 onion, chopped
1 garlic clove, crushed
½ cinnamon stick
6 cardamoms
1 bay leaf
250 g/9 oz/generous 1 cup basmati
  rice, rinsed and drained
50 g/2 oz/⅓ cup sultanas
1 tbsp oil
50 g/2 oz/½ cup cashew nuts

1 Add the saffron strands to the hot stock and set aside. Heat the butter in a large saucepan and fry the onion and garlic for 5 minutes. Stir in the cinnamon stick, cardamoms and bay leaf and cook for 2 minutes.

COOK'S TIP

To rinse the rice, stir it round in several changes of water until the water is clear. Drain thoroughly before cooking.

2 Add the rice and cook, stirring, for 2 minutes more. Pour in the stock and add the sultanas. Bring to the boil, stir, then lower the heat, cover and cook gently for 15 minutes or until the rice is tender and the liquid has all been absorbed.

3 Meanwhile, heat the oil in a frying pan and fry the cashew nuts until browned. Drain on kitchen paper. Scatter over the rice and serve.

Couscous Salad

This is a spicy variation on a classic tabbouleh, which is traditionally made with bulgur wheat, not couscous.

SERVES 4

3 tbsp olive oil
5 spring onions, chopped
1 garlic clove, crushed
1 tsp ground cumin
350 ml/12 fl oz/1½ cups
  vegetable stock
175 g/6 oz/1 cup couscous
2 tomatoes, peeled and chopped
4 tbsp chopped fresh parsley
4 tbsp chopped fresh mint
1 fresh green chilli, seeded and
  finely chopped
2 tbsp lemon juice
salt and ground black pepper
toasted pine nuts and grated lemon
  rind, to garnish
crisp lettuce leaves, to serve

1 Heat the olive oil in a saucepan. Add the spring onions and garlic. Stir in the cumin and cook for 1 minute. Add the stock and bring to the boil.

2 Remove the pan from the heat, stir in the couscous, cover the pan and leave it to stand for 10 minutes, until the couscous has swelled and all the liquid has been absorbed. If using instant couscous, follow the instructions on the packet.

3 Tip the couscous into a bowl. Stir in the tomatoes, parsley, mint, chilli and lemon juice, with salt and pepper to taste. If possible, leave to stand for up to an hour to allow the flavours to develop fully.

4 To serve, line a bowl with lettuce leaves and spoon the couscous salad into the centre. Scatter the toasted pine nuts and grated lemon rind over, to garnish.

Bulgur Wheat and Lentil Pilaff

Bulgur wheat is a very useful store-cupboard ingredient. It has a nutty taste and texture and only needs soaking before serving in a salad or warming through for a hot dish.

SERVES 4

115 g/4 oz/½ cup green lentils
115 g/4 oz/⅔ cup bulgur wheat
1 tsp ground coriander
1 tsp ground cinnamon
1 tbsp olive oil
225 g/8 oz rindless streaky bacon
 rashers, chopped
1 red onion, chopped
1 garlic clove, crushed
1 tsp cumin seeds
2 tbsp roughly chopped
 fresh parsley
salt and ground black pepper

COOK'S TIP

Look out for Puy lentils, which have a superior flavour, aroma and texture.

1 Soak the lentils and bulgur wheat separately in cold water for 1 hour, then drain. Tip the lentils into a pan. Stir in the coriander, cinnamon and 475 ml/16 fl oz/2 cups water. Bring to the boil, then simmer until the lentils are tender and the liquid has been absorbed.

2 Meanwhile, heat the olive oil and fry the bacon until crisp. Remove and drain on kitchen paper. Add the red onion and garlic to the oil remaining in the pan and fry for 10 minutes until soft and golden brown. Stir in the cumin seeds and cook for 1 minute more. Return the bacon to the pan.

3 Stir the drained bulgur wheat into the cooked lentils, then add the mixture to the frying pan. Season with salt and pepper and heat through. Stir in the parsley and serve.

BREADS, BUNS AND TEABREADS

Focaccia with Green Peppercorns and Rock Salt

The combination of green peppercorns and a fruity olive oil gives these open-textured Italian flatbreads a delectable flavour.

MAKES 1 LOAF

350 g/12 oz/3 cups strong white bread flour

½ tsp salt

2 tsp easy-blend dried yeast

2 tsp drained green peppercorns in brine, lightly crushed

1½ tbsp fruity extra virgin olive oil

about 250 ml/8 fl oz/1 cup hand-hot water

4 tsp roughly crushed rock salt, for the topping

basil leaves, to garnish

1 Sift the flour and salt into a mixing bowl. Stir in the yeast and crushed peppercorns. Make a well in the centre and stir in 1 tbsp of the olive oil, with enough of the hand-hot water to make a soft dough.

2 Turn the dough out on to a lightly floured surface and knead for about 10 minutes until smooth and elastic. Return to the clean, lightly oiled bowl, cover with clear film and leave in a warm place until doubled in bulk.

3 Turn the dough out on to a lightly floured surface and knead lightly for 2-3 minutes. Place on an oiled baking sheet and pat out to a rough oval. Cover with a clean cloth and leave for 30 minutes until the dough puffs up.

4 Preheat the oven to 190°C/375°F/ gas 5. With your fingers, make a few dimples in the surface of the dough. Drizzle the remaining olive oil over, then sprinkle with the crushed rock salt. Bake the focaccia for 25-30 minutes until pale gold. Scatter with basil leaves and serve warm.

COOK'S TIP

Instead of one large loaf, you could make two medium or four individual loaves.

Spiced Naan Bread

*Indian naan bread is
traditionally baked in
a fiercely hot tandoori
oven. However, good results
can be achieved at home by using a
combination of a hot oven and a grill.*

MAKES 6

450 g/1 lb/4 cups plain flour
1 tsp baking powder
½ tsp salt
1 sachet easy-blend dried yeast
1 tsp caster sugar
1 tsp fennel seeds
2 tsp black onion seeds
1 tsp cumin seeds
**150 ml/¼ pint/⅔ cup
  hand-hot milk**
**2 tbsp oil, plus extra
  for brushing**
**150 ml/¼ pint/⅔ cup natural
  yogurt**
1 egg, beaten

VARIATION

*Vary the spices used by adding chopped
chilli to the mixture, or sprinkling with
poppy seeds before baking.*

1 Sift the flour, baking powder and
salt into a mixing bowl. Stir in the yeast,
sugar, fennel seeds, black onion seeds
and cumin seeds. Make a well in the
centre. Stir the hand-hot milk into
the flour mixture, then add the oil,
yogurt and beaten egg. Mix to form
a ball of dough.

2 Turn the dough out on to a lightly
floured surface and knead it for
10 minutes until smooth. Return to
the clean, lightly oiled bowl and roll the
dough to coat it with oil. Cover the bowl
with clear film and set aside until the
dough has doubled in bulk.

3 Put a heavy baking sheet in the oven
and preheat the oven to 240°C/
475°F/gas 9. Also preheat the grill.
Knead the dough again lightly and
divide it into six pieces. Keep five pieces
covered while working with the sixth.
Quickly roll the piece of dough out to
a tear-drop shape (see right), brush
lightly with oil and slap the naan on to
the hot baking sheet. Repeat with the
remaining dough.

4 Bake the naan in the oven for
3 minutes until puffed up, then place
the baking sheet under the grill for
about 30 seconds or until
the naan are lightly
browned. Serve
hot or warm as
an accompani-
ment to an
Indian curry.

Chilli Cheese Muffins

These muffins are flavoured with chilli purée, which is available in tubes or jars.

MAKES 12

115 g/4 oz/1 cup self-raising flour
1 tbsp baking powder
1 tsp salt
225 g/8 oz/2 cups fine cornmeal
150 g/5 oz/1¼ cups grated mature
  Cheddar cheese
50 g/2 oz/4 tbsp butter, melted
2 large eggs, beaten
1 tsp chilli purée
1 garlic clove, crushed
300 ml/½ pint/1¼ cups milk

1 Preheat the oven to 200°C/400°F/gas 6. Thoroughly grease 12 deep muffin tins or line the tins with paper cake cases. Sift the flour, baking powder and salt into a bowl, then stir in the cornmeal and 115 g/4 oz/1 cup of the grated cheese.

2 Pour the melted butter into a bowl and stir in the eggs, chilli purée, crushed garlic and milk.

3 Pour on to the dry ingredients and mix quickly until just combined.

4 Spoon the batter into the prepared muffin tins, scatter the remaining cheese on top and bake for 20 minutes until risen and golden brown. Leave to cool for a few minutes before turning the muffins out on to a wire rack to cool completely.

COOK'S TIP

Take care not to over-mix the muffin mixture or they will be heavy. Stir the mixture just enough to combine the ingredients roughly.

Chilli Cornbread

This golden yellow cornbread spiked with chilli makes an excellent accompaniment to soups and salads.

MAKES 9 SLICES

2 eggs
450 ml/¾ pint/1⅞ cups
  buttermilk
50 g/2 oz/¼ cup butter, melted
65 g/2½ oz/½ cup plain flour
½ tsp ground mace
1 tsp bicarbonate of soda
2 tsp salt
250 g/9 oz/2¼ cups fine cornmeal
2 fresh red chillies, seeded and
  finely chopped
shredded red chillies and
  sea salt, to serve

1 Preheat the oven to 200°C/400°F/gas 6. Line and grease a 23 x 7.5 cm/9 x 3 in loaf tin. In a large bowl, whisk the eggs until frothy, then whisk in the buttermilk and melted butter.

2 Sift the flour, mace, bicarbonate of soda and salt together and gradually stir into the egg mixture. Fold in the cornmeal a little at a time, then stir in the fresh chillies.

3 Pour the mixture into the prepared tin and bake for 25-30 minutes until the top is firm to the touch.

4 Leave the loaf to cool in the tin for a few minutes before turning out. Scatter over the red chillies and sea salt, then cut into slices and serve warm.

COOK'S TIP

For a loaf with a more rustic appearance, use medium or coarse cornmeal.

Chelsea Buns

These traditional sticky buns, packed with spice and fruit, are always popular.

<u>MAKES 9</u>

225 g/8 oz/2 cups strong white
  bread flour
2 tsp easy-blend dried yeast
1 tsp caster sugar
½ tsp salt
25 g/1 oz/2 tbsp unsalted
  butter, softened
120 ml/4 fl oz/½ cup
  hand-hot milk
1 egg, beaten
75 g/3 oz/¾ cup icing sugar,
  for the glaze

> ### COOK'S TIP
>
> *Don't be tempted to try to hurry the rising process by putting the dough in an oven or similar hot place to rise. Excessive heat will kill the yeast.*

FILLING
50 g/2 oz/¼ cup unsalted
  butter, softened
50 g/2 oz/¼ cup soft light
  brown sugar
115 g/4 oz/⅔ cup mixed dried fruit
1 tsp ground cinnamon
½ tsp ground nutmeg
¼ tsp ground cloves

1   Grease an 18 cm/7 in square cake tin. Sift the flour into a mixing bowl. Stir in the yeast, caster sugar and salt. Rub in the butter until the mixture resembles breadcrumbs, then make a well in the centre and pour in the milk and beaten egg. Beat together vigorously to make a soft dough.

2   Knead the dough on a floured surface for 5-10 minutes until smooth. Return it to the clean, lightly oiled bowl, cover with clear film and leave in a warm place until doubled in bulk. Turn out on to a floured surface. Knead lightly and roll out the dough to give a rectangle. This should measure about 30 x 23 cm/12 x 9 in.

3   Spread the dough with the softened butter and sprinkle with the brown sugar, dried fruit, cinnamon, nutmeg and ground cloves. Roll up from a long side and cut into 9 pieces. Place in the prepared tin, cut sides up. Cover with lightly oiled clear film and leave in a warm place for 45 minutes or until the buns are well risen.

4   Preheat the oven to 190°C/375°F/ gas 5. Bake the buns for 30 minutes until golden. Leave to cool in the tin for 10 minutes, then transfer, in one piece, to a wire rack to cool. Mix the icing sugar with enough water to make a thin glaze and brush over the buns. Pull the buns apart to serve.

Cornish Saffron Buns

Saffron gives these buns a brilliant golden colour and a distinctive flavour.

<u>MAKES 12</u>

175 ml/6 fl oz/¾ cup milk
½ tsp saffron strands
50 g/2 oz/¼ cup caster sugar
400 g/14 oz/3½ cups strong white
  bread flour
1 sachet easy-blend dried yeast
½ tsp salt
40 g/1½ oz/3 tbsp butter, melted
2 eggs, beaten

1   Put the milk and saffron strands in a saucepan and slowly bring to the boil. Remove from the heat, stir in the sugar and leave for about 5 minutes until the mixture is hand hot.

2   Sift the flour into a bowl and stir in the yeast and salt. Make a well in the centre. Add the melted butter and half the egg to the milk, then mix with the dry ingredients to make a dough. Turn the dough out on to a lightly floured surface and knead for 10 minutes.

> ### COOK'S TIP
>
> *Buy fresh saffron for the best flavour and do not keep it for too long.*

3   Divide the dough into 12 pieces and roll into balls. Place on greased baking sheets and cover with a cloth. Leave to rise until the buns have doubled in size.

4   Preheat the oven to 190°C/375°F/ gas 5. Glaze the tops of the buns with the remaining beaten egg and bake for 15-20 minutes until they are golden and sound hollow when rapped with your knuckle underneath. Cool on a wine rack.

Barm Brack

This traditional Irish spiced bread is made and eaten at Hallowe'en. It used to be traditional to bake a wedding ring in the mixture in the belief that whoever retrieved it would be married within the year.

MAKES 1 x 23 CM/9 IN ROUND LOAF

675 g/1½ lb/6 cups plain flour
½ tsp mixed spice
1 tsp salt
1 sachet easy-blend dried yeast
50 g/2 oz/¼ cup caster sugar
300 ml/½ pint/1¼ cups hand-hot milk
150 ml/¼ pint/⅔ cup hand-hot water
50 g/2 oz/¼ cup butter, softened
225 g/8 oz/1⅓ cups sultanas
50 g/2 oz/⅓ cup currants
50 g/2 oz/⅓ cup chopped mixed peel
milk, for glazing

1 Sift the flour, mixed spice and salt into a bowl. Stir in the yeast and 1 tbsp of the caster sugar. Make a well in the centre and pour in the milk and water.

2 Mix well, gradually incorporating the dry ingredients to make a sticky dough. Place on a lightly floured board and knead the dough until smooth and no longer sticky. Put into a clean bowl. Cover with clear film and leave in a warm place for 1 hour until well risen and doubled in bulk.

3 Preheat the oven to 200°C/400°F/ gas 6. Knead the dough lightly on a floured surface. Add the remaining ingredients, apart from the milk, to the dough and work them in. Return the dough to the bowl, replace the clear film and leave to rise for 30 minutes.

4 Grease a 23 cm/9 in round cake tin. Pat the dough to a neat round and fit it in the tin. Cover and leave in a warm place for about 45 minutes until it has risen to the top of the tin. Brush lightly with milk and bake for 15 minutes. Cover the loaf with foil, reduce the oven temperature to 180°C/350°F/ gas 4 and bake for 45 minutes more, or until the bread is golden and sounds hollow when rapped underneath. Cool on a wire rack.

Swedish Spice Bread

Cardamom and caraway seeds are widely used in Scandinavian cooking. At Christmas, dried fruit and candied peel are added to this recipe to make a traditional julekake.

MAKES 1 x 23 CM/9 IN ROUND LOAF

25 g/1 oz/2 tbsp butter
45 ml/3 tbsp well-flavoured
  clear honey
225 g/8 oz/2 cups strong white
  bread flour
225 g/8 oz/2 cups rye flour
½ tsp salt
1 sachet easy-blend dried yeast
1 tsp ground cardamom
1 tsp ground caraway seeds
½ tsp ground star anise
2 tbsp caster sugar
grated rind and juice of
  1 small orange
175 ml/6 fl oz/¾ cup lager
1 egg, beaten
4 tbsp boiling water
GLAZE
1 tbsp clear honey

COOK'S TIP

For a more decorative loaf, scatter chopped crystalized citrus peel or browned flaked almonds over the top, after brushing with honey. As the dough tends to be rather sticky, knead it in a mixer or food processor if you have one, using a dough hook or blade.

1 Melt the butter with the honey in a small saucepan, then leave to cool. Sift the flours and salt into a bowl. Tip any rye remaining in the sieve into the bowl. Stir in the yeast, cardamom, caraway, star anise, caster sugar and orange rind.

2 Mix the lager with the boiling water in a jug. Stir the orange juice and beaten egg into the melted butter and honey, then stir the mixture into the flour. Add enough of the warm lager to make a soft and slightly sticky, but manageable dough.

3 Place the dough on a lightly floured surface and knead for 5 minutes until smooth and elastic. Place in an oiled bowl, cover and leave to rise until doubled in bulk. Knead briefly, then divide the dough in two. Roll out each piece into a long snake.

4 Grease a 23 cm/9 in round cake tin. Starting at the edge of the prepared tin, coil the dough round and round to the centre, joining the second piece to the first with a little water. Cover with oiled clear film and leave until doubled in size. Preheat the oven to 190°C/ 375°F/gas 5. Bake the bread for 10 minutes, then turn the oven down to 160°C/325°F/gas 3 and bake for 40-50 minutes more, until the bread is lightly browned and sounds hollow when rapped underneath.

5 Make the glaze by mixing the honey with 1 tbsp hot water, then brush the mixture over the hot bread. Leave the loaf on a wire rack to cool. Cut into slices and serve with butter.

Stollen

Stollen is an Austrian spiced fruit bread with a marzipan filling. Although it is traditionally served at Christmas, it is delicious at any time, served warm or cold or toasted and buttered.

SERVES 10

50 g/2 oz/¼ cup currants
75 g/3 oz/½ cup raisins
40 g/1½ oz/¼ cup chopped
  mixed peel
40 g/1½ oz/¼ cup glacé cherries,
  rinsed, dried and quartered
2 tbsp rum
50 g/2 oz/¼ cup butter
175 ml/6 fl oz/¾ cup milk
25 g/1 oz/2 tbsp caster sugar
375 g/12 oz/3 cups strong white
  bread flour
¼ tsp salt
½ tsp ground nutmeg
½ tsp ground cinnamon
seeds from 3 cardamoms
1 sachet easy-blend dried yeast
grated rind of 1 lemon
1 egg, beaten
40 g/1½ oz/⅓ cup flaked almonds
175 g/6 oz marzipan
melted butter, for brushing
sifted icing sugar, for dusting

1 Place the currants, raisins, mixed peel and cherries in a bowl. Stir in the rum and set aside. Combine the butter, milk and caster sugar in a saucepan and heat gently until the sugar has dissolved and the butter has just melted. Cool until hand-hot.

2 Sift the flour, salt, nutmeg and cinnamon into a bowl. Crush the cardamom seeds and add them to the flour mixture. Stir in the dried yeast. Make a well in the centre and stir in the milk mixture, lemon rind and beaten egg. Beat to form a soft dough.

3 Turn on to a floured surface. With floured hands, knead the dough for about 5 minutes. It will be quite sticky, so add more flour if necessary. Knead the soaked fruit and flaked almonds into the dough until just combined.

4 Return the dough to the clean, lightly oiled bowl, cover with clear film and leave in a warm place for up to 3 hours until doubled in bulk.

5 Turn the dough on to a floured surface. Knead for 1-2 minutes, then roll out to a 25 cm/10 in square. Roll the marzipan to a sausage shape slightly shorter than the length of the dough and place in the centre. Fold one side over to cover the marzipan and repeat with the other side, overlapping in the centre. Seal the ends.

6 Place the roll, seam side down, on a greased baking sheet. Cover with oiled clear film and leave in a warm place until doubled in bulk. Preheat the oven to 190°C/375°F/gas 5.

7 Bake the stollen for 40 minutes, or until it is golden and sounds hollow when rapped underneath. Brush the hot stollen generously with melted butter and dredge heavily with sifted icing sugar.

Orange and Coriander Brioches

The warm spicy flavour of coriander combines particularly well with orange.

<u>MAKES 12</u>

225 g/8 oz/2 cups strong white bread flour

2 tsp easy-blend dried yeast

½ tsp salt

1 tbsp caster sugar

2 tsp coriander seeds, coarsely ground

grated rind of 1 orange

2 eggs, beaten

50 g/2 oz/¼ cup unsalted butter, melted

1 small egg, beaten, to glaze

1 Grease 12 individual brioche tins. Sift the flour into a mixing bowl and stir in the yeast, salt, sugar, coriander seeds and orange rind. Make a well in the centre, pour in 2 tbsp hand-hot water, the eggs and melted butter and beat to make a soft dough. Turn the dough on to a lightly floured surface and knead for 5 minutes until smooth and elastic. Return to the clean, lightly oiled bowl, cover with clear film and leave in a warm place for 1 hour until doubled in bulk.

2 Turn on to a floured surface, knead again briefly and roll into a sausage. Cut into 12 pieces. Break off a quarter of each piece and set aside. Shape the larger pieces of dough into balls and place in the prepared tins.

3 With a floured wooden spoon, press a hole in each dough ball. Shape each small piece of dough into a little plug and press into the holes.

COOK'S TIP

These individual brioches look particularly attractive if they are made in special brioche tins. However, they can also be made in bun tins or muffin tins.

4 Place the brioche tins on a baking sheet. Cover with lightly oiled clear film and leave in a warm place until the dough rises almost to the top of the tins. Preheat the oven to 220°C/425°F/gas 7. Brush the brioches with beaten egg and bake for 15 minutes until golden brown. Scatter over extra shreds of orange rind to decorator, if you like, and serve the brioches warm with butter.

CAKES AND BISCUITS

Spiced Caribbean Christmas Cake

There's a taste of the tropics in this spicy fruit cake spiked with brandy, rum and port.

MAKES 1 x 23 CM/9 IN CAKE

675 g/1½ lb luxury dried mixed fruit

115 g/4 oz/⅔ cup ready-to-eat prunes, chopped

115 g/4 oz/⅔ cup ready-to-eat dried mango or papaya pieces, chopped

50 g/2 oz/½ cup glacé cherries, quartered

3 tbsp brandy

3 tbsp rum

3 tbsp port

4 tbsp cherry brandy

1 tbsp mixed spice

½ tsp salt

2 tsp vanilla essence

1 tbsp treacle

250 g/9 oz/2¼ cups self-raising flour

250 g/9 oz/1½ cups demerara sugar

250 g/9 oz/generous 1 cup butter, softened

6 eggs, beaten

1 Combine the mixed fruit, prunes, mango or papaya pieces and glacé cherries in a saucepan. Add the brandy, rum, port, cherry brandy, mixed spice, salt, vanilla essence, treacle and 4 tbsp water. Bring to the boil, then simmer gently for 15 minutes.

2 Set the fruit mixture aside to cool. Leave overnight or, if time allows, place in a large screwtop jar and chill for up to 1 week.

3 Preheat the oven to 140°C/275°F/gas 1. Grease and line a 23 cm/9 in round cake tin. Sift the flour into a large mixing bowl. Add the demerara sugar, softened butter and eggs. Beat the mixture thoroughly until well combined. Gradually fold in the macerated fruit mixture.

> **COOK'S TIP**
>
> *This is a very rich moist cake and does not need marzipan or icing, but, if you do want to decorate it, a glazed nut and glacé fruit topping looks good and tastes delicious.*

4 Pour the mixture into the prepared tin, leave the surface and bake for 3½–4 hours until cooked through. Place a sheet of greaseproof paper over the cake after about 3 hours if it appears to be browning too quickly.

5 Leave the cake to cool in the tin for 45 minutes, then transfer it to a wire rack to cool completely. Wrap in greaseproof paper and store in an airtight tin. If possible, keep the cake for 1 month before cutting.

Honey Spice Cake

Use a strongly flavoured honey such as chestnut honey, which will not be over-whelmed by the spices.

MAKES 8-10 SLICES

150 g/5 oz/⅔ cup **butter**
115 g/4 oz/½ cup **soft light brown sugar**
175 g/6 oz/¾ cup **clear honey**
200 g/7 oz/1¾ cups **self-raising flour**
½ tsp **ground ginger**
½ tsp **ground cinnamon**
¼ tsp **caraway seeds**
¼ tsp **ground cloves**
2 **eggs, beaten**
350 g/12 oz/3 cups **icing sugar**
crushed sugar, to decorate

COOK'S TIP

This cake benefits from being kept for a day before eating.

1 Preheat the oven to 180°C/350°F/ gas 4. Grease a 900 ml/1½ pint/ 3¾ cup fluted mould. Put the butter, sugar, honey and 1 tbsp water into a saucepan. Heat gently until the butter has melted and the sugar has dissolved. Remove from the heat and cool for 10 minutes.

2 Sift the flour into a bowl and mix in the ginger, cinnamon, caraway seeds and ground cloves. Make a well in the centre. Pour in the honey mixture and the eggs and beat well until smooth. Pour the batter into the prepared tin.

3 Bake for 40-50 minutes until the cake is well risen and a skewer inserted into the centre comes out clean. Leave to cool in the tin for 2-3 minutes, then remove to a wire rack to cool.

4 Make the icing. Sift the icing sugar into a bowl. Stir in enough warm water to make a smooth, flowing icing. Spoon carefully over the cake so that it is evenly coated. Decorate with sugar.

Lemon Poppy Seed Cake

Pouring lemon syrup over this makes it marvellously moist, while the poppy seeds add texture and extra flavour.

MAKES 12 SQUARES OR DIAMONDS
40 g/1½ oz/⅓ cup poppy seeds
115 g/4 oz/½ cup butter, softened
175 g/6 oz/¾ cup caster sugar
2 eggs, beaten
finely grated rind of 1 lemon
175 g/6 oz/1½ cups self-raising
 flour, sifted
4 tbsp milk
TOPPING
juice of 1 lemon
115 g/4 oz/½ cup granulated sugar
lemon rind, to decorate

1   Preheat the oven to 180°C/350°F/ gas 4. Grease a 23 x 18 cm/9 x 7 in cake tin, about 2.5 cm/1 in deep. Line it with non-stick baking paper. Grind the poppy seeds in a clean coffee grinder or place between 2 sheets of clear film and crush with a rolling pin.

2   Beat the butter and sugar in a bowl until light and fluffy. Gradually beat in the eggs. Stir in the lemon rind. Fold in the flour, alternately with the milk, then fold in the poppy seeds.

3   Spoon the mixture into the prepared tin and level the surface. Bake for about 45 minutes until the cake is well risen and pale golden.

COOK'S TIP

If you warm the lemon in a microwave for a few seconds on High, it will yield more juice.

4   While the cake is baking mix the lemon juice and sugar in a bowl. Remove the cake from the oven and, without taking it out of the tin, immediately pour the mixture evenly over the surface.

5   Leave the cake in the tin until completely cold, then cut into squares or diamonds. Decorate with fine strips of lemon rind.

Ginger Cake

Three forms of ginger make this the ultimate cake for all lovers of the versatile spice.

MAKES 12 SQUARES
225 g/8 oz/2 cups self-raising flour
1 tbsp ground ginger
1 tsp ground cinnamon
½ tsp bicarbonate of soda
115 g/4 oz/½ cup butter
115 g/4 oz/½ cup soft light brown sugar
2 eggs
1½ tbsp golden syrup
1½ tbsp milk
TOPPING
6 pieces stem ginger, plus 4 tsp syrup, from the jar
115 g/4 oz/1 cup icing sugar
lemon juice

1 Preheat the oven to 160°C/325°F/ gas 3. Grease a shallow 18 cm/7 in square cake tin and line with non-stick baking paper.

2 Sift the flour, ginger, cinnamon and bicarbonate of soda into a bowl. Rub in the butter, then stir in the sugar.

3 Make a well in the centre. In a bowl, whisk together the eggs, syrup and milk. Pour into the dry ingredients and beat until smooth and glossy.

4 Spoon into the prepared tin and bake for 45-50 minutes until well risen and firm to the touch. Leave in the tin for 30 minutes, then remove to a wire rack to cool completely.

COOK'S TIP

This cake benefits from being kept in an airtight tin for a day before eating.

5 Cut each piece of stem ginger into quarters and arrange the pieces on top of the cake.

6 Sift the icing sugar into a bowl and stir in the ginger syrup and enough lemon juice to make a smooth icing. Put the icing into a greaseproof paper icing bag and drizzle over the top of the cake. Leave to set, then cut the cake into squares.

Ginger-topped Shortbread Fingers

Topping a ginger shortbread base with a sticky ginger topping may be gilding the lily, but it tastes delicious!

MAKES ABOUT 40
225 g/8 oz/2 cups plain flour
1 tsp ground ginger
75 g/3 oz/6 tbsp caster sugar
3 pieces stem ginger,
  finely chopped
175 g/6 oz/¾ cup butter
TOPPING
1 tbsp golden syrup
50 g/2 oz/¼ cup butter
4 tbsp icing sugar, sifted
1 tsp ground ginger

1 Preheat the oven to 180°C/350°F/ gas 4. Grease a shallow rectangular 28 x 18 cm/11 x 7 in baking tin. Sift the flour and ground ginger into a bowl and stir in the sugar and stem ginger.

2 Rub in the butter until the mixture begins to stick together. Press the mixture into the prepared tin and smooth over the top with a palette knife. Bake for 40 minutes until the ginger shortbread base is very lightly browned.

3 Make the topping. Put the syrup and butter in a small saucepan. Heat gently until both have melted. Stir in the icing sugar and ginger. Remove the cake tin from the oven and pour the topping over the base while both are still hot. Allow to cool slightly, then cut into fingers. Remove to wire racks to cool completely.

COOK'S TIP
Use the syrup from the jar of stem ginger instead of golden syrup in the topping, if you prefer.

Apple and Cinnamon Muffins

These spicy muffins are quick and easy to make and are perfect for serving for breakfast or tea.

MAKES 6 LARGE MUFFINS
1 egg, beaten
40 g/1½ oz/3 tbsp caster sugar
120 ml/4 fl oz/½ cup milk
50 g/2 oz/¼ cup butter, melted
150 g/5 oz/1¼ cups plain flour
1½ tsp baking powder
¼ tsp salt
½ tsp ground cinnamon
2 small eating apples, peeled,
  cored and finely chopped
TOPPING
12 brown sugar cubes,
  roughly crushed
1 tsp ground cinnamon

1 Preheat the oven to 200°C/400°F/ gas 6. Line six large muffin tins with paper cases. Mix the egg, sugar, milk and melted butter in a large bowl. Sift in the flour, baking powder, salt and cinnamon. Add the chopped apple and mix roughly.

2 Spoon the mixture into the prepared muffin cases. Make the topping by mixing the crushed sugar cubes with the cinnamon. Sprinkle over the uncooked muffins. Bake for 30-35 minutes until well risen and golden. Cool on a wire rack.

COOK'S TIP
Do not overmix the muffin mixture – it should be lumpy.

Vanilla Streusel Bars

The crumbly topping on this cake makes a crunchy contrast to the moist vanilla-flavoured sponge underneath.

MAKES ABOUT 25
175 g/6 oz/1½ cups self-raising
  flour
1 tsp baking powder
175 g/6 oz/¾ cup butter, softened
175 g/6 oz/¾ cup vanilla sugar
3 eggs, beaten
1½ tsp pure vanilla essence
1-2 tbsp milk
STREUSEL TOPPING
115 g/4 oz/1 cup self-raising flour
75 g/3 oz/6 tbsp butter
75 g/3 oz/6 tbsp vanilla sugar
icing sugar, to finish

1 Preheat the oven to 180°C/350°F/gas 4. Lightly grease and line a shallow 23 x 18 cm/9 x 7 in baking tin.

2 Make the topping. Sift the flour into a bowl and rub in the butter until the mixture resembles coarse breadcrumbs. Stir in the vanilla sugar and set aside.

3 Sift the flour and baking powder into a bowl. Add the butter, vanilla sugar and eggs. Beat well until the mixture is smooth, adding the vanilla essence and just enough milk to give a soft dropping consistency.

4 Spoon the mixture into the prepared tin. Sprinkle the streusel topping over the surface and press down to cover. Bake for 45-60 minutes until browned and firm. Cool in the tin for 5 minutes, then turn out on to a wire rack to cool completely. Cut into bars when cool.

> **COOK'S TIP**
> *Cover the cake loosely with foil if the topping browns too quickly.*

Chocolate Lebkuchen

Cut this nutty spice cake into small squares to serve with after-dinner coffee instead of chocolates.

MAKES 24

3 eggs
200 g/7 oz/ 1 cup caster sugar
115 g/4 oz/1 cup plain flour
1 tsp ground cinnamon
¼ tsp ground cloves
¼ tsp ground nutmeg
¼ tsp ground cardamom
275 g/10 oz/2 cups unblanched almonds, coarsely ground
25 g/1 oz/¼ cup candied lemon peel, finely chopped
25 g/1 oz/¼ cup candied orange peel, finely chopped
40 g/1½ oz plain chocolate, grated
½ tsp grated lemon rind
½ tsp grated orange rind
2 tsp rosewater

ICING

1 egg white
2 tsp cocoa powder, mixed with 1 tbsp boiling water and cooled
115 g/4 oz/generous 1 cup icing sugar
2 tbsp sugar crystals

1 Preheat the oven to 160°C/325°F/gas 3. Base-line a 30 x 23 cm/12 x 9 in Swiss roll tin with rice paper.

2 Whisk the eggs and caster sugar in a large bowl until thick and pale. Sift the flour, cinnamon, ground cloves, nutmeg and cardamom. Stir in all the remaining dry ingredients.

3 Spread in the prepared tin and brush with the rosewater. Bake for 30-35 minutes until firm.

4 Make the icing. Stir the egg white into the cocoa mixture, sift in the icing sugar and mix. Spread over the cake while still warm. Sprinkle with sugar crystals. Return to the oven for 5 minutes. Cut into squares when cold.

COOK'S TIP

Do not worry when the top of the cake cracks when you cut it; it is meant to be like that!

Spiced Cocktail Biscuits

These savoury biscuits are ideal for serving with pre-dinner drinks. Each of the spice seeds contributes to the flavour.

MAKES 20-30
150 g/5 oz/1¼ cups plain flour
2 tsp curry powder
115 g/4 oz/½ cup butter
75 g/3 oz/¾ cup grated
  Cheddar cheese
2 tsp poppy seeds
1 tsp black onion seeds
1 egg yolk
cumin seeds, to decorate

> **COOK'S TIP**
>
> *These biscuits are at their best when freshly baked. Make the dough in advance and chill until required.*

1 Grease two baking sheets. Sift the flour and curry powder into a bowl.

2 Rub in the butter until the mixture resembles breadcrumbs, then stir in the cheese, poppy seeds and black onion seeds. Stir in the egg yolk and mix to a firm dough. Wrap the dough in clear film and chill for 30 minutes.

3 Roll out the dough on a floured surface to a thickness of about 3 mm/⅛ in. Cut into shapes with a biscuit cutter. Arrange on the prepared baking sheets and sprinkle with the cumin seeds. Chill for 15 minutes.

4 Preheat the oven to 190°C/375°F/gas 5. Bake the biscuits for about 20 minutes until crisp and golden. Serve warm or cold.

Cinnamon-spiced Pastelitos

These melt-in-the-mouth cinnamon and vanilla biscuits are traditionally served at Mexican weddings. They are perfect for serving with coffee.

MAKES ABOUT 40
225 g/8 oz/1 cup butter, softened
50 g/2 oz/¼ cup caster sugar
225 g/8 oz/2 cups plain flour
115 g/4 oz/1 cup cornflour
1 tsp pure vanilla essence
50 g/2 oz/½ cup icing sugar
1 tsp ground cinnamon

1 Preheat the oven to 160°C/325°F/gas 3. Grease two or three baking sheets. In a bowl, cream the butter with the caster sugar until light and fluffy. Sift the flour and cornflour together and gradually work into the creamed butter and sugar mixture with the vanilla essence.

2 Roll heaped teaspoons of the mixture into balls and place on the baking sheets. Bake for 30 minutes or until pale golden.

3 Sift the icing sugar and ground cinnamon into a bowl. While the biscuits are still warm, toss them in the icing sugar mixture. Leave on a wire rack to cool, then store in an airtight tin for up to 2 weeks.

> **COOK'S TIP**
>
> *The biscuit mixture can be prepared in a food processor.*

DESSERTS

Pear Tart Tatin with Cardamom

Cardamom is a spice that is equally at home in sweet and savoury dishes. It is delicious with pears.

SERVES 2-4

50 g/2 oz/¼ cup butter, softened
50 g/2 oz/¼ cup caster sugar
seeds from 10 cardamoms
225 g/8 oz puff pastry, thawed
** if frozen**
3 ripe pears

1   Preheat the oven to 220°C/425°F/ gas 7. Spread the butter over the base of a 18 cm/7 in heavy-based cake tin or an ovenproof omelette pan. Spread the sugar evenly over the bottom of the tin or pan. Scatter the cardamom seeds over the sugar. On a floured surface, roll out the pastry to a circle slightly larger than the tin or pan. Prick the pastry lightly, support it on a baking sheet and chill.

2   Peel the pears, cut out the cores and slice them lengthways into halves. Arrange the pears, rounded side down, on the butter and sugar. Set the cake tin or omelette pan over a medium heat until the sugar melts and begins to bubble with the butter and juice from the pears. If any areas are browning more than others, move the pan, but do not stir.

3   As soon as the sugar has caramelized remove the tin or pan carefully from the heat. Place the pastry on top, tucking the edges down the side of the pan. Transfer to the oven and bake for 25 minutes until the pastry is well risen and golden.

4   Leave the tart in the tin or pan for 2-3 minutes until the juices have stopped bubbling. Invert the tin over a plate and shake to release the tart. It may be necessary to slide a spatula underneath the pears to loosen them. Serve the tart warm with cream.

COOK'S TIP

Choose fairly large round pears for this tart rather than the more elongated varieties.

American Pumpkin Pie

This spicy sweet pie is traditionally served at Thanksgiving, or at Hallowe'en to use the pulp from the hollowed-out pumpkin lanterns.

SERVES 8

200 g/7 oz/1¾ cups plain flour

½ tsp salt

**90 g/3½ oz/scant ½ cup
  unsalted butter**

1 egg yolk

FILLING

900 g/2 lb piece of pumpkin

2 large eggs

75 g/3 oz/6 tbsp light brown sugar

4 tbsp golden syrup

250 ml/8 fl oz/1 cup double cream

1 tbsp mixed spice

½ tsp salt

icing sugar, for dusting

1 Sift the flour and salt into a mixing bowl. Rub in the butter until the mixture resembles breadcrumbs, then mix in the egg yolk and enough iced water (about 1 tbsp) to make a dough. Roll the dough into a ball, wrap it up in clear film and chill it for at least 30 minutes.

2 Make the filling. Peel the pumpkin and remove the seeds. Cut the flesh into cubes. Place in a heavy-based saucepan, add water to cover and boil until tender. Mash until completely smooth, then leave in a sieve set over a bowl to drain thoroughly.

3 Roll out the pastry on a lightly floured surface and line a 23-25 cm/ 9-10 in loose-bottomed flan tin. Prick the base and line with greaseproof paper and baking beans. Chill for 15 minutes. Preheat the oven to 200°C/400°F/gas 6. Bake the flan case for 10 minutes, remove the paper and beans, return the flan case to the oven and bake for 5 minutes more.

4 Lower the oven temperature to 190°C/375°F/gas 5. Tip the pumpkin pulp into a bowl and beat in the eggs, sugar, syrup, cream, mixed spice and salt. Pour the mixture into the pastry case. Bake for 40 minutes or until the filling has set. Dust with icing sugar and serve at room temperature.

Clementines with Star Anise and Cinnamon

This fresh dessert, delicately flavoured with mulling spices, makes the perfect ending for a festive meal.

SERVES 6

**350 ml/12 fl oz/1½ cups sweet
  dessert wine**
75 g/3 oz/6 tbsp caster sugar
6 star anise
1 cinnamon stick
1 vanilla pod
2 tbsp Cointreau
1 strip of thinly pared lime rind
12 clementines

1 Put the wine, sugar, star anise and cinnamon in a saucepan. Split the vanilla pod and add it to the pan with the lime rind. Bring to the boil, lower the heat and simmer for 10 minutes. Allow to cool, then stir in the Cointreau.

2 Peel the clementines, removing all the pith and white membranes. Cut some clementines in half and arrange them all in a glass dish. Pour over the spiced wine and chill overnight.

VARIATION

Tangerines or oranges can be used instead of clementines.

Pistachio Halva Ice Cream

Halva is made from sesame seeds and is available in several flavours. This ice cream, studded with chunks of pistachio-flavoured halva, is as unusual as it is irresistible.

SERVES 6

3 egg yolks
115 g/4 oz/½ cup caster sugar
**300 ml/½ pint/1¼ cups
  single cream**
**300 ml/½ pint/1¼ cups
  double cream**
**115 g/4 oz pistachio halva
chopped pistachio nuts,
  to decorate**

1 Turn the freezer to its lowest setting. Whisk the egg yolks with the caster sugar in a bowl until thick and pale. Pour the single cream into a small saucepan and bring to the boil. Stir the hot cream into the egg yolk mixture.

2 Transfer the mixture to a double boiler or a heatproof bowl placed over a pan of boiling water. Cook, stirring continuously, until the custard is thick enough to coat the back of a spoon. Strain into a bowl and leave to cool.

COOK'S TIP

Use an ice cream machine, if you have one, to make the ice cream.

3 Whisk the double cream lightly, then whisk in the cooled custard. Crumble the halva into the mixture and stir in gently.

4 Pour the mixture into a freezer-proof container. Cover and freeze for 3 hours or until half set. Stir well, breaking up any ice crystals, then return to the freezer until frozen solid.

5 Remove the ice cream from the freezer about 15 minutes before serving so that it softens enough for scooping, and to allow the full flavour to develop. Decorate with chopped pistachio nuts.

Ginger and Lemon Puddings with Vanilla Custard

The flavours of lemon and ginger complement each other perfectly in these light little puddings.

SERVES 8

3 lemons
75 g/3 oz drained stem ginger plus 2 tbsp syrup from the jar
4 tbsp golden syrup
175 g/6 oz/1½ cups self-raising flour
2 tsp ground ginger
115 g/4 oz/½ cup butter, softened
115 g/4 oz/½ cup caster sugar
2 eggs, beaten
3-4 tbsp milk

VANILLA CUSTARD
150 ml/¼ pint/⅔ cup milk
150 ml/¼ pint/⅔ cup double cream
1 vanilla pod, split
3 egg yolks
1 tsp cornflour
25 g/1 oz/2 tbsp caster sugar

1 Preheat the oven to 160°C/325°F/gas 3. Grease eight individual pudding basins. Set one lemon aside for the sauce. Grate the rind from the remaining lemons and reserve in a bowl. Remove all the pith from one of the grated lemons and slice the flesh into eight thin rounds. Squeeze the juice from the second grated lemon. Chop the stem ginger.

2 In a small bowl, mix 1 tbsp of the ginger syrup with 2 tbsp of the golden syrup and 1 tsp of the lemon juice. Divide among the greased pudding basins. Place a slice of lemon in the base of each basin.

3 Sift the flour and ground ginger into a bowl. In a separate bowl, beat the butter and sugar together until pale and fluffy. Gradually beat in the eggs, then fold in the flour mixture and add enough milk to give a soft dropping consistency. Stir in the reserved grated lemon rind. Spoon into the pudding basins.

4 Cover each basin with foil and stand in a roasting tin. Add boiling water to come halfway up the basins. Overwrap with foil, sealing well. Bake for 30-45 minutes, until cooked through.

5 Meanwhile make a lemon and ginger sauce. Grate the rind and squeeze the juice from the remaining lemon. Place in a saucepan with the remaining ginger syrup and golden syrup. Bring to the boil, lower the heat and simmer for 2 minutes. Keep warm.

6 Make the custard. Mix the milk and cream in a pan. Add the vanilla pod. Heat to just below boiling. Remove from the heat and leave for 10 minutes. Whisk together the egg yolks, cornflour and sugar until light, then strain in the hot milk and cream. Whisk until blended, then return to the clean pan and heat, stirring, until thick. Turn out the puddings, spoon over the sauce and serve with the custard.

Churros with Cinnamon Syrup

Deep-fried choux puffs tossed in sugar flavoured with star anise are a popular Mexican dessert. They are traditionally served with a cinnamon syrup.

SERVES 4-6

50 g/2 oz/¼ cup unsalted butter
65 g/2½ oz/⅔ cup plain flour, sifted
2 eggs, beaten
oil, for deep frying
shreds of pared orange rind, to decorate
STAR ANISE SUGAR
5 star anise
75 g/3 oz/6 tbsp caster sugar
CINNAMON SYRUP
115 g/4 oz/½ cup caster sugar
2 star anise
1 cinnamon stick
2 tbsp orange juice

1 Make the star anise sugar. Put the star anise and sugar into a mortar and grind with a pestle until very fine. Sift into a bowl.

2 To make the cinnamon syrup, mix the sugar and 150 ml/¼ pint/⅔ cup water in a saucepan. Add the star anise and cinnamon stick. Heat, stirring occasionally until the sugar has dissolved, then boil without stirring for 2 minutes. Stir in the orange juice and set aside.

3 Melt the butter in a saucepan. Add 150 ml/¼ pint/⅔ cup water and bring to the boil. Add the flour, all at once, and beat thoroughly until the mixture leaves the sides of the pan. Cool slightly, then vigorously beat in the eggs, a little at a time. Spoon the churro mixture into a large piping bag fitted with a large star nozzle.

4 Heat the oil to 180°C/350°F or until a cube of bread browns in 1 minute. Fry a few churros at a time: pipe the paste into the oil, cutting off 2.5 cm/1 in lengths with a knife. Each batch will take 3-4 minutes. The churros are ready when they float to the surface of the oil and are golden. Drain the churros on kitchen paper and keep hot while you are cooking successive batches.

5 Toss the churros in the star anise sugar. Decorate with the shreds of orange rind. Pour the cinnamon syrup into a small bowl and serve with the hot churros.

Kulfi with Cardamom

Kulfi is a delicately spiced Indian ice cream, which is traditionally made in individual containers. Yogurt pots or dariole moulds are ideal, but it can be made like other ice cream in a large container if you prefer.

SERVES 6

**2 litres/3½ pints/8 cups
  creamy milk**
12 cardamoms
175 g/6 oz/¾ cup caster sugar
**25 g/1 oz/¼ cup blanched
  almonds, chopped**
**toasted flaked almonds and
  cardamoms, to decorate**

1 Place the milk and cardamoms in a large heavy-based pan. Bring to the boil then simmer vigorously until reduced by one-third. Strain the milk into a bowl, discarding the cardamoms, then stir in the sugar and almonds until the sugar is dissolved. Cool.

> COOK'S TIP
>
> *Use a large pan for reducing the milk as there needs to be plenty of room for it to bubble up.*

2 Pour the mixture into a freezer-proof container, cover and freeze until almost firm, stirring every 30 minutes. When almost solid, pack the ice cream into six clean yogurt pots. Return to the freezer until required, removing the pots about 10 minutes before serving and turning the individual ices out. Decorate with toasted almonds and cardamoms before serving.

Pears in Mulled Wine

The red wine gives the pears a deep ruby colour, and the spices contribute a lovely warm flavour.

SERVES 4

1 bottle full-bodied red wine
1 cinnamon stick
4 cloves
½ tsp grated nutmeg
½ tsp ground ginger
8 peppercorns
175 g/6 oz/¾ cup caster sugar
thinly pared rind of ½ orange
thinly pared rind of ½ lemon
8 firm ripe pears

1 Pour the wine into a heavy-based saucepan into which the pears will fit snugly when standing upright. Stir the cinnamon stick, cloves, nutmeg, ginger, peppercorns, caster sugar and citrus rinds into the wine.

> COOK'S TIP
>
> *Serve the pears with a mascarpone cream, made by combining equal quantities of mascarpone cheese and double cream, and adding a little vanilla essence for flavour.*

2 Peel the pears, leaving the stalks intact, and stand them in the pan. The wine should only just cover the pears. Bring the liquid to the boil, lower the heat, cover and simmer very gently for 30 minutes or until the pears are tender. Using a slotted spoon, transfer the pears to a bowl.

3 Boil the poaching liquid until it has reduced by half and is syrupy. Strain the syrup over and around the pears and serve hot or cold.

Fruit Platter with Chat Masala

The spicy sour flavour of chat masala may seem a little strange at first, but it can become quite addictive!

SERVES 6

1 pineapple
2 papayas
1 small melon
juice of 2 limes
2 pomegranates
chat masala, to taste
sprigs of mint, to decorate

COOK'S TIP

If you haven't time, or the spices to hand, to make chat masala, simply season the fruit with ground black pepper.

1   Peel the pineapple. Remove the core and any remaining 'eyes', then cut the flesh lengthways into thin wedges. Peel the papayas, cut them in half, and then into thin wedges. Halve the melon and remove the seeds from the middle. Cut it into thin wedges and remove the skin.

VARIATION

The selection of fruit can be varied according to what is available. Apples and bananas make a simple salad, or guava and mango a more exotic combination.

2   Arrange the fruit on six individual plates and sprinkle with the lime juice. Cut the pomegranates in half and scoop out the seeds, discarding any pith. Scatter the seeds over the fruit. Serve, sprinkled with a little chat masala to taste. Scatter over a few sprigs of mint if you have some.

Caribbean Bananas with Ground Allspice and Ginger

Tender baked bananas in a rich and spicy sauce – a dessert for those with a sweet tooth!

SERVES 4

25 g/1 oz/2 tbsp butter
8 firm ripe bananas
juice of 1 lime
75 g/3 oz/scant ½ cup soft dark brown sugar
1 tsp ground allspice
½ tsp ground ginger
seeds from 6 cardamoms crushed
2 tbsp rum
pared lime rind, to decorate
crème fraîche, to serve

1   Preheat the oven to 200°C/400°F/ gas 6. Use a little of the butter to grease a shallow baking dish large enough to hold the bananas snugly in a single layer. Peel the bananas and cut them in half lengthways. Arrange the bananas in the dish and pour over the lime juice.

VARIATION

For a version which will appeal more to children, use orange juice instead of lime and omit the rum.

2   Mix the sugar, allspice, ginger and cardamom in a bowl. Scatter the mixture over the bananas. Dot with the remaining butter. Bake, basting once, for 15 minutes, or until the bananas are soft.

3   Remove the dish from the oven. Warm the rum in a small pan or metal soup ladle, pour it over the bananas and set it alight. As soon as the flames die down, decorate the dessert with the pared lime rind and serve each portion with a dollop of crème fraîche.

PRESERVES AND CHUTNEYS

Moroccan Spiced Preserved Lemons

Salt is all that you need to preserve lemons, but adding spices gives them an aromatic flavour.

MAKES ABOUT 900 G/2 LB

6 unwaxed lemons, washed
6 tbsp sea salt
2 tbsp black peppercorns
4 bay leaves
6 cardamoms
1 cinnamon stick
sunflower oil

1 Cut the lemons lengthways into quarters. Layer the lemon quarters and salt in a sieve, place over a bowl and leave to drain for 2 days.

> ### COOK'S TIP
>
> *The chopped preserved peel from preserved lemons is used in couscous, tagines and other Middle Eastern chicken and fish dishes.*

2 Pack the lemon quarters tightly into one or two clean preserving jars with the peppercorns, bay leaves, cardamoms and cinnamon stick.

3 Pour in sunflower oil to cover the lemons, seal the jar and leave for 3-4 weeks before using.

Roasted Red Pepper and Chilli Jelly

The hint of chilli in this glowing red jelly makes it ideal for spicing up hot or cold roast meat. The jelly is also good stirred into sauces.

MAKES ABOUT 900 G/2 LB

8 red peppers, quartered
  and seeded
4 fresh red chillies, halved
  and seeded
1 onion, roughly chopped
2 garlic cloves, roughly chopped
250 ml/8 fl oz/1 cup water
250 ml/8 fl oz/1 cup white
  wine vinegar
1½ tsp salt
450 g/1 lb/2 cups preserving sugar
13 g/½ oz sachet powdered pectin
  (about 5 tsp)

1 Place the peppers, skin side up, on a rack in a grill pan. Grill until the skins blister and blacken. Place in a polythene bag until cool enough to handle, then remove the skins.

2 Purée the red peppers with the chillies, onion, garlic and water in a blender or food processor. Press the purée through a nylon sieve set over a bowl, pressing hard with a wooden spoon, to extract as much juice as possible. There should be about 750 ml/1¼ pints/3 cups.

3 Scrape the purée into a large stainless steel pan. Add the vinegar and salt. In a bowl, mix the sugar and pectin, then stir into the liquid. Heat gently until both the sugar and pectin have dissolved, then bring to a full rolling boil. Boil, stirring frequently, for exactly 4 minutes.

4 Remove the jelly from the heat and pour into warm sterilized jars. Leave to cool and set, then cover.

> ### COOK'S TIP
>
> *It is not essential to use preserving sugar, but it produces less scum.*

Clementine and Coriander Marmalade

Coriander has a warm spicy flavour, which goes particularly well with clementines and lemons.

MAKES ABOUT 2.75 KG/6 LB

1.5 kg/3-3½ lb clementines
6 unwaxed lemons
2 tbsp coriander seeds, roasted and roughly crushed
3 litres/5¼ pints/12 cups water
1.5 kg/3-3½ lb/6 cups preserving sugar

1 Wash the clementines and lemons, then cut them in half. Squeeze all the fruit and pour the juice into a large saucepan.

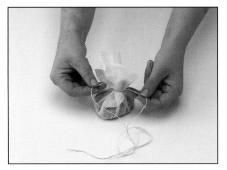

2 Scrape all the pith from the citrus shells and tie it, with the pips and half the crushed coriander seeds, in a piece of muslin. Add the bag to the juice.

3 Slice the clementine and lemon peels into fine shreds and add them to the pan with the water.

4 Bring the water to the boil, lower the heat and simmer for 1½ hours, or until the clementine and lemon peel is very soft. Remove the muslin bag. Holding it over the pan, squeeze it between two saucers.

5 Add the sugar and the remaining coriander seeds to the pan and stir over a low heat until dissolved. Boil rapidly until setting point is reached. Skim the surface of the marmalade, then leave it to stand for 30 minutes, stirring occasionally to distribute the peel evenly. Pour into warm sterilized jars and cover with waxed paper discs. Seal the jars when cool and store them in a cool dry place.

> **COOK'S TIP**
>
> *To test for a set, spoon a little marmalade on to a cold saucer. If a wrinkled skin forms within a few minutes it is ready for skimming.*

Spiced Kumquats

Cloves and other spices are combined with kumquats to make a perfect accompaniment for baked ham.

MAKES ABOUT 900 G/2 LB

500 g/1¼ lb kumquats
350 ml/12 fl oz/1½ cups white wine vinegar
500 g/1¼ lb/2½ cups granulated sugar
1 cinnamon stick
15 cloves
6 allspice berries

1 Cut the kumquats into quarters and remove the pips. Place the kumquats in a large heavy-based saucepan and pour in just enough water to cover. Bring to the boil, then lower the heat and simmer gently until the fruit is tender.

> **COOK'S TIP**
>
> *If you prefer, tie the spices in a muslin bag and remove them before bottling.*

2 With a slotted spoon, remove the kumquats and set them aside. Add the vinegar, sugar, cinnamon stick, cloves and allspice berries to the cooking liquid. Bring to the boil, stirring occasionally. Return the kumquats to the pan, lower the heat and simmer for 30 minutes.

3 With a slotted spoon, remove the kumquats from the syrup and place in warm sterilized jars. Boil the syrup until thick and syrupy. Pour over the kumquats, cover and leave for at least 2 weeks before using.

Fresh Tomato, Onion and Coriander Chutney

Indian chutneys of this type are not meant to be kept, but are used in much the same way as salsas, and eaten when freshly made. Fresh chilli is used with cayenne pepper to make the relish quite hot.

SERVES 4-6

2 tomatoes

1 red onion

1 fresh green chilli, seeded and finely chopped

4 tbsp chopped fresh coriander

juice of 1 lime

½ tsp salt

½ tsp ground paprika

½ tsp cayenne pepper

½ tsp cumin seeds, roasted and ground

1 Dice the tomatoes and onion finely. Place them in a bowl.

2 Add the chilli, coriander, lime juice, salt, paprika, cayenne and ground cumin seeds. Mix well and serve as soon as possible.

Bread and Butter Pickles

This is a traditional American pickle with a distinctive blend of whole spices. The celery seeds combine particularly well with the cucumber, and the mustard seeds add a little fire and also look attractive in the jar.

MAKES ABOUT 1.75 KG/4-4½ LB

900 g/2 lb cucumbers, cut into 5 mm/¼ in slices

2 onions, thinly sliced

50 g/2 oz/¼ cup salt

350 ml/12 fl oz/1½ cups cider vinegar

350 g/12 oz/1½ cups granulated sugar

2 tbsp white mustard seeds

2 tsp celery seeds

½ tsp ground turmeric

½ tsp black peppercorns

1 Put the cucumbers and onions in a large bowl. Add the salt and mix well. Fit a plate inside the bowl, pressing down on the cucumber mixture. Add a weight to compress the vegetables even more, and leave for 3 hours. Drain the cucumber and onions, rinse under cold running water and drain again.

2 Put the vinegar, sugar, mustard seeds, celery seeds, ground turmeric and peppercorns in a large saucepan. Bring to the boil, stirring to dissolve the sugar. Add the drained cucumber and onions. As soon as the mixture comes to the boil again, remove the pan from the heat.

3 Spoon the pickle into warm sterilized preserving jars, making sure the vegetables are covered with the liquid. Cover with airtight, vinegar-proof lids and store for at least 1 month before using.

Christmas Chutney

This savoury mixture of spices and dried fruit takes its inspiration from mincemeat, and makes a delicious addition to the Boxing Day buffet.

MAKES 900 G-1.5 KG/2-3½ LB

450 g/1 lb cooking apples, peeled, cored and chopped

500 g/1¼ lb/3 cups luxury mixed dried fruit

grated rind of 1 orange

2 tbsp mixed spice

150 ml/¼ pint/⅔ cup cider vinegar

350 g/12 oz/2 cups soft light brown sugar

1 Place the apples, dried fruit and orange rind in a large saucepan. Stir in the mixed spice, vinegar and sugar. Heat gently, stirring until all the sugar has dissolved.

COOK'S TIP

Watch the chutney carefully towards the end of the cooking time, as it has a tendency to catch on the bottom of the pan. Stir frequently at this stage.

2 Bring to the boil, then lower the heat and simmer, for 40-45 minutes, stirring occasionally, until the mixture is thick. Ladle into warm sterilized jars, cover and seal. Keep for 1 month before using.

Green Tomato Chutney

This is a classic chutney to make at the end of summer when the last tomatoes on the plants refuse to ripen. Preparing your own pickling spice makes it easy to add exactly the right amount of spiciness to balance the sweet and sour flavours.

MAKES ABOUT 2.5 KG/5½ LB

1.75 kg/4-4½ lb green tomatoes, roughly chopped

450 g/1 lb cooking apples, peeled, cored and chopped

450 g/1 lb onions, chopped

2 large garlic cloves, crushed

1 tbsp salt

3 tbsp pickling spice

600 ml/1 pint/2½ cups cider vinegar

450 g/1 lb/2 cups granulated sugar

1 Place the tomatoes, apples, onions and garlic in a large saucepan. Add the salt. Tie the pickling spice in a piece of muslin and add to the pan.

2 Pour in half the vinegar and bring to the boil. Lower the heat and simmer for 1 hour, or until the chutney is thick, stirring frequently.

3 Dissolve the sugar in the remaining vinegar and add to the chutney. Simmer for 1½ hours until the chutney is thick, stirring. Remove the muslin bag from the chutney. Spoon the hot chutney into warm sterilized jars. Cover with airtight, vinegar-proof lids and store for at least 1 month before using.

COOK'S TIP

Use a jam funnel to transfer the chutney into the jars. Wipe the jars and label them when cold.

Index

Acknowledgements

Sallie Morris would like to thank her family:
Johnnie, Alex and James for their support;
Beryl Castles for her help in typing the
manuscript; and John Phengsiri at the Wang
Thai Supermarket, 101-103 Kew Road,
Richmond, Surrey, Tel. 020 8332 2959 for
providing advice, information, and a wonderful
selection of fresh and dried spices.

Lesley Mackley would like to thank her
family and friends for their willingness to
try out new recipes, with special thanks
to Edward Shaw of Bart Spices for his
invaluable help and advice.

The publishers would like to thank the
following companies who supplied spices
and equipment for photography:
Cool Chili Company, PO Box 5702, London
W10 6WE, Tel. 020 7229 9360; Bart Spices
Limited, York Road, Bedminster, Bristol,
BS3 4AD, 0117 977 3474; Pepper Alley Herbs,

Fiddes Payne Limited, The Spice
Warehouse, Banbury, Oxfordshire,
OX16 8JB, Tel. 01295 253 888; Magimix
UK Limited, 115A High Street Godalming,
Surrey, GU7 1AQ, Tel. 01483 427411;
HP Foods Limited for supplying Maille
and Grey Poupon mustards.

Photographs: With the exceptions noted
below, all photographs are by William
Adams-Lingwood: Tony Stone Worldwide,
p6, 8, 9 (top left and bottom right), 10 and
11; Image Bank, p7, 12, 13 (bottom right);
Zefa Picture Library, p9 (centre); and
Anthony Blake Photo Library, p 13 top.